Brazil and Latin America

Brazil and Latin America

Between the Separation and Integration Paths

José Briceño-Ruiz and Andrés Rivarola Puntigliano

LEXINGTON BOOKS
Lanham • Boulder • New York • London

Published by Lexington Books
An imprint of The Rowman & Littlefield Publishing Group, Inc.
4501 Forbes Boulevard, Suite 200, Lanham, Maryland 20706
www.rowman.com

Unit A, Whitacre Mews, 26-34 Stannary Street, London SE11 4AB

British Library Cataloguing in Publication Information Available
The hardback edition of this book was previously catalogued by the Library of Congress as follows:

Library of Congress Cataloging-in-Publication Data

Names: Briceño Ruíz, José, author. | Rivarola, Andrés, author.
Title: Brazil and Latin America : between the separation and integration paths / José Briceño-Ruiz and Andrés Rivarola Puntigliano.
Description: Lanham, Maryland : Lexington Books, 2017. | Includes bibliographical references and index.
Identifiers: LCCN 2017027968 (print) | LCCN 2017028196 (ebook) | ISBN 9781498538459 (cloth : alk. paper) | ISBN 9781498538473 (pbk. : alk. paper) | ISBN 9781498538466 (Electronic)
Subjects: LCSH: Brazil--Foreign relations--Latin America. | Latin America--Foreign relations--Brazil. | Brazil--Foreign relations--1985- | Latin America--Foreign relations--1980-
Classification: LCC F1416.B73 B75 2017 (print) | LCC F1416.B73 (ebook) | DDC 327.8108--dc23
LC record available at https://lccn.loc.gov/2017027968

ISBN 9781498538459 (cloth : alk. paper)
ISBN 9781498538473 (pbk. : alk. paper)
ISBN 9781498538466 (electronic)

Contents

Acknowledgments

We would like to express our sincere thanks and appreciation to all those who helped us to complete and improve this book. A special gratitude goes to the Institute of Latin American Studies at Stockholm University for providing resources to proofread chapters of the book as well as to the scholars at the institute's research seminar for their comments and contributions. We are also deeply grateful to the colleagues at the Research Group on Regional Integration, at the University of the Andes, for some insights that became part of this book. We are greatly indebted to Dr. Raphael Padula, which made a second reading of the book and helped in this way to improve its quality. Finally, yet importantly, we thank the anonymous reviewer for a careful reading of our manuscript as well as insightful comments and suggestions. Naturally, any faults and mistakes that remain in the text are the sole responsibility of the authors.

List of Acronyms and Abbreviations

ABC	Argentina, Brazil and Chile
ABV	Argentina, Brazil and Venezuela
ACT	Amazonian Cooperation Treaty
ALBA	Alianza Bolivariana para los Pueblos de Nuestra América/Bolivarian Alliance for the Peoples of Our America.
BRICS	Brazil, Russia, India, China, South Africa
CACM	Central American Common Market
CARICOM	Caribbean Community
CAUCE	Argentine-Uruguayan Economic Complementarity Agreement
CELAC	Latin American and Caribbean Community of States
CEPAL	Comisión Económica para América Latina y el Caribe/ Economic Commission for Latin America and the Caribbean
CSN	Companhia Siderúrgica Nacional
ECLA	Economic Commission for Latin America
ECOSOC	Economic and Social Council
EEC	European Economic Communities
EFTA	European Free Trade Association
FONPLATA	Financial Fond for the Development of the Plata Basin Countries
FTAA	Free Trade Area of the Americas
GATT	General Agreement on Tariffs and Trade
IEA	Initiative Enterprise for the Americas
IIRSA	Iniciativa para la Integración de la Infraestructura Regional Suramericana/Initiative for the Integration of the South American Infrastructure

ISEB	Instituto Superior de Estudos Brasileiros
LAIA	Latin American Integration Association
LAFTA	Latin American Free Trade Association
Mercosul/Mercosur	Mercado Comum do Sul/Southern Common Market
NAFTA	North American Free Trade Agreement
UNSTAMIH	The United Nations Stabilization Mission in Haiti
OAS	Organization of American States
OPA	Pan American Operation
PEC	Protocol for Trade Promotion
PEI	Política Externa Independente
PEIC/PICE	Program of Economic Integration and Cooperation between Argentina and Brazil
SACN	South American Community of Nations
SAFTA	South America Free Trade Area
SELA	Sistema Económico Latinoamericano/Latin American Economic System
UDUAL	Universidad de América Latina
UN	United Nations Organization
UNASUR	União de Nações Sul-Americanas/Unión de Naciones Suramericanas/Union of South American Nations
UNCTAD	United Nations Conference on Trade and Development

Introduction

The mainstream approach to the study of the relations between Brazil and other Latin American countries highlights cultural, geographic, political, economic and state power issues that in different forms have created a deep cleavage between this country and the rest of the region. By the end of the 19th century, along with the idea of Brazil as an "immense island," Eduardo Prado asserted that "looking inward the rising sun—with its populations centers located closer to Europe than to other Latin America countries and separated from these by differences of origin and language—neither the physical Brazil nor the spiritual one, forms a system with these nations."[1] In our days, this argument is retaken by specialists such as Leslie Bethell, arguing that Brazilians are aware of what separated Brazil from Spanish America, "geography, history (Portugal's long struggle to maintain its independence from Spain and the different colonial experiences of Portuguese America and Spanish America), an economy and society based on plantation agriculture and African slavery and, above all, language culture and political institutions."[2] We describe this way to understand the relations between Brazil and Latin American as the "path of separation."

An underlying historical view behind the "path of separation" has its roots in the confrontations between the Spanish and Portuguese states in, for example, the well-known dispute concerning the distribution of the "new world." This led to what could be seen as the first geopolitical division of the world system in a papal bull issued by Pope Alexander VI in 1493. It granted to Spain and Portugal all lands west and south of a pole-to-pole line one hundred leagues west and south of any of the islands of the Azores or Cape Verde islands. From here, it is argued that Iberian rivalry was transferred to the American continent, as part of their global struggle for the control of trade and colonies. The main territorial stage of this dispute was fundamentally in the southern part of the continent, where there was natural point of geographic connection and colonization. To the north and west of Brazil there were natural barriers, such as the Amazonas, that prevented a more fluid contact between the colonizing forces. For this reason, the River Plate (*Río de la Plata*) basin has become one of the cases most studied in the analysis of the relationship between Brazil and its neighboring countries.

Following the "path of separation" until the present time, Bethell concludes that while the political and economic integration has been a focal point in the government of Luiz Inacio Lula da Silva (2003–2011), this trend toward integration and cooperation generally occurs more in the South American region, and not with regard to Latin America.[3] South America is here seen as a platform from which Brazil intends to exercise the role of "regional power" by way of positioning itself as a new "global power." To be sure, Bethell is skeptical about integration across the whole region, and particularly concerning the integration of Brazil and the Latin American region. If there is any possibility of integration, although not with doubts and ambivalence, it would be reserved to the new South American space[4]. Moreover, Bethell not only takes distance from the idea of integration in terms of foreign or economic policy, but even the concept that has functioned as a national common ground for the region, that is, "Latin America." For Bethell, this concept is not original to the region but a French invention. This view is not a minor issue when analyzing Brazil's relation with its neighbors. According to Bethell, "none of the Spanish-American intellectuals and writers who first used the expression '*América Latina*,' or their French and Spanish counterparts, thought Brazil was included in it. '*América Latina*' was simply another name for '*América Española*.'"[5]

Bethell is not alone in this view, which has, in different forms, been the fundament of the mainstream view regarding a "path of separation." In a famous study on global politics and civilizations, Samuel Huntington holds that Latin America has the potential to establish a civilization in itself, separated from the "West," but that the region is currently no more than a "sub-civilization." To become a civilization, according to Huntington, Latin American countries need to establish an internal order that includes what is called a "core state"—a role that in the case of the "West" is played by the United States. In his view, size, resources, population, and economic and military capacity make Brazil eligible to be the leader in Latin America. However, for Huntington, Brazil is to Latin America what Iran is to Islam, "otherwise well-qualified to be a core state, sub-civilizational differences (religious in Iran, linguistic with Brazil) make it difficult for it to assume that role. Latin America thus has several states, Brazil, Venezuela, and Argentina, which cooperate and compete for leadership."[6]

There are indeed historical arguments to sustain the idea of a "path of separation." One of the elements used in the construction of Brazilian identity in the first decades of independent life was the description of Hispanic America as the "other." The Brazilian Empire was characterized by political stability, territorial unity and peace guaranteed by the monarchy. The Hispanic American republics, in contrast, were perceived to live in a political turmoil, controlled by *caudillos* and territorially dismembered because of the adoption of the Republican regime. Thus, in the Brazilian view, the factor that distinguished Brazil from Latin America was not race or geography but a different political regime. As a result, Brazil looked to Europe when searching for an identity reference due to the monarchic tradition of the old continent. As the Brazilian scholar and diplomat Luís Cláudio Villafañe Santos argues, by conserving the dynastic principle as a source of legitimation, Brazil established a distinction from the Latin American Republics. Thus, "in the metaphoric rupture between America and Europe [argued in those years], Brazil was placed ideologically on the side of the European powers."[7] During the empire, Brazil created a self-image based on alleged superiority—in terms of civilization— by connecting the country's political regime to the European monarchies. As argued by Villafañe Santos: "even if a backward, slavish and distant, that "tropical monarchy" felt superior to its neighbors, that were perceived as anarchic and savages."[8]

An example of this view is *the História Geral do Brasil* published between 1854 and 1857 by Francisco Adolfo Varnhagen, Visconde de Porto Seguro, in which the opposition between Brazil and the rest of Hispanic America was stressed. The major argument was that different political conceptions about the political regime and internal organization (Monarchic and Unitarian in Brazil, Republican and Federal in Hispanic America) made an approximation to nations described as chaotic unadvisable. Thus, a clear difference should be established between "us" (the monarchic and stable Brazil) and "them" (the republican and chaotic Hispanic American states).

However, historical analysis on the issue is not unanimous in confirming the arguments presented by the followers of the "path of separation." Pundits such as Arturo Ardao (1986; 1993) and Miguel Rojas Mix[9] have, for example, contested the French origin of the expression Latin America, as argued by Bethel. Bethel actually subscribes to the argument presented by John Leddy Phelan that Latin American was an expression first used by Michel Chevallier in his *Lettres d'Amérique du Nord*, published in 1836, and then by Napoleon III to justify the concept of *latinité*, on which basis Maximilian was crowned as emperor of Mexico. It is undeniable that Chevallier was the first to use the term, and he influenced the idea of *Pan-latinité* as fostered by Napoleon III. [10] Yet, other narratives on the emergence of Latin America were skeptical toward Phelan's approach to the issue. Arturo Ardao, for example, argued that José María Torres Caicedo (1856) used the expression in his poem *Las dos Américas* already in 1856. Another example is Miguel Rojas Mix, who asserted that some months before the publication of Caicedo's poem. Francisco Bilbao (1856) in *La iniciativa para América* described the region as Latin America. In other words, at least two important regional pundits used the expression before the French invasion of México. For both Caicedo and Bilbao, "Latin America" was a concept related to identity that emerged as a response to the US expansionism in Mexico and Central America. Bilbao, in another book published in 1862 called *La América en Peligro*, rejected the French pretension to use the idea of *Latinité* to justify imperialist actions. Latin America remained as an identity notion not only in opposition to Anglo America but also to Europe. As we explain further below, Brazil was neither included nor excluded from the notion of Latin America.

BRAZIL AND LATIN AMERICA: THE "INTEGRATION PATH"

The aim of this book is to challenge the "separatist" bias of this perspective by exploring the parallel existence of its opposite, which Jaguaribe calls the "path of integration." From this point of view, the focus is on those forces that have intended to forge different forms of alignment, integration and sometimes union among the states. These positions have changed form and strengthened in different periods of time. Yet, as this book intends to address, this is a perspective of long data, which was inherent in the mind-set of elites even before independence. We agree with the mainstream view in that the "path of integration" has most of the time not been the dominant position; still, our point is that there are moments in which it has been influential. Moreover, research should focus not only on "results" or "dominating positions" but on the complexity surrounding policy-making and debates on national positions, which, as Ori Preuss rightfully holds, conforms this to the "history of defining what Brazil is and what it is not, the history of construction of the Brazilian self."[11]

A guiding argument behind this book is that current decision-making in terms of national identity and foreign or economic policies cannot be understood without a more open analysis of the past. Along these lines, we argue, for example, that the integration efforts that mainstream views point out as emerging since the late 1980s have a much longer history, where we identify supporters of the "paths of integration" since emancipation. Moreover, we also address that these supporters have not been "outsiders" in Brazilian politics, but highly representative members of the commanding heights and sometimes even chiefs of state. Furthermore, we not only analyze political or economic forces and representatives, but also intellectuals, including those considered as pivotal in the shaping of the "Brazilian self."

There are, of course, scholars pointing out this issue from different perspectives. Nevertheless, there is as of yet no book that addresses the whole set of dimensions that exist. Some are, for example, concentrated in the field of economics with others focusing on international relations, ideas and culture. However, more importantly, nobody has yet intended to analyze this issue in terms of *longue dureé,* namely, by identifying and contextualizing the process of changes and continuities in ideas and initiatives along the "path of integration" as the other side of the coin of the "path of separation." This makes this book unique, as well as timely. The current debate on Brazilian foreign policy and economic strategies, as the very definition of the nation's place in the world, is centered around some key questions such as: Is Brazil part of the region? In that case, what is the "region," South America, Latin America or America (with the latter term referring to the Western Hemisphere)? Shall Brazil, in that case, remain separate? Does it belong to the "West," or should the country seek autonomy by joining other emerging countries such as Brazil, Russia, India, China and South Africa (BRICS)? Along a *longue durée* historical analysis of Brazil's relations with Latin America, this book intends to provide new insights to find answers in this debate, particularly concerning arguments that neglects the existence of the path of integration.

Before declaring Brazilian independence in 1822, Silvestre Pinheiro Ferreira, Minister of Foreign Affairs and War of the United Kingdom of Portugal, Brazil and Algarves, proposed the signing of a Confederation Treaty between the United States, Brazil and the Hispanic American countries; Haiti, Spain, Portugal and Greece. The aim of such a treaty was to guarantee the independence and mutual defense of all those states[12]. Afterward, José Bonifácio de Andrade e Silva, the first Brazilian Minister of Foreign Affairs, sent a representative to Buenos Aires with the instructions to propose to the Argentinean government the creation of a confederation between Brazil and the United Provinces of the River Plate. In instructions sent to Antonio Manuel Correa da Camara, Trade and Political representative of Brazil in the River Plate, Bonifácio pointed out:

> After ably convinced them that the interests of our Kingdom are the same that those of the other states of this hemisphere and let them know that they are part our destiny (...) you expose them the immeasurable benefits which may result from the creation of a Confederation or a defensive and offensive treaty with Brazil, in order to oppose, with other governments of Hispanic America, to singular political maneuvers of the European politics; you demonstrate that none of those governments could win a loyal and closer ally than the Brazilian government.[13]

This idea of regional unity was defended by Bonifácio on different occasions, to the point that the French Admiral Roussinin sent a letter to Paris asserting that: "José Bonifácio dreamed with a confederation of all free states of America, with the aim of counterbalance the European confederation. He explained his idea with great vehemence given details with an emphasis on the prosperity it would give to Brazil"[14]. There were, of course, sectors of society, both in Brazil and among its neighbors, which were reluctant to the idea of regional unity. In Brazil, for example, the influential scholar and member of government João Pandiá Calógeras criticized Bonifácio's initiatives and preferred a continuation of the policy developed during the period of 1808–1822, particularly regarding a more distant and, at times, conflicting relation with the countries of the River Plate Basin[15]. Beyond Brazil, it is also well known that the *Libertador* of the Spanish-speaking South American colonies, Simón Bolivar, was reluctant to invite Brazil to the Amphictyonic Congress of Panamá in 1826. In reality, Bolivar's negative stance was not based on a rejection of cultural arguments, but on the political organization of Brazil and the fears that its territory would be used by the Holy Alliance in an attempt to reestablish Spanish power in America.

Since the beginning of its independent life, Brazil's relations with Latin America, and particularly with those in South America, have been a complex issue. Pinheiro Ferreira and Bonifácio have had followers, and so also has Calégoras. It is, however, the later view that has been the mainstream approach, particularly in what concerns the description of bilateral relations as based on mistrust or, in the best of cases, indifference. Somewhat schematically, one could say that there are two major perspectives on the analysis of the relations between Brazil and the other Latin American countries. On the one side, there are those who emphasize what Helio Jaguaribe has called the "path of separation,"[16] that is, the predominance of the elements of opposition and rivalry between Brazil and the countries of the region. This is principally in relation to Argentina, for example, Calégoras' reluctance on Bonifácio's initiatives.

Along this line, it is argued that due to "history" (the Spanish-Portuguese split and Brazil's imperial tradition), "size" (Argentina as a potential rival for regional power) or "culture" (Luso-Hispanic differences), Brazil has always had, and perhaps always will have, a complicated relationship with Argentina and, in extension, its other neighbors in the Rio the Plata. Geography has also been stressed as a factor causing "separation," for example, in relation to the Andean countries and the northern South American countries such as Venezuela and the Guianas. The geographic distance toward Central America, the Caribbean and Mexico can also be added here, as well as the fact that these states became part of United States' sphere of influence. A central theme in this narrative of conflict is that "indifference" and "distance" have been the general rule of Brazilian relations with the rest of Latin America. To validate this perspective, the following events are always mentioned: the Brazilian-Argentinean conflict concerning the Cisplatine Province in the 1820s; the Brazilian involvement in the Uruguayan civil war between 1838 and 1851; the non-participation of Brazil in the Hispanic American Congresses held in Lima (1847), Santiago (1856) and Lima (1854); the Triple Alliance War; and the Brazilian non-written alliance with the United States since the influential José Maria da Silva Paranhos Júnior, also known as Barão do Rio Branco, took office as Minister of Foreign Affairs in 1902.

There are, on the other hand, those pundits who emphasize what Jaguaribe has called the "path of integration," which focuses more on the approximation between Brazil and its neighbors due to "cultural" (common Hispanic heritage), "economic" (to overcome underdevelopment) or "geopolitical" (union to confront common and greater rivals and achieve autonomy) reasons. This view was closer to popular movements such as a *Conjuração dos Alfaiates* (Bahia, 1798), a *Revolução Pernambucana* (Recife, 1817), *Confederação do Equador* (Pernambuco, Ceará, Rio Grande do Norte, Paraíba, 1824) and the *Revolução Praieira* (Recife, 1848) led by figures such as Cipriano Barata, José Abreu e Lima, Frei Caneca, and Domingos José Martins e Antônio Gonçalves da Cruz "Cabugá." All of them belonged to a liberal, republican, constitutionalist and anti-Lusitanian movement that was connected to other Hispanic American leaders. Thus, Martins was in contact with Francisco de Miranda[17]. Ferreira Pinheiro, De Andrada e Silva and Miguel Maria Lisboa, even if they were monarchists, also fostered closer relations with their Latin America neighbors, and Celso Furtado, Helio Jaguaribe, Luiz Alberto Moniz Bandeira, Darcy Ribeiro, Gilberto Freyre and Samuel Pinheiro Guimarães continued this path of integration in the twentieth century.

In other words, forces highlighting separation and integration have coexisted since the early years of Latin American independence up until the current time. Many would probably have doubts about the existence of the "path of integration." That is, comprehensible since most research has been made along the "path of separation" perspective. It would be fair to say that this is a mainstream view in the study of Brazilian history, international relations and culture, but also in the way to understand the relations between Brazil and Latin American countries. There is no doubt, plenty of arguments that maintain that there has been and still is a "path of separation" and that this has been predominant for long periods in Brazil's foreign policy. However, this can also be said of countries such as Argentina, which particularly in the 19th century was committed to the "path of separation." Thus, the paths of separation and integration can be found in Brazil and also in other South American countries. In this book, we are devoted to the analysis of how the path of integration has developed in Brazil, and the analysis will at times require that we consider the views and perceptions of Latin American countries.

Bethell was right when arguing that Brazil was not part of the notion of Latin America in the 1850s and 1860s. However, no documents by Bilbao, Caicedo or Arosemena described Brazil as something outside that. Even if one would accept Phelan's view on the origins of Latin America as part of the idea of *Latinité*, France considered Brazil as part of the *Amérique Latine*. The reasons for the exclusion of Brazil from the early debates on the idea of Latin America are not necessarily related to culture, but to the political context of that period, in which dichotomies such as Republic vs. Monarchy and civilization vs. anarchy were used to differentiate Brazil from its neighbors. Michel Gobat argues that "because the Brazilian Empire sided with Europe's monarchical powers, its elites did not embrace 'Latin America' in the 1860s, when the idea gained further strength with the upsurge in French and Spanish intervention."[18] However, this narrative on separation began to be weakened gradually in Brazil in the last third of the nineteenth century. On the one hand, the stereotype of the Hispanic (Latin) American countries as unstable, as opposed to a civilized and stable empire, began to be contested. One reason for this contestation was slavery, an element that denied the alleged superiority of the empire in terms of civilization. This was argued during the time of the Triple Alliance, where Brazil as a slave country alleged it was fighting to liberate Paraguay from the Solano Lopez regime. At the same time, Chile and Argentina (particularly after the demise of Rosas) had achieved political stability and an increasing Eurocentric view that began to interest the Brazilian elites. In other words, the argument concerning Monarchic superiority did not fit with reality. In that context, the narrative of the monarchy as civilization, and its corollary of separation with the Latin America countries, began to be rejected, particularly by the Republican movement that began to emerge in the 1870s. Leaders and thinkers like Quintino Bocaíuva and Francisco Xavier da Cunha objected the "empire's foreign policy toward its southern neighbors, and more significantly (...) the perceptions underlying it as well."[19]

The instauration of the Republic in 1889 led to a review of that narrative of separation from Latin America. In the new narrative, "the Brazilian identity was to be forged as part of a broader American identity based on common values and political forms that unified the New World and distinguished it from the Old."[20] However, this view was not followed by all the academic and political circles in Brazil. An example could be Eduardo Prado, who wrote *A Ilusão Americana* in 1893. This book is very well known for its criticism to the US imperialism in the region, but also for its rejection of any involvement with the Hispanic American nations. However, views on the Hispanic American countries by other Brazilian pundits began to change in the early years of the twentieth century. Thus, Joaquin Nabuco expressed in his book

Balmaceda a positive opinion of Chile. Moreover, new regards vis-á-vis Buenos Aires emerged during the period of economic prosperity in Argentina and initial steps of approximation, such as the visits of Julio Argentino Roca to Rio de Janeiro in 1899 and Manoel Ferraz de Campo Salles to Buenos Aires, took place in 1900. This led in the following decades to initiatives such the ABC treaty.[21]

Events such as the end of the Brazilian Empire and the Declaration of the Republic, the Spanish-American war and US expansionism in the Caribbean, the announcement of the Roosevelt Corollary and the emergence of a new Latin American movement led by José Martí and José Enrique Rodó marked a period of redefinitions of identities in the region. Brazil was not excluded from this movement, and the narrative of separation furthered by the empire was substituted by another one in which the country was perceived as sharing traits with its neighbors of the region. A particular case was that of Manoel Bomfim, a thinker from the northeastern state of Sergipe, who published in 1905 *A America Latina: Males de Origem*, a book in which he rejects the alleged distinction between the Brazilian and Hispanic American historical experiences. According to Bomfim, the problems of all the Latin American countries (he used that expression), including Brazil, were actually the same, and they originated in what he called "social parasitism," a common heritage of the colonial period.[22] However, contesting the separation path narrative did not mean that such narrative disappeared. Manoel Bomfim, for example, published in 1929 *Brasil e América Latina*, a book that contradicted his earlier arguments in *A América Latina: Males de Origem.*

What is crucial to argue is that the view of Latin America as the "other" began to be replaced by the United States in the perception of many political leaders and intellectuals in Brazil, such as Manuel Oliviera Lima and José Veríssimo. It is normally highlighted, as in the case of Joaquin Nabuco, that this new identity meant a closer approximation to the United States and Pan-Americanism than to Latin America. However, as Ori Preuss has argued, the Brazilian shift toward the Americas also meant "closer encounters of peripheral kind," especially but not exclusively with Argentina and Chile.[23] Veríssimo through literature and Oliveira Lima through diplomacy criticized Pan-Americanism. However, even if their perception of Latin American neighbors was not that positive, they established contacts with intellectual and political leaders in the region.

The link between Brazil and the idea of Latin America was consolidated in the new identitarian wave that took place in the region in the late 1890s after the Spanish-American war and the conquest of Cuba and Puerto Rico by the United States. One key element of this new Latin Americanism, represented by José Martí, José Enrique Rodó and Manuel Ugarte, is that Brazil began to be considered part of Latin America. Martí did not write about Brazil, but the country was included in his idea of "Our America." In fact, the very emergence of the concept Latin America in this period implied the inclusion of Brazil. In the case of Rodó, that became a leading figure in the Latin Americanist movement of the early 20th century, he argued that Brazil was also part of Hispanic America, but Hispanic in his view was not referred to Spain, but to the Roman territories of the Iberian Peninsula that belonged during the Roman Empire. This was Rodo's argument in "Iberoamerica," an essay published in 1909, to justify Brazil's place in the region.[24] This was, however, one of his last texts and not so known texts. Along the line of Martí and Rodó, the straightforward inclusion of Brazil into a common idea of nationhood was made by Ugarte, who argued that "Brazil is part of Hispanic America and its destiny as a nation is inseparable from the rest of the continent."[25] Ugarte was also, probably, the first to write of Latin America, as a nation. A nation that cannot be, without Brazil.[26]

It is this historical process that led us to the current defenders of the integration path, the most important of them Helio Jaguaribe who, earlier than other, pointed out the "impracticability of the separate track and the need and convenience of undertaking the integration road."[27] Another prominent name along this line of thought is Luiz Alberto Moniz Bandeira. Taking a stand on a solid historical perspective, he rejects the "stereotypes" surrounding the "rivalry" with Argentina, as well as the "traditional friendship" between Brazil and the United States.[28]

As said before, the divide between the two perspectives of "separation" or "integration" paths cannot in the academic field be seen in a schematic way. Jaguaribe, for example, shared a negative view in relation to the "romantic" elements found in the "path integration" perspective. In this sense, he sees the "integrationist romanticism, of Bolivarian style" as one of the reasons for the failure of Latin American integration projects[29]. Moniz Bandeira rejects the concept of "Latin America," which describes it as a creation of the French (following Phelan's narrative) and "generic and without consistency with the geo-economic and geopolitical reality."[30] The concept "Latin America" has been, and still is, difficult to accept for many Brazilians. Probably, for this reason, those in favor of the "path of integration" have preferred expressions such "poles" (Atlantic, Andean and Mesoamerican), or the "South American path," with the aim of making South America a world power[31].

METHODOLOGICAL ISSUES

From a methodological perspective, we are aware of the contextual problems that exist when analyzing "integration" or "divergence." For example, the conception of integration has changed over the different periods of time. If one looks at Latin America since independence, political integration was predominant in the 19th century, while economic integration was so in the 20th century. Hence, contextual differences must always be highlighted to avoid "tempocentrism," namely, the "set of illusions that represent the present as an autonomous, natural, spontaneous and immutable system."[32] To understand these contextual differences, our analyses considered three elements: 1) a conceptualization of the categories "region" and "regional"; 2) an analysis of the influence of the global, systemic context; and 3) the importance of domestic policies. All these elements refer to the level of analysis in which our research is located.

Starting with the first element, the category "regional" is used when referring to, for example, "Brazil and its neighbors" or "Brazil and the region." However, region is a changing concept, an artifact of human geography and human history.[33] Recent literature on the issue highlights that regions are socially constructed. Constructivist scholars such as Iver Neumann argue that two approaches exist to explain the construction of a region. The first one is described as the "inside-out" approach in which regions are constructed by identity and cultural factors that exist in a geographic space, such as tradition, language or religion. The second one is called the "outside-in" approach, in which regions are constructed due to external factors such as geopolitics or struggle for power.[34] Neumann proposes a "genealogical" approach, according to which regions are political projects constructed through a narrative focus on geography, shared history and external threads. By using Benedict Anderson's argument that nationalism is a mechanism to "invent nations," Neumann asserts that a similar process occurs with the creation "of international regions." Thus, regions are also "imaged communities" where some leading actors behave as "region-builders."[35] The process is managed by the "region-builders," who are the forces (normally political and economics elites) that create such regional imaged communities. In Neumann's words: "The existence of regions is preceded by the existence of region-builders. They are political actors who, as part of a political project, see it in their interest to imagine a certain spatial and chronological identity for a region and to disseminate this imagination to as many other people as possible."[36] Region builders not only propose their views but they also try to eliminate any competing projects in the process of constructing a region. Region builders "use the other," namely an external reference or someone who due to its differences has the condition of other, differences that are converted "into otherness in order to secure its own self-certainty."[37]

As a constructivist, Neumann's approach is centered on ideas, identities and narratives. This approach is rejected by both the liberal and realist traditions in which interests are the main forces that influence the decisions made by political actors' interests. Andrew Moravcsik, for example, argues that although ideas "are ubiquitous and necessary tools to coordinate social life (...) major integration decisions by invoking variables that alter the instrumental calculations of social actors and states: economic interests, relative power and the need for credible commitment."[38] Thus, "ideas are present but not causally central. They may be irrelevant and random, or, more likely, they are transmission belts for interests."[39]

In this book, we aim to go beyond this debate. The complexity of the regional processes shows that a diversity of motivations exists. Some of them are ideational, while others are linked to the interests the actors promote and still others are related to the international system. From our point of view, the analysis of the construction of a region implies recognizing the role played by the narratives and discourses but also the material interests fostered by the region builders in Brazil. The idea of otherness is also crucial for understanding the way Brazil considers its relations with its neighbors. In this sense, we adopt three elements proposed by Neumann in order to understand the process of the construction of regions.

Firstly, the explanation of the process of the construction of regions is incomplete if the role of the interests of political actors and the influence of systemic variables are not included in the explanatory framework. The strategies of the region builders are influenced by ideas, narratives and identities as well as by power and interests. Thus, in this book, we argue that although the ideational motivations matter, they are mostly intervening variables, because the logic of the construction of South American regionalism, and the role Brazil has played in such a process, also depends on in the interests of the region builders (political elites or figures such as José Bonifácio de Andrada e Silva or José Maria da Silva Paranhos Junior *Barão* of Rio Branco).

Secondly, we see each period as shaped by a particular systemic context which sets a framework that conditions and influences the perceptions of national (local) actors in terms of their foreign policy, geopolitical strategies and the framework set by the international economy. This is a crucial variable for explaining the role of Brazil in the construction of region in Latin America. For example, during the colonial period, Brazil was perceived as a region in itself, demanding measures for regional integration. The Spanish colonial state was the neighbor state, sometimes in communion with the Portuguese and at other times a rival.

Thirdly, the understanding of regional processes in South America requires not only adopting, as explained in the previous paragraph, a systemic view, but also an agent-based analysis. Thus, in the book, factors related to the international system, such as European imperialism, the expansion of the United States and rise as a regional and global power or the North-South asymmetries, are considered crucial to understand the national choices adopted by Brazil. However, these choices are not conceived as mere responses of passive actors that are compelled to accept the systemic influence. The national political system matters—and the social and economic structure, ideas, perceptions and prejudices of the elites, as well as political and social movements—are crucial for understanding the complex process of the construction of "regionhood" in South America.

Based on these premises, we propose three key elements of analysis in order to explain the reasons that have led to the Brazilian elites to foster regional cooperation and integration with the rest of Latin America: autonomy, development and identity. The first two, autonomy and development, are the independent variables and are based on interests; the third (identity) is an intervening variable and is mostly ideational. Our argument is that, like the case of the rest of Latin America, Brazilian forces favorable to the path of integration perceive regional integration as a mechanism that could help in the achieving those objectives. Autonomy was implicit in the confederation proposed by the founder of Brazilian diplomacy, Jose Bonifacio de Andrade e Silva, the ABC treaty fostered by Rio Branco or, more recently, by the Union of South American Nations (UNASUR). "Development" is more related to the processes of economic integration that have been developed since the 1960s, from the Latin American Free Trade Association (LAFTA) to the creation of Southern Common Market (Mercosur). "Identity" is an ideational variable that has been present in the debate of the relations between Brazil and Latin America. It is also part of the construction and "imagination" of three distinct national visions: the 1) Pan-American, 2) Latin American or the 3) "Brazilian island."[40]

ORGANIZATION OF THE BOOK

Chapter 1 of the book, "A Prologue of Integration: The Pan-Hispanic Dream," is concerned with what we see as antecedents of the Brazilian path of integration. Our long-term approach takes us to the period before, and during, independence. As said above, "integration," means different things at distinct periods of time, and are promoted by different kinds of political forces. One element to highlight here is the "Iberian Union" (1580–1640), which was the designation of the federation between the Crown of Portugal and the Spanish Crown through a dynastic union under the Spanish monarchy of the Hapsburg king Philip III of Spain 1578–1621. There were of course many rejections and conflicts around the integration of these states that we will consider. Yet, our point is to explore the elements which promote cohesion and cooperation. One example is the level of Portuguese participation in the creation and consolidation of the city of Buenos Aires (1580) and Iberian colonization in the River Plate Basin.[41] Another issue here is to explore the role of diplomats such as, Alexandre de Gusmão, the so-called founder of Brazilian diplomacy. The analysis here goes from the promotion of a peaceful understanding with neighboring territories toward straightforward proposals for the creation of common state building. An example of this was the "Carlotist" movement, where leading personalities from Argentina and Brazil promoted the creation of a South American kingdom under the rule of Carlota Joaquina, the sister of King Fernando VII of Spain and wife of King Dom João VI of Portugal (1816–1826).[42] This part will also explore the antecedents of Brazilian sub-national initiatives and leaders who promoted "republicanism" and a closer alignment to the Spanish-speaking republics, which was the case of the republican movement in the state of Pernambuco, in 1817.[43]

Chapter 2, "Distant but not Absent: Brazil and Latin America from The Independence to the International American Congresses," deals with the 19th century during the domain of the Brazilian Empire. In this period, the study focused on the origins of the path of separation based in the different political systems. A first factor analysis in this section is the Brazilian involvement in regional conflicts in the River Plate, in particular in the Uruguayan civil war, the internal fight in Argentina against Juan Manuel de Rosas and the War of Paraguay. A particular issue analyzed in this chapter is the initial construction of the path of integration in the early days of the empire and the re-emergence of the path of integration in the middle of the century. In contrast to its South American (and Hispanic American) neighbors, Brazil adopted the monarchy and closer relation with the European monarchic dynasties. One of the effects of the adoption of this form of government was a political stability unknown in other Latin American countries, which were to a large extent experiencing political turmoil, civil wars and caudillo-led governments. As a result, the Brazilian imperial elites defended the separation with a region that was considered unstable and turbulent. However, by the middle of the century and especially after the war of Paraguay this perception began to change, and an embryonic path of integration began to be developed. Firstly, although the empire had political stability, slavery was being increasingly rejected in other countries of the region, which meant Brazil was perceived more as an enslaving empire than a political model. Secondly, the political stability achieved by countries such as Argentina and Chile also demonstrated that a republic could succeed in avoiding the chaos and caudillos. These two factors (the image of a slave nation and the success of republicanism in other South American states) began to influence some sectors of Brazilian society, especially those favorable to adopt a republican form of government. These sectors were quite influential when the Brazilian Republic was established and the process of gradual rapprochement with some South American countries began.

Chapter 3, "Brazil and the making of Latin America," covers the period from the last decade of the 19th century to the rise of power by

Getulio Vargas in the early 1930s. This is a period in which one observes moments of rapprochement and initiatives of regional cooperation, as well as moments of distancing. An example of rapprochement was the visits of Justo Argentina Roca to Brazil in 1899 and Manoel Ferraz de Campo Salles to Argentina in 1900. A leading figure of this period is José Maria da Silva Paranhos Junior, Barão de Rio Branco. Considered the founder of the Brazilian modern diplomacy, Rio Branco developed a diplomatic strategy based on three pillars: the maintenance of special relations with Europe, closer links with the United States and a rapprochement with Brazil's South American neighbors. This later aspect implied, on the one hand, the delimitation of borders with most of the countries of the region; on the other hand, Rio Branco promoted a mechanism of regional cooperation such as the ABC treaty, a framework to initiate political dialogue and the solution of conflicts between Argentina, Brazil and Chile. This process at the political and diplomatic level went together with an intellectual discussion on the relation of Brazil with Latin American led by pundits such as Bomfim, José Veríssimo or Manuel de Oliviera Lima. These debates are also analyzed in this chapter.

Chapter 4, "Setting the path for integration: Developmentalism, Nationalism and Integration," is devoted to the Brazilian relations with Latin American from 1930 to the beginning of bilateral integration with Argentina in the mid-1980s. This chapter deals with the change of course during the Vargas administration, in relation to Brazil's insertion in the region. One aspect of this was the drawing nearer to Argentina and the government of Juan Domingo Perón. Another was the position of Vargas's government to support the creation and existence of the United Nation's Economic Commission for Latin America (ECLA, in Spanish CEPAL[44]), which also became one of the most important promotors of Latin American regional integration. Vargas was successful in this case, but not concerning an alliance with Argentina, which faced strong reactions from anti-integrationist groups in Brazil. Yet, this line of action was not forgotten. It was in part followed by the posterior government of Juscelino Kubitschek (1956–1961) and, particularly, by Vargas's former minister of Labor (and Kubitschek's vice president), João Goulart (1961–1964). Even if there was a break of integration-oriented initiatives after the military coup in 1964, this chapter outlines a return of integration-oriented initiatives since the government of Artur da Costa e Silva (1967–1969).

Chapter 5, "Brazil and the contemporary path of integration: from MERCOSUR to CELAC," examines the recent period of the Brazilian relations with Latin America, in which the path of integration became hegemonic. This period began in 1979, when Argentina and Brazil subscribed the Treaty Itaipú Corpus that terminated the conflict surrounding the Itaupú dam. That was the beginning of an increasing bilateral relation that coincided with the end of the authoritarian governments in both countries. A paramount moment was the Summit held in 1985 in Foz de Iguaçu, Brazil, between the Presidents of Argentina and Brazil, Raúl Alfonsín and José Sarney, which triggered a process of bilateral cooperation that was deepened in the following years through the so-called Program of Bilateral Cooperation and Integration (known in Spanish as PICE). As the bilateral process was deepened, other countries of the region began to show interest in participating in it. This was the case of Uruguay, which began to be involved in the PICE since 1988. The result was the creation of the Mercosur, in which Argentina, Brazil, Paraguay and Uruguay decided to create a common market. Mercosur was a crucial moment in the consolidation of the path of integration because it not only allowed the overcoming of hypothesis of conflict in the Southern Cone but also implied the construction of a common project of international insertion in the changing world of the early 1990s.

Mercosur was the beginning of a process of region construction in South America, a category that became increasingly important for the Brazilian diplomacy. The initial success of Mercosur led to debate in Itamaraty on the need to establish a similar process of cooperation between Brazil and the countries such as Colombia, Ecuador, Perú and Venezuela. An initial proposal was the creation of a Northern Common Market (known in Spanish as Merconorte), but the idea was rejected in some sectors in Itamaraty because it implied an artificial division of South America in two areas. Then, the idea of Merconorte was substituted in 1994 by a South American Free Trade agreement (SAFTA), a sort of counterweight to the North American Free Trade Agreement (NAFTA). SAFTA should be achieved through the convergence between Mercosur, Andean Community and Chile. SAFTA was relaunched and transformed in 2000, when President Fernando Henrique Cardoso convened for the first time in history a Summit of South American Heads of State and Governments that included Guyana and Surinam, two countries traditionally more linked with the English-speaking Caribbean countries member of the Caribbean Community (CARICOM). In this Summit, the project of SAFTA was substituted by the South American Community of Nations (SACN), a regional initiative that went beyond free trade as its main goal and included new objectives such as the promotion of a common infrastructure, the fight against drug trafficking and the consolidation of South America as a zone of peace.

The rise to power of Luiz Inácio Lula da Silva led to a consolidation of the South American strategy of Brazil. In alliance with leaders such as Néstor Kirchner and Hugo Chávez, Lula transformed the SACN into the Union of South American Nations, a more ambitious regional scheme with specific goals in areas such as defense and security, the defense of democracy, solutions to national and regional crises, financial cooperation and social issues. Thus, UNASUR meant the consolidation and paramount moment for the path of integration. Similarly, the Brazilian promotion (with Mexico) of the Latin American and Caribbean Community of States (CELAC) showed that the efforts of cooperation and integration went beyond the South American neighborhood to include the whole of Latin America and the Caribbean, such as the Brazilian participation in the coordination of the United Nations Stabilization Mission in Haiti (MINUSTAH), and its involvement in the Honduran political crisis in 2010 after the coup d'état of the President Manuel Zelaya. However, this impetus was lost during Dilma Rousseff's government, which showed a interest in developing links with emerging powers, especially in the framework of the BRICS group with Russia, India, China and South Africa.

The book closes with a chapter of conclusions that summarize the findings derived from the *longue durée* analysis of the relations between Brazil and Latin America.

NOTES

1. Eduardo Prado, *A Ilusão Americana* (São Paulo: Editora e Officinas Magalhães, 1917), 5.
2. Leslie Bethell, "Brazil and 'Latin America'" *Journal of Latin American Studies,* vol. 42, no. 3 (2010), 461.
3. Ibid, 484.
4. Ibid.,
5. Ibid., 460.
6. Samuel Huntington, *The Clash of Civilizations and the Remaking of World Order* (London: Simon & Schuster UK Ltd., 2002 [1997]), 135–6.
7. Luís Cláudio Villafañe G. Santos, *A América do Sul no Discursos Diplomático Brasileiro* (Brasilia: FUNAG, 2014), 64
8. Ibid., 64.
9. Arturo Ardao, "Panamericanismo y Latinoamericanismo," in Leopoldo Zea (ed.) *América Latina en sus Ideas,* (México D.F: Siglo XXI, 1986); Arturo Ardao, *América Latina y la Latinidad* (México D.F: UNAM, 1993); Rojas Mix, Miguel, "América Latina: integración e identidad", available at: http://miguelrojasmix.net/wp/?p=127 (accessed: April 16, 2014).
10. John Leddy Phelan, "Pan-Latinism, French Intervention in Mexico (1861–1867) and the genesis of the Idea of Latin America," in Juan Antonio Ortega y Medina (ed.) *Conciencia y Autenticidad Históricas. Escritos en homenaje a Edmundo O'Gorman,* (México D.F: UNAM, 1968).
11. Ori Preuss, *Bridging the Island: Brazilians' Views of Spanish America and Themselves, 1865–1912* (Madrid: Iberoamericana – Vervuert, 2011).
12. José Carlos Brandi Aleixo, "O Brasil e o Congresso Anfictiônico do Panamá," *Revista Brasileira de Política Internacional,* vol. 43, no. 2 (2000), 170–191.
13. José Bonifácio, Instruções de José Bonifácio de Andrada e Silva, ministro dos Negócios Estrangeiros, a Antônio Manuel Correa da Câmara, agente comercial e

político no Rio da Prata, Despacho y 30 maio 1822 - AHI 267/03/14, in *Cadernos do CHDD*, Fundação Alexandre de Gusmão, vol. 7, no. 2 (2008), 14.

14. João Alfredo dos Anjos, *José Bonifácio, Primeiro Chanceler do Brasil* (Brasilia: Fundação Alexandre de Gusmão, 2007), 83.

15. Ibid., 16.

16. Helio Jaguaribe, "Brasil y la América Latina," in Luciano Tomassini (ed.), *Las Relaciones Internacionales de la América Latina*, (México, DF: Fondo de Cultura Económica 1981), 431.

17. Tiago Coelho Fernandes, "Entre Bolívar e Monroe: o Brasil nas Relações Interamericanas," in Luis Suárez Salazar and Tania García Lorenzo (eds.), *Las Relaciones Interamericanas: Continuidades y Cambios* (Buenos Aires: CLACSO, 2008), 216.

18. Michel Gobat, "The Invention of Latin America: A Transnational History of Anti-Imperialism, Democracy, and Race," *The American Historical Review*, vol. 118, no. 5 (2013): 1371.

19. Ori Preuss, "Brazil into Latin America: The Demise of Slavery and Monarchy as Transnational Events," *Luso-Brazilian Review*, vol. 49, no. 1 (2012), 101.

20. Ori Preuss, "Discovering 'Os Ianques do Sul': Towards an Entangled Luso-Hispanic History of Latin America," *Revista Brasileira de Política Internacional*, vol. 56, no. 2 (2013), 161.

21. This was a treaty between Ministers of Foreign Affairs from Argentina, Brazil and Chile signed on May 25, 1915 to facilitate the peaceful solution of international controversies.

22. Manoel Bomfim, *América Latina: Males de Origem* (Rio de Janeiro: Centro Edelstein de Pesquisas Sociais, 2008).

23. Ori Preuss, *Bridging the Island: Brazilians' Views of Spanish America and Themselves, 1865–1912*, 117.

24. José Enrique Rodó, "Iberoamérica," in *Obras completas* José Enrique Rodó (Aguilar: Madrid, 1967).

25. Manuel Ugarte, *El Porvenir de América Española* (Valencia: Prometeo Sociedad Editorial, 1910), 17.

26. Manuel Ugarte, *La Nación Latinoamericana* (Caracas: Biblioteca Ayacucho, 1978).

27. Helio Jaguaribe, "Brasil y la América Latina," 445.

28. Luiz Alberto Moniz Bandeira, "Brasil, Estados Unidos y los Procesos de Integración Regional. La lógica de los pragmatismos," *Nueva Sociedad*, no. 186 (2003), 144.

29. Helio Jaguaribe, "Brasil y la América Latina," 435.

30. Luiz Alberto Moniz Bandeira, "América Latina o Sudamérica?" *Diario Clarin.com*, Buenos Aires, May 16, 2005, available at: http://edant.clarin.com/diario/2005/05/16/opinion/o-01901.htm, accessed: 11 November 2016.

31. Helio Jaguaribe, "Brasil y la América Latina," 435.

32. J. M. Hobson, "What's at Stake in 'Bringing Historical Sociology Back into International Relations'?" Transcending "Chronofetishism" and "Tempocentrism," in Stephen. Hobden and John M. Hobson (eds.) *Historical Sociology of International Relations*, (Cambridge: Cambridge University Press, 2002), 12.

33. Martin W. Lewis & Kären E. Wigen, *The Myth of Continents. A Critique of Metageography* (Berkeley: University of California Press, 1997), 187.

34. Iver B. Neumann, "A Region-Building Approach to Northern Europe," *Review of International Studies*, vol. 20, no. 1 (1994), 58.

35. Iver B. Neumann, "A Nordic and/or a Baltic Sea Region? The Discursive Structure of Region-Building" in Christian Wellmann (ed.), *Baltic Sea Region: Conflict or Cooperation?* (Kiel: Kiel Peace Research Series, 1992), 69–70.

36. Iver B. Neumann, "A Region-Building Approach to Northern Europe," 58.

37. Iver B. Neumann, *Uses of the Other: "The East" in European identity* (Manchester: Manchester University Press, 1999), 228.

38. Andrew Moravcsik, "Bringing Constructivist Integration Theory of EU out of the Clouds: Has it Landed Yet?," *European Union Politics*, vol. 2, no. 2. (2001), 229.

39. Ibid., 229.

40. Ori Preuss. *Bridging the Island: Brazilians' Views of Spanish America and Themselves, 1865–1912*, 164.

41. Eduardo Azcuy Ameghino and Carlos Maria Birocco, "Las Colonias del Río de la Plata y Brasil: Geopolítica, Poder, Economía y Sociedad (Siglos VIII y XVIII)," in Mario Rapoport and Amado L. Cervo (eds.), *El Cono Sur: Una Historia Común*, (Buenos Aires: Fondo de Cultura Económica de Argentina, S.A., 2001), 11–70.

42. De Carvalho, Delgado, *Historia Diplomática do Brasil* (São Paulo: Companhia Editora Nacional, 1959), 54.

43. José Carlos Brandi Aleixo, "O Brasil e o Congresso Anfictiônico do Panamá," 170–191.

44. The United Nations Commission for Latin America (ECLA)—the Spanish acronym is CEPAL—was created in February 1948. The scope of the Commission's work was decades later broadened to include the countries of the Caribbean. As a result, the Economic Council changed in 1984 the name to the the United Nations Economic Commission for Latin America and the Caribbean (ECLAC). Yet, the Spanish acronym, CEPAL, was not modified. We use in this book the Spanish acronym.

Chapter 1

A Prologue of Integration

The Pan-Hispanic Dream

One of the strongest pillars behind arguments sustaining the "path of separation" is the historical dimension concerning a constant "rivalry" between Brazil and its Spanish-speaking neighbors. Particularly relevant is the case of Argentina, which took over the role of Spain in relation to Portugal. As this argument goes, the rivalry is deeply rooted in pre-colonial times, even going back all the way to the very formation of the modern Iberian states. In this pre-colonial period, the Portuguese nation struggled for autonomy *vis-à-vis* its bigger, and in many ways stronger, Iberian Castilian neighbors. A problem, however, with the "path of separation" perspective, is generally the bias in focusing on "separation" while overlooking, completely ignoring, or simply failing to explain the initiatives that occur along the "path of integration."

If one studies the history of the formation of the modern Iberian states, there is no doubt about the validity of arguments concerning the "path of separation"; the creation of the Portuguese kingdom is in itself proof of that. However, the main point addressed in this chapter is that the "path of integration" has roots in this same period. Before delving into this, it is important to first make clear that the origins of state making in the Iberian Peninsula have nothing to do with the modern nation-states that we currently know. It was fundamentally related to Greek, Phoenician and Carthaginian cities. When searching for a notion of common Iberian statehood, one must look to the unification of the peninsula under a long period of Roman rule and civilization. After considerable struggle, the Romans finally conquered central Portugal in 140 BC, which was habited by a people of Celtic origin called the Lusitani[1], which later lent its name to the Luso (Portuguese) culture. Much of what is known about this people did, however, came from their Roman conquerors through the poet Rufus Festus Avienus or via Strabo's *Geography*.[2] Through the organization of the Roman Empire, this ethnic group was Romanized and forged a common identity through clans, which were grouped around ethnic confederations called *populous* or *gens*.[3] Nevertheless, this was a long process since the Lusitanians resisted domination, and even supported the Carthaginian invasion of Spain in 218 and 201 BC.

It was not until 61–44 BC that Hispania was successfully occupied, joining what the Romans called Hispania Ulterior and Hispania Citerior. This common Roman past is not irrelevant. As Anthony Rendell Disney explains, for around 450 years, a complex and sustained process of Romanization took place, where the Iberian peoples adopted Roman civilization and many colonists settled across the Iberian Peninsula. Another element of Iberian convergence, according to Disney, was the acceptance of a common official Roman religion that changed into "Christianity through the conversion of Emperor Constantine in AD 312 and the declaration of Nicene Christianity (Catholicism) by Emperor Theodosius I, in AD 392."[4]

The end of Roman dominance in the Iberian Peninsula did not appear to be driven by a major internal upheaval or general discontent with Roman authorities. It could be regarded as a traumatic period, followed by plague, famine and invaders, such as the Visigoths. Nevertheless, even if Rome by early 460 AD appeared to have lost control over its Iberian territories, this did not occur in the cultural realm. "Latinity" remained strong in language, religion, the legal code and social organization, leading to a form of national re-creation through an accelerating trend toward what Disney calls, Hispano-Romanization.[5] The idea of Portugal as a political entity did, however, not have any direct link to the Roman administration. There was a Province of Lusitania, but that occupied only a part of the current Portuguese territory, and there was no administrative unit corresponding to Portugal during the Muslim domination, where Iberia was called *al-Andalus*.

Besides centuries of stability and relative peace, the new Muslim state gave something else very important to the Christian population: a common enemy. In the year 722, around 300 years after the disintegration of the Roman (Christian) Empire, a common Christian force finally won a small victory against the Muslims in a place called Covadonga. This event was part of a long and sustained process of liberation that, in the case of Portugal, lasted until 1249. It is from this period the word Portugal originated.

The Catholic Church was fundamental to the consolidation process, and the Portuguese kings of the twelfth and thirteenth centuries accorded high priority to restoring the church in re-conquered territory. As Disney holds, new settlers were seldom prepared to put down roots without a visible church presence.[6] In spite of that, the process of national consolidation took time and was not peaceful, partly because of the continuous re-conquest against the Moors, but also due to conflicts among the different Christian nations. The Lusitanians were rivals of the Castilians, who strengthened their position in a union with the Kingdom of Leon, consolidated in 1230, and the later union with the Kingdom of Aragon in 1479. This was geopolitically difficult for Portugal since it was now territorially surrounded in the Iberian Peninsula, something that probably encouraged a further move toward the west, where the sea was the only alternative. Yet the situation on the mainland was difficult, something described quite dramatically by the Brazilian historian João Pandiá Calógeras, according to whom: "during four centuries, from XII to XVI, Castile and Leon where, for Portugal, synonymous with wars without truce, ferocity, insidiousness, persecutions, and grief."[7]

Such a negative view is not without reason. There were several wars and mutual invasions between 1348 and 1349, where Lisbon itself was briefly occupied by Castilian troops. A decisive moment took place on August 1385, when the army of King João of Avis, proclaimed João I (1385–1433), confronted a Castilian invasion on a ridge called Aljubarrota. The result was a staunch Portuguese victory. If not decisive enough to end the conflicts among neighbors, it was a milestone in the constitution of Portugal as nation-state, confirming the rule of João I and the house of Avis. One of the factors behind Portuguese success in this battle was the introduction of new military technology through the crossbow and a contingent of soldiers and archers recruited in England. This linkage to England was an element that would mark Portugal's foreign policy into the future. Once proclaimed as king, João rapidly sought an alliance with England, of which the outcome was the Treaty of Windsor, signed in May 1386, where each king agreed to grant reciprocal military assistance and trading rights to their respective citizens. This treaty laid the ground for a long-lasting Anglo-Portuguese alliance, which would have an important effect in Iberian and American affairs.

Still, despite intra-Iberian conflicts, there were also strong and relevant links of cooperation and effort to reach a peaceful coexistence. One example was a Treaty of Friendship between Alfonso IV of Portugal (1325–1357) and Alfonso XI of Castile in 1327. Alfonso himself aided Castilians and participated personally in the great victory of the Christian forces against the Moors at Rio Salado in 1340.[8] Thus we would like to raise a caveat concerning easy answers in relation to the dividing lines between friends and foes during this period, which was characterized by a highly complex geopolitical situation. There were many different actors involved, cutting across shifting alliances within unclear political and territorial units. Besides Portugal and Castile, we also have France, León, Aragon, Catalonia, Galicia, al-Ándalus and different Italian states. Indeed, by the early 1380s, the Genovese had "become the most important financiers in the Iberian region."[9]

Moreover, despite conflicts, every Portuguese king from Sancho I to Alfonso IV chose his partner from either the royal house of Castile or that of Aragon, while Castilian kings often choose their brides among Portuguese princesses. Thus, as Disney points out, the possibility of dynastic unification "was always lurking." Unionist ideas went beyond marriage arrangements and dynastic ideals. Even if a separate Portuguese identity was steadily growing in the 14th century, there were parts of the elite that continued to think in terms of a Pan-Hispanic world. An explanation for this, according to Disney, is that the physical frontiers with Castile remained permeable and was transcended by ecclesiastical jurisdictions.[10] Even at the battle of Aljubarrota, there were a large number of Portuguese nobles on the side of Castile.[11]

In line with the spirit of King Alfonso, João I understood that a peace with Castile was necessary, in his case due to the focus on overseas expansion, starting with the invasion of Moroccan territory in 1415. Even if there were sometimes intentions to avoid dynastic entanglements there was a growing need to reach an agreement with Castile. A step into that direction was the Treaty of Alcaçovas in 1479. This meant an end of efforts to unite Portugal and Castile by force, and a recognition of new overseas possessions and territorial domains in the Iberian Peninsula.

The dynastic links with Castile—now united with Aragon to form Spain—grew steadily closer under the government of Manuel I of Portugal (1495–1521). His reign started with the most important and long-lasting Luso-Spanish agreement for peaceful coexistence after Alcaçovas. After the arrival of the Spaniards to America, Pope Alexander VI's edict, *inter caetera divinae*, divided the world into two separate spheres, one for Spain and one for Portugal. This was confirmed in the famous Treaty of Tordesillas (1494), in what Carl Schmitt called the "first global lines" of history; where the two "Catholic powers agreed that all newly discovered territories west of the line would belong to Spain and those east of the line to Portugal." This line was called a *partition del mar océano*, and was sanctioned by Pope Julius II.[12] Within the framework of a new Iberian world order in coexistence with Spain, Portugal now had the door open for the expansion and consolidation of its overseas empire. In 1549, a royal colony was formally established in Brazil, which was followed by the rapid growth of a Brazilian plantation industry. This created a demand for African slaves, further stimulating the continuous expansion of the Portuguese Atlantic trade.

PORTUGUESE AMERICAN EXPANSION

After the initial "discovery" of Brazil in 1500, a fleet left Lisbon for that territory in 1502 and brought back the following year a cargo with Brazilwood and Indian slaves. The issue here was, however, not of temporal extracting of resources. The first factory (*feitoria*) was created in 1504, and the crown had a firm intention to take direct control of Brazilian trade, firstly through the establishment of strategic points along the coast: in Pernambuco, Bahia, Porto Seguro, Cabo Frio and São Vicente.[13] By the end of the 1520s, sugar cane had been established in Pernambuco and this would rapidly expand to become one of the major economic driving forces of the Atlantic economy between the sixteenth and seventieth centuries.[14]

During the first period of establishment, the French represented a fundamental challenge to Portugal's exclusive rights to Brazil since they, as the Dutch, did not recognize the papal bulls and the Spanish-Portuguese Treaty of Tordesillas. By 1530, King João III (1521–1557) and his advisers concluded that some kind of permanent colony would have to be planted in Brazil. To counter French attacks, the Portuguese decided to move the line of defense from the sea to the land. Thus, "instead of attempting to keep the French ships from reaching the Brazilian coast, the Portuguese would instead establish several settlements to prevent the Indian population from direct trading with the French."[15] Portugal could now claim "effective possession" of Brazil and extended its explorations toward the mouths of the Amazon and River Plate rivers. The plans of permanent settlement included the creation of new administrative units through the establishment of captaincies. This paved the way for the royal bureaucracy, which stepped in to administer the new domains. In 1549, the new general governor (*governador-geral*) departed from Lisbon to found the new captaincy of Bahía, from which the crown attempted to control the process of colonization.[16] Along with the governor was a group of Jesuits representing Ignatius of Loyola's Society of Jesus that, according to Pandiá Calógeras, "would prove its value, as a backbone of the establishment of Portuguese civilization in American soil."[17]

The other side of the *conquista* was the establishment of the *bandeiras*, which also played a crucial role in the *entradas* into the interior, as organized slaving expeditions.[18] While the Jesuits dealt with the more peaceful and spiritual part, the *bandeiras* organized the defense, captured slaves, fought against indigenous people and made geographic and mineral explorations.[19] However, the resources extracted from Brazil were not yet of great value, at least not compared to the great mining assets produced by the Spanish American colonies. Hence, despite a successful territorial establishment and defense against foreign powers, Portugal increasingly moved under the economic influence of Spain. The main catalyst for this was Spanish American silver, which flowed into Portugal at a rapidly growing rate from the middle of the sixteenth century. This silver was badly needed by Portugal to pay for wheat imports and to maintain its trade with India and China, where there was a high demand of this metal. According to Disney, even though Portuguese merchants managed to obtain Japanese silver through Japan, the main source of supply was Spanish America, where a reciprocal market developed in Peru and Mexico for Portuguese-procured African slaves. Even in Macau, the Portuguese accessed Mexican silver by linking indirectly into the trans-Pacific through Manila. In North Africa, the Portuguese fortresses were also heavily dependent on Andalusia for supplies.[20] In short, the Portuguese and Spanish economic systems were becoming increasingly interdependent.

This convergence also appeared in a political and institutional dimension. When King Henrique finally accepted that he was not going to marry and have his own heir in 1579, there were four possible successors to the Portuguese throne. One of them was Felipe II of Spain, who was the son of Manuel's oldest daughter. As said above, the dream of a united Hispania under a single monarch, as in Roman and later Visigoth times, was still attractive to many Portuguese. In the sixteenth century, with the recent union of crowns between Castile and Aragon, the emergence of a united France and the trend toward unity in the British Isles, it seemed an attractive geopolitical move to avoid a vulnerable position. The result of this was the Iberian Union in 1580, when Felipe II (1554–1558) became the king of Spain, Portugal, Naples and Sicily, and the Seventeen Provinces of the Netherlands. It was, without a doubt, the most important empire that the world had ever seen, where the sun never set.

The union implied that Portugal would retain its traditional liberties, customs and uses; that all offices would remain under the Portuguese crown; that trade and navigation with and within the empire were to be reserved exclusively for the Portuguese; that Portuguese would remain the official language; and that the kingdom would keep its own coinage. At least in appearance, Portugal would retain its autonomy within the frame of a "dual monarchy" where Felipe II of Spain also became Felipe I of Portugal. Among the expected benefits for Portugal, there was an abolition of customs barriers on the frontier with Castile, as well as a provision in the form of a cash injection of Castilian silver to reanimate Portuguese trade. There were also hopes of better military protection for overseas territories.[21] In sum, the dream of a Hispanic union appeared to have finally become true, leading to the much more ambitious dream of a Catholic global empire. This was indeed the moment of splendor of Spanish power. As Disney explains, there was in Portugal a tendency to regard all things of the Spanish court as somehow exemplary. This included the Spanish language that, according to Disney, appealed strongly to the Portuguese elite: "most Portuguese writers of the era, including Camões himself, spoke fluent Castilian and frequently chose to write in that language."[22] Cooperation and association appeared to be the key to consolidate the Iberian state and a global position.

THE IBERIAN UNION

The focus here is on the effect of the Iberian Union in American territory. Since this was at a rather early stage in the process of colonization, this common Iberian form of statehood had effects with implications for future processes of state formation. It is, however, important to note that when the union was formed the Portuguese were already an essential part of the River Plate region. The first European expedition to reach this place was a Spanish expedition led by the Portuguese explorer Juan Díaz de Solís in 1516. After two failed attempts to settle in what later became the city of Buenos Aires, there was a third and successful attempt that took place the same year as the creation of the Iberian Union, that is, in 1580. Buenos Aires could therefore be regarded as part of a common Luso-Spanish projection toward the River Plate basin. It is then not a coincidence that the Portuguese were influential in this region, assisting in issues that would also benefit the Spanish settlements, such as introducing (from Paraguay) what was to become one of the great sources of wealth, namely cattle.[23]

There was then, as Azcuy Amegino and Birocco point out, a vast network of intertwined interests and identities which acted as unifying elements beyond state boundaries.[24] This can be extended to language, culture and a sense of belonging that was not necessarily divided by the boundaries of the empires. There were, for example, numerous indigenous nations that did not identify with either of them. Moreover, among those who had already accepted living within the framework of European civilization, there could be a stronger attachment to Catholic orders, such as the Jesuits. During the Iberian Union, the Jesuits strengthened their establishment and influence through their missions, benefiting greatly from the collaboration among its members in different parts of the continent. The leaders of the Peruvian Jesuit province, for example, begged the Brazilian Jesuits to send missionaries to the River Plate region since it was easier "to reach Paraguay and Buenos Aires from Brazil than from Peru."[25] The case of the missions is of great importance due to the economic influence they had on trade in goods such as yerba mate, cotton, tobacco and handicraft products. Furthermore, it was also important for framing a common form of Catholic identity that went beyond being Spanish or Portuguese.

There was a real attempt in the Iberian Union to abolish former boundaries within the American continent. Spanish America was now open to Portuguese trade, even though Brazil remained a Portuguese monopoly market. This meant new possibilities for Portuguese businessmen, which gained easier access to Spanish American silver and the Spanish trans-Pacific trade route between Manila and Acapulco. There was also a stimulus for increased migration across former borders. That happened within the Iberian Peninsula as well as in America. In the case of the former, around 25 percent of the population of Seville consisted of Portuguese, and the so-called new Christians (converted Jews) were permitted to settle anywhere in Castile as well as to participate in official trade between Seville and America.[26] In the case of America, there were some 6000 Portuguese in Peru, while the Portuguese comprised 7 percent of the population of Mexico and up to 40 percent in Buenos Aires (in 1640).[27] According to Darcy Ribeiro, much of the colonization of current Argentina, as well the forces leading to independence, were led by around 800 thousand *mamelucos*.[28] There were also a large number of Spaniards living in São Paulo and about two-thirds of the habitants of Bahia in 1641 were Spanish and Neapolitan.[29] In the case of São Paulo, the Spanish-speaking population was so important that there even was an influential Spanish party, called the *Camargos*.[30]

A further dimension of the benefits of the Iberian Union was the, in some aspects, relatively efficient standards of the Spanish administration that left a legacy in terms of legislation. King Felipe II of Spain ordered the formidable task of codifying the law, which resulted in the *Ordenações Filipinas* of 1603, a legal code that served as the foundation of the Portuguese statute of law well into the nineteenth century.[31]

Yet, beyond all this, what is probably the most important effect of the Iberian Union for the establishment of what later became Brazil is how it opened a door for further Portuguese territorial expansion with Spanish assistance. This was directed to the north during the 1580s, from Pernambuco into Paraíba, at the expense of the French and the Indigenous nations, and later expanded into Ceará. Along this line of expansion, in 1616 the Portuguese founded *Forte do Presépio*, which would later become the city of Belem do Pará. This city was the key to further expansion into the Amazon, a region that until then had been within the Spanish sphere of interest.[32] In 1621, a separate *Estado do Maranhão* was formed from the recently established crown captaincies of Ceará, Maranhão and Pará.[33] The expansion was continued during the 1620s, when Felipe IV of Spain (Felipe III of Portugal) authorized further exploration of the Amazon River. Scholars are, however, somewhat puzzled about the Spanish passivity toward this Portuguese expansion. Under the banner of "unification," and in practice suspending the Treaty of Tordesillas, the new Iberian government probably sought to promote Portuguese sympathies toward the empire.

Nevertheless, what is clear, as recognized by Brazilian historians such as Pandía Calógeras, is that the opening of borders provided great opportunities for the Portuguese. In fact, it is pointed out as the very start of the Brazilian *drang nach westen*[34]—an idea of great geopolitical significance concerning the formation of the current Brazilian nation-state. However, not everything was a bed of roses. The union also implied new kinds of problems, such as bringing Portugal into a global power conflict with other European powers, which entailed a break with former allies such as the English. According to Disney, these nations now saw Portuguese shipping and possessions as legitimate targets, and with good reason since Lisbon was, for example, a base for Felipe I's "invincible" Armada in 1588, to which Portugal contributed twelve warships and thousands of men. The British, on their side, responded by landing an expeditionary force near Lisbon and moved aggressively into the Asian market.[35] Another major threat came from the Dutch East India Company, which by 1640 had decisively replaced the Portuguese *Estado da India* as the principal European force east of the Cape of Good Hope.

In response to the challenge from hostile powers, the Habsburg crown imposed a series of embargos on trade, something that affected Portugal since they were a major overseas customer. One of the most formidable threats for the Portuguese was, however, the arrival of the Dutch West India Company (*West-Indische Compagnie*, WIC) on American soil by. In its strive for control over sugar production, the WICs captured the Portuguese captaincy of Bahia in 1624. Although they later lost it, the Dutch did not give up and successfully seized Pernambuco in 1630, which remained in Dutch hands for the rest of the Portuguese Habsburg era. At the same time, Portugal was losing its Asian Empire, which meant a heavy blow to the Portuguese economy and serious disruptions of their control of sugar imports into Europe.

After the death of Felipe III of Spain in 1621, he was succeeded by his son Felipe IV (Felipe III of Portugal), but the administration of government was largely in the hands of the Count-Duke of Olivares. With steadfast rule, Olivares drew up reform proposals geared toward a more centralized structure and recommended a process of gradual integration. Much of this was related to the military dimension due to the growing conflicts and challenges that the Hapsburgs were facing in Europe and elsewhere. Olivares called this a "union of arms," "which meant creating a single army to serve the whole monarchy, to which all parts of the empire would contribute."[36] Yet, for the Portuguese, the reality was that the Hapsburg monarchy showed a lack of capacity to protect their overseas interests. By the 1630s the French had begun to seek approximation to the Portuguese in order to undermine their Spanish enemy. At the same time, Olivares was suffering disastrous military defeats as well as a revolt in Catalonia. Thus, supported by other powers, there was a kind of *coup d'État* in Portugal in 1640 that restored the House of Bragança at the throne, with João IV as the new monarch.

The political separation from the Habsburg monarchy meant that Portugal lost its formal status as part of the Spanish economic bloc and regained its capacity to develop an independent trade policy. One of the first steps of the Bragança monarch was to return to a renewed alliance with the British through a series of Anglo-Portuguese agreements signed in 1642, 1654 and

1662. Such treaties guaranteed Portugal English protection, opened Lisbon to the Cromwellian navy for repairs and replenishment, and conceded wide privileges to English merchants in the Portuguese colonial trade. This treaty also assured Portugal's maritime communications, something that was crucial in the ongoing conflict with the Dutch. It probably also contributed to the great success for the Portuguese in the war against the Dutch, who faced serious defeats in Pernambuco and were finally forced to sign a peace treaty recognizing Portuguese sovereignty over Brazilian soil.[37] However, the alliance with the British could be regarded as what Pandía Calógeras has called an "unequilibrated union," where the weakest country received a condescending protection from the more powerful one.[38] Already by 1670, English exports to Portugal, primarily in the form of textiles, were worth more than twice the Portuguese exports to England.[39] This negative trade pattern was later on consolidated through the Methuen Treaty signed in 1703.[40] From this moment forward, almost all Portuguese merchandise exported from Portugal was carried on English ships.[41]

After the Iberian split, the Hapsburg monarchy continued a sustained period of decline resulting in a new defeat in the later War of the Spanish Succession (1701–1714). During this period, the Portuguese, supported by their British allies, conducted a renewed expansionary wave toward the South, causing new conflicts with the Spaniards. A major target for the *bandeiras* new direction was the River Plate basin. It was regarded as strategically important, not only as an outlet for trade goods from inland South American territories, but particularly for control of the access to the silver flow from Peru and Alto Peru (current Bolivia). The Portuguese knew very well that a control of the River Plate implied access to a back door to the Peruvian mines.[42] Nevertheless, the Spaniards were also aware of that and were prepared to offer a strong resistance.

One of the nodes for this renewed conflict was the foundation, by the Portuguese, of Colonia del Sacramento in 1668, on the eastern shore of the River Plate River, with Buenos on the opposite side. There is no place here to deepen the details about this conflict, which falls, without doubt, within a period where the path of separation is predominant. It should be sufficient to say that, due to this conflict, there was an overall expansion toward this region, with the creation of new provinces and cities that would become of great importance in the future. For example, the foundation of the city of Montevideo by the Spaniards in 1724, and the foundation of Rio Grande in 1725 by the Portuguese, also created the Captaincies of Rio Grande and Santa Catarina.[43] Despite the conflict, there was still intense cultural, commercial and religious contact among the inhabitants of this region, regardless of their side of the border. There were also common issues among the states; one was, for example, their shared interest and cooperation in the slave trade, and another was the war against the Jesuits, but there were also more important things.

TREATY OF MADRID

There was an increasing view, in Portugal as well as in Spain, on the problems with the continuous conflict and wars. One was related with the heavy economic burden. For the Portuguese this was particularly true regarding the maintenance of Colonia del Sacramento, which was far away from their lines of supply. Another was the awareness of the weak economic position of each Iberian state, and their increasingly subordinate position in relation to an emerging British economic and military power. One of the promoters of economic reform in Portugal was Dom Luís de Meneses, third Count of Ericeira. During the late 17th century, he attempted to introduce a kind of import substitution system to favor the Portuguese textile industry, silk production, and develop a more sophisticated metal industry.[44] Some of his ideas and policies were later continued by a prominent member of the Portuguese government, the Secretary of State of Internal Affairs of the Kingdom, Sebastião José de Carvalho e Melo, the Marquis of Pombal (1699–1782). Suspicious about the Spanish, he was also aware of the imperial ambitions of the British Empire, with its desire to control the enormous resources of Brazil.[45] Despite a period of Bonanza facilitated by the discovery of gold in Minas Gerais, by the early eighteenth century, Portugal's constant wars and economic backwardness were causing an increasing number of economic problems for state finances.

This motivated a growing consciousness around the need to find a permanent settlement with the Spaniards, which once again opened up the search for peaceful coexistence. A central idea for this was a treaty that would establish, once and for all, the territorial boundaries. One impediment, which was also a constant source of renewed conflict, was the lack of clarity concerning these borders; another was the outdated Treaty of Tordesillas which was neither precise in geographic terms nor took into account demographic realities and changes. The great name behind the establishment of such a treaty was the Brazilian-born Alexandre de Gusmão, who had a pivotal role as adviser to the government in the process behind what later became the Treaty of Madrid in 1750.

Alexandre de Gusmão personally knew the Count of Ericea, who advocated a solution to the problem concerning Colonia del Sacramento. Both knew very well that the Spaniards would never cease to reclaim control over the River Plate, for the geopolitical reasons outlined earlier, but also because the Portuguese brought with them their British allies. At least for the Spaniards, this might have been perceived as an even greater threat.[46] The solution was to search for an equilibrium of powers through mutual recognition. What became the key behind the Treaty of Madrid was the exchange of Colonia and the monopoly of navigation at the River Plate for equivalent territory elsewhere.

One of the interesting issues surrounding this treaty was the important forms of collaboration developed by both states in, for example, the common expeditions of technical experts, fundamentally astronomers and geographers. There were several expeditions along the rivers Ibiquy, Paraná and Jauru.[47] Later on, in 1784, near a frontier city named Chuy, a group of 198 Portuguese experts (*technicos*) joined around 240 Spaniards to work with the recognition of territory and border areas. This is not an irrelevant matter, since it shows the level of cooperation reached by both crowns, as well as the seriousness in which geographical matters and the knowledge about the continuous process of colonization was conducted. This attachment to geographical technique, as well as an awareness of territorial matters, was to become a central characteristic and concern for chancellors and Brazilian diplomacy into the future. Along the spirit of the Treaty of Madrid and the ideas of Alexandre de Gusmão, this went hand in hand with the concern for peaceful coexistence with the Spanish-speaking neighbors. Moreover, this was not only the position of de Gusmão but also, perhaps fundamentally, that of the Portuguese monarchs themselves.

The policies concerning intermarriage with Hapsburg monarchs continued despite the, by the year 1700, Spanish dynastic transition toward the Bourbon family. In this case, the royal marriages approximated Portugal toward the so-called Family Pact in 1733 between the Spanish and French royal houses. As examples of these marriages we have the case of Dom João V (1689–1750) marrying the Hapsburg, Maria Anna of Austria, and the marriage of José I (1714–1777) with the daughter of Felipe V of Spain, one of the most relevant for our analysis. There was also the marriage of Dom João VI (1767–1826) with Doña Carlota Joaquina of Spain (1775–1830), who was the eldest daughter and surviving child of King Carlos IV of Spain.

The Treaty of Madrid, signed six months before Pombal became secretary of state for foreign affairs and war, was, however, not ratified. Consequently, the conflicts around Luso-Spanish border areas continued, particularly in relation to Colonia del Sacramento and the territory around what later became the province of the Banda Oriental (which later developed into what today is the Oriental Republic of Uruguay). This also included a separate conflict with the Jesuits, which lead to their expulsion from American territory, in this case amidst a close Luso-Spanish cooperation.[48] The delay in ratification did not imply, however, an end in the search of cooperation, which was probably stimulated by the new framework of the Family Pact. A final breakthrough finally came with the Luso-Spanish Treaty of San Ildefonso (1777) and El

Pardo (1778). These resolved a number of territorial disputes, proclaiming a "permanent peace" between both countries. The Treaty of El Pardo also established the principle of *uti possidetis* and regulated the settlement of fortifications and borders by trying to establish guaranties for a "perpetual harmony." Moreover, the Treaty of Santo-Ildefonso also contained principles related to a perpetual and indissoluble alliance and trade.[49] Thus, all these royal marriages should be regarded as part of a process of increasing cooperation, where Portugal intended to settle things with Spain as well as mark a distance to Great Britain. One example of that was recognizing, six months before Britain, the independence of the United States.[50]

Not everybody was favorable toward this on the Portuguese side, and there were doubts about leaving the Portuguese positions at the shores of the River Plate. On the other hand, it secured the control of all territories that had been occupied by the Portuguese, far beyond the Tordesillas line and toward the Amazonas Basin, as well as toward the south in Rio Grande and the Lagoa Mirim. The retirement of the Portuguese from the River Plate region was, however, just a temporary issue. As we will see in the next section, they would return, but with local support. In a way, it could be argued that they did so without breaking the "spirit" of the Santo-Ildefonso treaty. By this time, the Portuguese, and who could already be identified at this time as Brazilians,[51] had established their territorial scope, where the "continental" notion became part of the worldview of both government and settlers. Perhaps a sign of this was that they called the new captaincy of Rio Grande do Sul, *Continente do Rio Grande*.[52]

By the early years of the 19th century, the political situation was radically changing in the European arena. Napoleon Bonaparte's French empire was creating a European continental system that took over Spain, and in 1808, Portugal. There was not much the Portuguese could do to oppose, since they lacked in both military and economic resources. By that time, Brazil was Portugal's only significant overseas outlet for industrial goods and, as such, it was of key importance for its progress toward industrialization.[53] After the devastating earthquake of 1755, Pombal had already evaluated the transfer of government to Rio de Janeiro. That finally took place in 1808, when the royal family and the rest of the government escaped to Rio de Janeiro, changing forever the fate of that colony and perhaps also the rest of South America.

A SOUTH AMERICAN REALM

By the time the Portuguese court moved to Rio de Janeiro, there had already been revolutionary upheavals of protest against the imperial government, and in some cases a search for independence. Nevertheless, even if making Brazil the seat of the central government was an unexpected turn, strengthening the monarchic position, it would prove impossible to restore the *status quo ante*.[54] The transfer to Rio had also major economic effects, for example, the "ending of the 300-year-old monopoly of colonial trade and the elimination of Lisbon as an *entrepôt* for Brazilian imports and exports."[55] The British, who had escorted the journey of the Portuguese court to Brazil with their navy, expected a price to be paid for British protection, that is, that the Portuguese would open Brazilian ports for British trade. King João VI did not disappoint them: "he revoked all the decrees prohibiting manufacturing, especially textile manufacturing, in the colony, exempted industrial raw materials from import duties, encouraged the invention or introduction of new machinery and offered direct subsidies to the cotton, wool, silk and iron industries."[56] Despite opposition from Portuguese interests in Rio and Lisbon, the direction was now settled. Rio de Janeiro was going to become a main destiny for British manufacturers and their *entrepôt* for further exports and trade expansion in the rest of South America. As outlined by Sergio Buarque de Holanda, British industry needed new markets for their goods and further expansion in order to follow its path from being European to becoming universal. In fact, all sorts of manufactured goods were exported to Brazil; it is said that even British ice skates reached the Brazilian market.[57]

New trade rules were established in the British-Portuguese Treaty of Navigation and Commerce of 1810, also known as the Strangford Treaty, which was also followed by a separate Treaty of Alliance and Friendship. The commercial treaty fixed a maximum tariff of 15 percent ad valorem on British goods imported into Brazil. This was, however, without British reciprocity in lowering its virtually prohibitive duties on Brazilian sugar or coffee entering the British market. A consequence of the Strangford Treaty was then, as explained by Leslie Bethell, cheap British imports becoming even cheaper and undermining the efforts being made after 1808 to promote the establishment of Brazilian industries. During this period, Portuguese trade with Brazil collapsed, with a downturn of some 30 percent of its 1800–4 level. The only trade to Brazil still dominated by the Portuguese was the trade in slaves from Portuguese Africa.[58]

One of the forms in which the Portuguese Empire dealt with the new situation was to reinvent its political structure, taking into account the new reality and confronting independence claims in Brazil. The result was the creation of the pluricontinental monarchy, the United Kingdom of Portugal and Brazil in 1808. In the Spanish colonies, the process took a very different path, where independence movements were gaining the upper hand after the upheavals of 1810. Nevertheless, not all these movements, nor many of its leaders, were republicans, at least in the beginning. That was, for example, the case of one of the earliest independence leaders, the Venezuelan Francisco de Miranda.

He was a great admirer of the British system and had plans for a South American government ruled by an Inca monarch.[59] This idea was later on also supported by Manuel Belgrano, one of the most influential members of the Buenos Aires Junta created in 1810. The idea, and the monarchic system as an institution, was also supported by one of the most important personalities of Latin American independence, the Argentinean José de San Martin.[60] At the north of the Iberian American limits, Mexico also entered the monarchic, imperial path during the brief rule of Augustin de Iturbide (1822–1823).

Concerning Brazil's relation to its neighbors, the French occupation of the Iberian Peninsula created a difficult situation in the River Plate region. With Spain without government and Napoleon claiming sovereignty of its American territory, there was a local reaction. Around 1810, local Juntas were created in the name of the deposed king Fernando VII (1784–1833) in the main Spanish American cities, each one intending to establish themselves as the head of the Spanish administrative units, Vice Royalties or Captaincies. In many of these there were also independency-oriented aspirations, and there would soon be an open break with Spain, leading to the, in many cases, prolonged process of independence wars and, for most, the even longer process of forming new nation-states. The centralizing and oligarchic-dominated Buenos Aires Junta attempted to liberate the rest of the Vice Royalty from Spanish control and take its place as the leading entity. However, Paraguay opposed this by creating its own independent state, while a Spanish army still had the control of Montevideo and parts of the Banda Oriental.

One of the main commanders of the Junta's liberation army in the Banda Oriental was José Gervasio Artigas (1764–1850). He successfully defeated the Spaniards, as well as united several provinces of the former Viceroyalty in support of a federalist, republican and progressive political and economic project. This included the abolition of slavery, agrarian reform with rights for indigenous peoples, the defense of local manufacturers and less concentration of power in Buenos Aires. This, and the growing popular support for Artigas, caused great fears, both in Buenos Aires and Rio de Janeiro.

In opposition to the perceived "anarchy" from leaders such as Artigas, and the overall fragmentation of the new states in the making, there was a search for conservative alternatives. One of these was the "Carlotist" movement, where leading personalities from Argentina and Brazil promoted the creation of a South American kingdom under the rule of Carlota Joaquina, the sister of King Fernando VII of Spain and wife of King Dom João VI of Portugal (1816–1826).[61]

What is the relevance of our study on this confusing period concerning the close alliances with the Spanish-speaking neighbors that were made by the Portuguese royal family and later continued by the independent Brazilian Empire? Perhaps the most relevant aspect concerned the Buenos Aires Junta, where many of its leading members were strong adherents of the idea of an independent South American monarchy under the rule of Princess Carlota Joaquina. One of the main reasons for this alternative was to fill the power vacuum left by the Iberian crisis and quell the oligarchic fears of unleashing popular forces under an inclusive and democratizing republican agenda. There was, however, also a relevant geopolitical reason that was perhaps clearer from a Brazilian perspective. Similarly, to what was expressed in the *Unión Ibérica*, the Pan-Hispanic dreams and the spirit behind the Treaties of Madrid and Santo-Ildefonso, there was a need to counterbalance the weakening of the state in its confrontation with rising powers, such as the British Empire or France, which had had such a devastating effect on the Iberian states. Moreover, with the European war, as well as the prior conflicts associated with the independence of the British North American colonies, the Spanish and Portuguese American regions took more interest in each other and the possibilities for trade. One such area was the slave trade and its ramifications for the export of food.[62]

As said before, the settlement of a European royal family shocked the political environment of the Ibero-American regions, particularly in the case of South America. It is interesting to observe here how there were, from the very start, voices that upheld Dom João as the "emperor for whole South America"[63]—a view that was probably also promoted by the Portuguese themselves.

One of the first measures of the king after his arrival was to make an official approximation to Buenos Aires by sending a representative with a direct message offering Portuguese protection and support against French threats as well as an intermediation with his British allies. Both these countries had attacked Buenos Aires and Montevideo between 1806 and 1807. In this case, as argued by João Paulo G. Pimenta and Adriana Salay Leme, one of the aims of the Portuguese was to avoid being drawn into a conflict between its closest neighbors and their closest allies, the British.[64]

Another form of reaching out to the Spanish subjects was the manifest issued in 1808 by Carlota Joaquina, where she declared herself a defender of monarchic values and pretended to be recognized as the legitimate successor of the Spanish king by the Spanish authorities in Europe, America and the Philippines. She here made a pledge for the need to maintain the unity of the Spanish Empire, however, in a way that presented herself as a legitimate alternative and a natural link between both houses.[65] The Princess' manifest was distributed by the Spanish authorities in the colonies and was an official document from the Portuguese court. In this sense, it could have been regarded as supported by the king. This is an important point made by G. Pimenta and Salay Leme, although it is still difficult to assess to what extent the movement led by the Princess was supported by the Portuguese monarch.[66]

With the turn of events in Buenos Aires after 1810, the new rulers were divided into two main currents; a liberal one, led by Mariano Moreno, and a more conservative one, under the leadership of Cornelio Saavedra. It was within the latter that we found Belgrano and those who saw the emergent Brazilian monarchy as an alternative to the continuity and stability that they could not find in Spain or the republican alternative.[67] The Portuguese had to maneuver here in a difficult diplomatic context. On the one hand, they avoided conflict with the Spanish authorities that still dominated Montevideo and other parts of the American continent. On the other hand, they also wanted to be in good terms with the new rulers of Buenos Aires. With a tacit support of the conservatives (also called Unitarians) in Buenos Aires, the Portuguese monarch chose to support the Spaniards and sent a military force to the Banda Oriental. This was the first Portuguese invasion of this territory in cooperation with local authorities, the Spanish. One of the reasons for the Luso-Spanish supremacy here was the split between Artigas' federalists and the Unitarians of Buenos Aires, who preferred conservative alliances with the Iberian states. This did, however, change. After the withdrawal of the Portuguese, Unitarians and Federalists joined forces and finally defeated the Spaniards in 1814.

By this time, the revolutionary forces of the former Spanish territory had, in a congress in 1813, agreed to the creation of a new state called the United Provinces of the River Plate. Except for the already autonomous Paraguay, this state was going to become the heir of the former Spanish Viceroyalty of the River Plate, including Alto Peru (current Bolivia). Yet, the internal confrontations between the more popular and politically liberal federalists clashed with the more politically conservative, although economically liberal, *Unitarians*. It was exactly this element, being politically conservative and economically liberal, that united the Unitarians with the Portuguese and with the British too. After a period of continuous military success by Artigas's forces, this alliance took a more real form through the Unitarian request of a second Portuguese invasion of the Banda Oriental in 1817.

In fact, according to the Uruguayan historian Washington Reyes Abadie, the aims of conservative Unitarians went far beyond only ceding the Banda Oriental. A Buenos Aires representative in Rio de Janeiro, Manuel José García, was, on the one hand, in contact with the British to make the United Provinces a British protectorate. On the other hand, in addition to giving guaranties for a Portuguese occupation of the Banda Oriental, he also offered the possibility of a Union between the United Kingdom of Portugal, Brazil and Algarve, and the United Provinces of the River Plate, with João VI as the "Emperor of South America."[68] As we can see here, the Carlotism was not an isolated proposal, but one of the alternatives that was seriously discussed with one goal that is of interest for our analysis: the integration of everything into one common Luso-Hispanic South American state.

A result of the contacts between Spanish- and Luso-speaking elites was the Portuguese occupation of the Banda Oriental in 1816 with the support of the Buenos Aires government—an invasion that was extended to the territories of the Misiones and the provinces of Corrientes and Entre Ríos. The goal was to defeat the federalist forces of José Gervasio Artigas. However, it was not only the Buenos Aires Unitarians that supported the Portuguese. Furthermore, the most relevant habitants of the city of Montevideo, the trade and urban node of the Federalist provinces—as well as some influential leaders of Artigas' army, as Fructuoso Rivera—joined the Portuguese side and saluted the proposal of a United Kingdom of South America. At this moment, the Carlotists increased their activity, both in Buenos Aires, Rio, and other parts of South America, by promoting Carlota Joaquina as the head of the new South American Empire.[69]

The Carlotism did not, however, prosper. In Pandiá Calógeras' view, there was a split between King João IV and his ambitious wife. He also argues that there was a strong British opposition toward the idea of a united South American state since it could interfere with their plans of controlling resources and opening markets for their goods.[70] That is not a far-fetched hypothesis. As also suggested by Delgado de Carvalho, another Brazilian pundit on the foreign policy of this country, the idea of a South American monarchy went along the prior initiatives of creating a Hispanic or Latin block that would provide a stronger geopolitical projection to confront other great powers, but neither of these initiatives found British support.[71] Yet, as shown here, in one form or another, this has been resilient aspiration among Portuguese and Spaniards, but that was also followed up by some of the new American leaders at the very start of the process of independence. Carlota Joaquina proposed an interesting alternative concerning the process surrounding independence. In spite of being a European Bourbon, she appeared to accept the idea of making South America the base of her imperial initiative; for this, Pandiá Calógeras called here a Brazilian *avant la lettre*.[72] Still, a major problem for the Carlotism at that particular moment might have been its reactionary profile. At a time when the Americans were dreaming of freedom, absolutist values were increasingly regarded as outdated and alien. Furthermore, at least in the Spanish-speaking parts of America, many years of war against the Spanish Empire probably contributed to a negative view of a Bourbon South American queen; it no longer seemed modern or legitimate.

Nonetheless, the view of Brazil as a "continental" state was not dependent on the Carlotism, since, as said before, João VI appeared to have his own plans for a continental kingdom.[73] More interestingly, however, he did consider a union with the new Spanish-speaking republics, at least with the dominating forces in Buenos Aires that were facing the challenge of Artigas's federalist forces. A challenge was also felt from the Portuguese side since Artigas' aims were to extend the reach of his revolutionary movement to southern Brazil, where the *gaúchos* of Rio Grande do Sul were already nourishing their own plans of independence and union with the Spanish-speaking federalists. Together with Artigas' intentions of giving rights to indigenous people and the abolition of slavery, this was an alarming threat to Portuguese and later imperial Brazil. The outcome of the Portuguese invasion from 1817 was the final defeat of Artigas, who went into lifelong exile in Paraguay.

After the independence of Brazil in 1822, the country managed, again, to make what might be one of its most relevant characteristics: balancing important institutional change with important institutional continuities while maintaining order. Although Dom João VI left the country with his family, the rule of the new independent Empire of Brazil was given to his son, Dom Pedro I (1798–1834). His government continued the line of involvement in the River Plate, where Brazil now controlled the Banda Oriental province that in 1822 was formally transformed into a part of the Empire of Brazil and named Cisplatina (Cisplatine). Even if this was resisted by the Federalists of the United Provinces, the Unitarians maintained good relations with the empire, and the citizens of Montevideo, who approved in a referendum the incorporation of Brazil.

There was, however, a great resentment among the Federalists of the United Provinces toward ceding the territory of the Banda Oriental to the Portuguese. Geopolitical motives and a deep anti-imperialist feeling (including toward the British) were surely part of the reason, but national feeling should not be underestimated, since many the Federalists of the United Provinces felt part of the same nation.[74] All the years of conflict surrounding Colonia and Montevideo in the past might also have played a role in this. By 1825, the bonds with Brazil had again been broken, and the United Provinces supported an insurrection that finally defeated the Brazilians, forcing them to give up this territory. Nevertheless, this did not put an end to then conflicts between Federalists and Unitarians, and the Banda Oriental continued to be a central part of this. At this moment, the United Provinces of the River Plate had changed their name to the Argentinean Republic, with Bernardino Rivadavia as the first president (1826–1827). Rivadavia sought, again, a closer relation with Brazil. Already as Minister of Government and Foreign Affairs of the Buenos Aires Province (since 1821), he sent a mission to Rio de Janeiro and contributed to make, in 1823, what might be the first official recognition of the newly created Empire of Brazil.[75] Later, as President of the United Provinces of the Río de la Plata, he sent Manuel José García as ambassador to Río de Janeiro, in 1828, to negotiate a peace treaty with Brazil. As pointed out earlier, García had been one of the firm supporters of a Luso-Argentinean union, as well as a close linkage to British trade interests. Thus, under the oversight of British diplomacy, he signed a treaty with the Brazilian government granting the independence of the Banda Oriental. This treaty later caused a major upheaval in Buenos Aires, with strong opposition from the federalists, who later forced Rivadavia to resign.

There is no room here to delve deeper into issues concerning the creation of the Uruguayan state. The point here is to reflect on the lines of cooperation and understanding between the Brazilian government and at least some of its neighbors. We want to raise a caveat here in terms of transplanting contemporary "national" notions to other historical contexts. None of the modern national identities were clearly established at that time, and would not be for several decades. This includes the case of Brazil. Both before and long after independence in 1822, this country had to face strong sub-national revolts with independence claims. In some of these, such as the revolution of the *Farroupilha* in Rio Grande do Sul (1835–1845), there were bonds of union directed toward Spanish-speaking neighbors. These links were actually incorporated into the Brazilian political system, playing a significant role for later efforts toward the path of integration (see chapter 3).

Hence, regarding the elements presented in this chapter, we raise a caveat centered on the idea that the new independent states would have inherited from the Iberian states a "mental system oriented towards dispute."[76] After the Treaty of San Ildefonso, none of the Portuguese or Brazilian military interventions into local conflicts in the south were made without approval from local authorities. The truth is that, in this region, there were more conflicts within Brazil and among the Spanish-speaking states (or states in formation), than between these states and Brazil. The first Brazilian intervention was made after the petition of the Spanish authorities in the Banda Oriental. After being repelled by the federalist *Orientales*, the Unitarians again sought an understanding with Brazil, which led to the creation of the Uruguayan state. This caused a major federalist revolt, but it did not revert that initiative.

As with the case of the Carlotism, the Unitarians were attracted by the conservative dimension of the Portuguese and later Brazilian Empire. They also shared a positive view of economic liberalism and a growing dependence on British trade, which also gave reason for concern. Consequently, the elites on both sides of the River Plate rejected Bolivar's appeals of a unification of Hispanic American countries; the Buenos Aires–based Unitarians was perhaps not less negative to this idea than Brazilian rulers. However, there was not just Unitarian cooperation. We mentioned above the relationship with Rio Grande do Sul, and could also add the case of Pernambuco in 1817,[77] but there was much more than that. For example, in the war against the governor of Buenos Aires, Manuel de Rosas intended to reincorporate the Banda Oriental into the United Provinces while at the same time seeking to centralize the provinces in

Buenos Aires. In this case, Brazilian troops even fought under the command of Argentinean federalists at the Battle of Monte Caseros in 1852, defeating Rosas. There was also local cooperation in successive Brazilian invasions of Uruguay afterward. The most important of these was in 1864 in support of a revolution involving the Colorado Party. Its victory laid the foundation of the so-called Triple Alliance between Uruguay, Argentina and Brazil, in a victorious but devastating war against Paraguay (1864–1870). This has been, perhaps, the only Brazilian invasion of a Spanish-speaking neighbor without a national convention. Yet, in this case it was done in alliance with the other countries of this South American sub-region. Moreover, once again, Brazilian troops fought under the command of an Argentinean leader, in this case the President of the Argentinean Republic, Bartolomé Mitre (1862–1868).

NOTES

1. Darc Costa, *Fundamentos para o Estudo da Estratégia Nacional* (São Paulo: Paz e Terra, 2009), 198.
2. A. R. Disney, *A History of Portugal and the Portuguese Empire: From Beginnings to 1807*, vol. 1 (Cambridge: Cambridge University Press, 2009), 13.
3. Ibid., 15, 21.
4. Ibid., 25.
5. Ibid., 43.
6. Ibid., 87.
7. Jõao Pandiá Calógeras, *A Política Exterior do Imperio*, vol. 1 (Brasilia: Senado Federal, 1998), 14.
8. A. R. Disney, *A History of Portugal and the Portuguese Empire*, 111.
9. Giovanni Arrighi, *The Long Twentieth Century* (London: Verso, 2006), 117.
10. A. R. Disney, *A History of Portugal and the Portuguese Empire*, 96–97.
11. Charles Ralph Boxer, *O Império Colonial Português* (São Paulo: Edições 70, 1969), 39.
12. Carl Schmitt, *The Nomos of the Earth in the Law of the Jus Publicum Europaeum* (New York: Telos Press, Ltd, 2003 [1950]), 89.
13. H. B Johnson, "Portuguese Settlement, 1500–1580," in Leslie Bethell (ed.), *Colonial Brazil* (Cambridge: Cambridge University Press, 1987), 8.
14. Charles Ralph Boxer, *O Império Colonial Português*, 127.
15. H. B Johnson, "Portuguese Settlement, 1500–1580," 12.
16. Charles Ralph Boxer, *O Império Colonial Português*, 110.
17. Jõao Pandiá Calógeras, *A Política Exterior do Imperio*, vol. 1, 61.
18. H. B Johnson, "Portuguese Settlement, 1500–1580," 27, 29.
19. Jõao Pandiá Calógeras, *A Política Exterior do Imperio*, vol. 1, 26.
20. A. R. Disney, *A History of Portugal and the Portuguese Empire*, 179.
21. Ibid., 197.
22. Ibid., 194.

23. Eduardo Azcuy Ameghino & Carlos Maria Birocco, "Las colonias del Río de la Plata y Brasil: geopolítica, poder, economía y sociedad (siglos VIII y XVIII)," in Mario Rapoport and Amado Luiz Cervo (eds.), *El Cono Sur. Una historia Común* (Buenos Aires: Fondo de Cultura Económica de Argentina, S.A., 2001), 19–20.

24. Ibid., 28.

25. Magnus Mörner, *The Political and Economic Activities of the Jesuits in the La Plata Region. The Hapsburg Era* (Stockholm: Library and Institute of Ibero-American Studies, 1953), 61.

26. A. R. Disney, *A History of Portugal and the Portuguese Empire*, vol. 1, 207.

27. Ibid., 206, 209; Eduardo Azcuy Ameghino and Carlos Maria Birocco, "Las colonias del Río de la Plata y Brasil," 17.

28. Darcy Riberio, *O Povo Brasileiro* (São Paulo: Companhia das Letras, 2006), 96, 98. The author defines *mamelucos* as the offspring European and Amerindian population, the concept to the Spanish word *mestizo*.

29. Sérgio Buarque de Holanda (ed.), *História Geral da Civilização Brasileira*. Tomo I, A Época Colonial, Administração, Economia, Sociedade (São Paulo: Difusão Eurpéia do Livro, 1960), 10.

30. Ibid., 10–11.

31. A. R. Disney, *A History of Portugal and the Portuguese Empire: From Beginnings to 1807*, vol. 2 (Cambridge: Cambridge University Press, 2009), 204.

32. Magnus Mörner, *The Political and Economic Activities*, 44.

33. Fréderic Mauro, "Political and Economic Structures of Empire," in Leslie Bethell (ed.), *Colonial Brazil* (Cambridge: Cambridge University Press, 1987), 44–5.

34. Jõao Pandiá Calógeras, *A Política Exterior do Imperio*, vol. 1, 155, 159.

35. A. R. Disney, *A History of Portugal and the Portuguese*, 211.

36. Ibid., 213.

37. Jõao Pandiá Calógeras, *A Política Exterior do Imp*erio, vol. 1, 136.

38. Ibid., 140.

39. A. R. Disney, *A History of Portugal and the Portuguese Empire: From Beginnings to 1807*, vol. I, 245.

40. Jõao Pandiá Calógeras, *A Política Exterior do Imperio*, vol. 1, 183.

41. Fréderic Mauro, "Political and Economic Structures of Empire," 61.

42. João Pandiá Calógeras, *A Política Exterior do Imperio*, vol. 1, 174.

43. João Paulo G. Pimenta & Adriana Salay Leme, " 'Imperador de toda a América do Sul.' D. João no Brasil e o Rio da Prata," *Revista USP*, São Paulo, no.79 (2008), 35.

44. A. R. Disney, *A History of Portugal and the Portuguese Empire*, vol. I, 246–7.

45. Jõao Lúcio Azevedo, *O Marquês de Pombal e a Sua Epoca* (São Paulo: Alameda, 2004), 48–9.

46. Jaime Cortesão, *Alexandre de Gusmão e o Tratado de Madrid*, Parte I – Tomo I (1695–1735) (Rio de Janeiro: Ministério das Relações Exteriores-Instituto Rio-Branco, 1952), 167, 176.

47. Jõao Pandiá Calógeras, *A Política Exterior do Imp*erio, vol. 1, 275.

48. Ibid., 226–7.

49. Carlos Calvo, *Colección Completa de los Tratados, Convenciones, Capitulaciones, Armisticios y Otros Actos Diplomáticos de todos los Estados de la América Latina Comprendidos entre el Golfo de Méjico y el Cabo de Hornos Desde el Año de 1493 Hasta Nuestros Días*, Tomo Tercero (Paris: Libreria de A. Durand, 1862), 131–2.

50. A. R. Disney, *A History of Portugal and the Portuguese Empire*, vol. I, 316.
51. Darcy Riberio, *O Povo Brasileiro* (São Paulo: Companhia das Letras, 2006).
52. Jõao Pandiá Calógeras, *A Política Exterior do Imperio*, vol. 1, 39.
53. A. R. Disney, *A History of Portugal and the Portuguese Empire*, vol. I, 333.
54. Leslie Bethell, *Brazil. Empire and Republic, 1822–1930* (Cambridge: Cambridge University Press, 1993 [1989]), 17.
55. Ibid., 17.
56. Ibid., 18–19.
57. Sérgio Buarque de Holanda (ed.), *História Geral da Civilização Brasileira*, Tomo I, 76, 311.
58. Leslie Bethell, *Brazil. Empire and Republic, 1822–1930*, 19–20.
59. Carmen L. Bohórquez Morán, *Francisco de Miranda. Precursor de las Independencias de la América Latina* (Caracas: Fundación Editorial el Perro y la Rana, 2006), 303.
60. Manuel Ángel de Marco, *Belgrano. Artífice de la Nación, Soldado de la Libertad* (Buenos Aires: Emecé, 2012); Jorge Abelardo Ramos, *Historia de la Nación Latinoamericana* (Buenos Aires: Senado de la Nación, 2006), 139.
61. Delgado De Carvalho, *Historia Diplomática do Brasil* (São Paulo: Companhia Editora Nacional, 1959), 54.
62. João Paulo G. Pimenta & Adriana Salay Leme, " 'Imperador de toda a América do Sul': D. João no Brasil e o Rio da Prata," 34–43, 35.
63. Ibid., 37.
64. Ibid., 39.
65. Carlota Juaquina, *Manifiesto Dirigido a' los Fieles Vasallos de su Magestad Católigca el Rey de las Españas é Indias* (Rio de Janeiro: Impressão Régia, 1808), available at http://purl.pt/23592(accessed: June 22, 2016).
66. João Paulo G. Pimenta & Adriana Salay Leme, "'Imperador de toda a América do Sul,'" 40.
67. Manuel Ángel de Marco, *Belgrano. Artífice de la Nación, Soldado de la Libertad*, 405, 416.
68. Washington Reyes Abadie, *Artigas y el Federalismo en el Río de la Plata, 1811–1820* (Montevideo: Ediciones de la Banda Oriental, 1987), 259.
69. Jõao Pandiá Calógeras, *A Política Exterior do Imperio*, vol. 1, 419, 425.
70. Ibid., 406, 412.
71. Delgado De Carvalho, *Historia Diplomática do Brasil*, 54.
72. Jõao Pandiá Calógeras, *A Política Exterior do Imperio*, vol. 1, 398.
73. Ibid., 433.
74. Vivan Trías, *Las Montoneras y el Imperio Británico* (Montevideo: Ediciones Uruguay, 1961).
75. Rodrigo Wiese Randing, "Argentina, Primer País en Reconocer la Independencia de Brasil," *Archivos del Presente. Revista Latinoamericana de Temas Internacionales*, n/d, 114.
76. Érica Christina Alexandre Winand, "A Rivalidade Como Sentimento Profundo: Origem, Evolução Histórica e Reflexos Contemporâneos do Padrão de Rivalidad entre Brasil e Argentina," *Historia e Cultura*, vol. 4, no. 1 (1995), 68–94, 72.
77. José Carlos Brandi Aleixo, "O Brasil e o Congresso Afictiônico do Panamá," 174.

Chapter 2

Distant But Not Absent

Brazil and Latin America from the Independence to the International American Congresses

The path of integration and separation in the relations between Brazil and Latin America existed in the early years of political independence in the first decades of the 19th century. As it is widely known, Brazil followed a quite different path to political independence from their former European metropolis. While Spanish territories were involved in a long military conflict, Brazil opted for a more peaceful way after the move of the Portuguese royal family in 1808. As explained in the first chapter, the presence of King João VI in Rio de Janeiro triggered a complex political process in Brazil that had effects on the relations with the neighbors, in particular, with those of the River Plate Basin. However, the impact of the presence of the Portuguese monarchy in Rio also had implications well beyond the River Plate in a moment when the rest of the region still struggled for political independence.

In consequence, the path of integration and separation began gradually to emerge in those years. On the one hand, the military conflict among the Spanish territories was perceived in the nascent Brazilian elites as a manifestation of chaos. This showed the superiority of monarchy over the republican model, defended by the leaders of former Spanish colonies. The perception that monarchy was synonymous of order and republic of chaos remains as a political imaginary of the Brazilian elites throughout the 19th century. Nonetheless, negative perceptions also existed in the Hispanic American side, where Brazil was seen as a kind of anomaly in a region that was fighting for the construction of new states with modern forms of political organization. That was the initial perception of Simón Bolívar about the Brazilian government: a monarchy considered an ally of the Holy Alliance' plans to restore the Spanish domain in the continent.

At the same time, the path of integration began also to develop, even if an embryonic way. One example was the "Carlotist" movement explained in the

25

first chapter but also some proposals of José Bonifácio de Andrada e Silva and of Silvestre Ferreira Pinheiro. We also must mention the connections that existed between the northeastern movements of independence in Brazil and some Hispanic American leaders such as Bolívar.

BRAZIL AND LATIN AMERICA: INTERACTIONS AND DIFFERENT PATTERNS OF INDEPENDENCE

Mainstream literature on the independence of Latin American countries has highlighted the different path followed by former Spanish and Portuguese colonies. Spanish America had chosen conflict, war and a rupture of monarchy to adopt republicanism, while Brazil opted for a peaceful way in which there was not a violent separation from Portugal and monarchy remained as the model of political organization. The corollary of that argument is that processes of independence were not only distinct but also separated and without major connections. This is part of the narrative of the Brazilian exceptionalism in Latin America based on which the path of separation has been constructed.

However, recent literature on the issue contests the arguments of lack of connections between Brazilian independence and the similar process that was taken place in the Spanish colonies. As the Brazilian scholar João Paulo G. Pimenta has argued, the processes of independence in Brazil and the rest of current Latin America "were articulated in quite precise way," namely, they were influenced by each other in different aspects.[1]

Both Portuguese and Spanish royal families were experiencing similar situations that produced political reactions in their territories in the American continent, even if subsequent developments of those situations led to different political trajectories. For that reason, Pimenta says that "Hispanic America taught Brazil to be independent", not by providing a model to be reproduced but giving examples of "positive and negative paradigms, warnings and prognostics" that, once received in Brazil, helped the political leaders to shape political projects that led to independence and separation from Portugal."[2]

The argument is quite interesting because it implies breaking away with the idea of Brazil as an island separated from the regional dynamics that was being developed in Latin America (and particularly in South America). Firstly, the Hispanic American revolution was well known and followed by leaders in Brazil. The reason is quite simple: The Portuguese emperor D. João VI succeeded in avoiding the fate of Carlos IV in Madrid, but the situation of his country was not different from Spain. Both countries were under French control but by moving the imperial government to Brazil, João VI impeded that the vacuum of power that took place in Spain after the abdication of

Carlos IV was to occur also in Portugal. Nonetheless, the establishment of the Portuguese crown in Rio de Janeiro created a link with the events that were beginning to be developed in territories still under Spanish control—and the crown was aware of that. Some weeks after the installation of the government in Rio de Janeiro, the Portuguese Minister of War and Foreign Affairs, Rodrigo de Sousa Coutinho, recommended to the Prince Regent João the adoption of a foreign policy especially devoted to Hispanic America.[3] Coutinho suggested the adoption of such policy strategy by raising the possibility that "the Spanish domains neighboring and adjacent to the states of H.R.H (…) fall in the hands of French of which could result in incalculable evils."[4] Similarly, diplomatic agents were sent to the diverse Hispanic American Viceroyalties.

French occupation of Spain was the beginning of the end of the Empire in America. Spaniards established the *Juntas de Gobierno*—local governing bodies—to deal with the power vacuum. This caused a reaction in the Spanish territories in America, firstly in Chuquisaca, Upper Peru in May 1809 and in Quito in August the same year. Caracas established a Junta on April 19, 1810, Buenos Aires on May 25, 1810, Santa Fe on 20 July and Santiago 18 September. Initially created with the aim of defending the rights of Spanish Emperor, these Juntas triggered the process of independence. In line with a Spanish legal and philosophical tradition, their argument was quite simple: as the link with the crown was broken, power should be reverted to the people, who were free to establish a new social contract and create a new government.[5] As a result, the Portuguese crown stayed safe of the Napoleonic troops that invaded Portugal but, at the same time, it was surrounded by territories in which the idea of rupture with the Spanish monarchy was being widespread. Thus, the destiny of the Portuguese territories in America was linked to that of the Spanish ones.

These movements in the Spanish domains did not go unnoticed for the Portuguese crown in Rio. They were followed by the official newspaper of the Crown the *Gazeta de Rio de Janeiro*[6] that in the issue of February 22, 1810 stated that "the Proclamations of Juntas in the peninsula and the Hispanic American territories should be followed, because it was of the interest of or every good Portuguese servant to know the public sprit of the Spanish nation, because of the state of that nation largely depends the fate of our nation."[7] In the following months, another influential newspaper, *O Correio Brasiliense*[8], also informed on the events in Caracas in April 1810 and Buenos Aires in May of the same year. The events were followed even with particular attention. Thus, *O Correio Brasiliense* in his edition of August 1810 analyzed the events in process initiated in Caracas in April. This deserved attention because Guayana was a border region of northern Brazil. Subsequent editions of *O Correio* dealt with the establishment of a Junta in Santa Fe and the political turmoil in the River Plate.[9]

In other words, the Portuguese government established in Brazil was since its early beginning closely connected with what went on in Hispanic America. "Since then, what happened in the Spanish America would not be ignored, or treated dismissively, by the Portuguese imperial helm"[10]. Obviously, the Portuguese authorities feared that the independence movement was spread in Brazil. Although the Juntas initially aimed at defending the rights of Ferdinand VII, they (the Juntas) quickly turned into a movement of independence that fostered the creation of republics and in some case the abolition of slavery. These ideas were contrary to the plan of the Portuguese crown to preserve the monarchy and defend the status quo. The problem was that, as shown in chapter 1, relations had been established with some parts of the Spanish domains, particularly those located in the River Plate and, indeed, it was in this region where the ideas of independence began "to be sold" to the Brazilians.

An example of this was the so-called Operational Plan[11] attributed to Mariano Moreno, the Secretary of the Junta of Buenos Aires. Actions related to the independence of Brazil are included in the Plan. By proposing a strategy to create animosities between Portugal and the United Kingdom, the Plan proposed actions to cause a revolt in Rio Grande do Sul and other Brazilian provinces.[12] A polemic exists on the authorship of this Plan and some pundits are skeptical about the possibility that Moreno had written the document. It is beyond the objective of this chapter to discuss that issue[13], but regardless of who wrote the Plan, what matters for our analysis is the fact that in some important sectors of the River Plate, the independence of their countries was linked to the political future of Brazil. Another example of this was the anonymous pamphlet *"Falla aos Americanos Brazilianos, em nome d'America por seus irmãos os habitantes das vastas Províncias do Rio da Prata,"*[14] that circulated in Rio Grande do Sul in 1811, in which an invitation to the Brazilians to join the independence movement was made. Furthermore, the document highlighted a commitment to defend the liberty of the "Brazilian brothers" and invited them to become a united independence province and join the *rioplatenses* [people of the River Plate] in single and united peoples in feelings and interest.[15]

Thus, one observes that both in the Portuguese government in Rio de Janeiro and in the South American countries that were struggling for the independence, "the other" was not being ignored. That is not certainly a discovery of this research because there were quite well known the Brazilian interaction with its neighbors of the River Plate but what is normally highlighted is the conflictive nature of those relations, example of which was the conflict in the Cisplatine Province, as it is argued by the narrative of the path of separation. Other kind of relations was created between Brazil and its neighbors as result of the establishment of the imperial government in Rio that showed the existence of early manifestations of the path of integration. One could present two examples: the first is a concrete attempt to unite the future of Brazil and the Hispanic American territories in a single common government—the so-called Carlotism, an issue analyzed in the previous chapter. As this initiative failed, the second is what Pimenta describes as the "spaces of experience," a process that certainly shows the way as the Hispanic American revolutions influenced on the independence of Brazil.

The establishment of the Junta in Buenos Aires on May 25, 1810 meant the failure of the Carlotist project but not the end of the interactions of Brazil and Hispanic America during the following years of the independence process. Certainly, Brazil and Hispanic America opted for different paths to achieve independence as it is widely examined in the literature on the issue and there are no doubts that each of them has their own particularities, strategies and results. However, this does not mean that no interaction among them existed. By using the argument put forward by Reinhardt Koselleck, Pimenta argues that the Latin American independence movement was a "space of experience" for the Brazilian elites. As beforehand explained, the Iberian Empires were interrelated after the Napoleonic invasions and the crown in Rio de Janeiro and intellectual, journalists and political leaders in Brazil were also were attentive to the events in the Spanish territories. This opened a new battleground in the war of independence where the weapons were the circulation of ideas through the press in order to influence the public opinion. As Pimenta argues, "whatever happened in Spanish America, was released in all its details, in the Portuguese world, by the press and other information channels. This was not only followed with deep interest by statesmen, but also by all those who, involved with the task of taming the cloudy future of the Portuguese political unity, saw in recent historical examples of their neighbors, warnings and parameters of actions."[16]

The role played by journals like the *Correio Brasiliense* or *Correo del Orinoco* in Venezuela was crucial in this process by creating channels of communication and information that allow leaders both in Brazil and Spanish America to be informed on the political processes that as being developed in the region. In consequence, Brazilians were informed about the establishment of local governments or Juntas, the military and political strategies of republican leaders, the reactions of the Spanish imperial authorities and even decisions as the abolition of slavery. It is hard to believe that the Brazilian were not interested in those events.

Thus, the *Correio Brasiliense* continuously informed on the events in Venezuela and the River Plate. Hipólito José da Costa, the director of the journal, was quite involved in the analysis of the Spanish American independence process in a section of the *Correio* called *Miscelaneas*, in which

Costa not only reported the most recent events but also presented his own analysis and conclusions about them. Since his early reports, Costa did not conceal his criticism to the way as Spanish colonial power was governing their domains in America. This certainly did not mean that Costa backed unconditionally the independence movement or that he adhered to republican ideas. Conversely, he perceived the establishment of local governments in Caracas or Buenos Aires as positive if he aimed at defending the rights of King Ferdinand VII that had been arrested in Bayonne by the Napoleonic troops. However, Costa also perceived in those movements a will of the Spanish American elites of constructing new modalities of relations with the colonial power.[17] Thus, Costa has an originally positive view of the Hispanic American movements. This initial interest on the independence movement remained after the attempts of restoration of the Spanish power in America once the King Ferdinand VII was restored in power in 1814. In general terms, Costa presented, in the *Correio Brasiliense*, as an inevitable movement of independence and criticized the strategy of the Spanish emperor after his return to power to repudiate the independence of Hispanic America. However, it was not an unconditional support, because Costa criticized the lack of experience of the leaders of that movement.[18]

The role played by Costa and the *Correio Brasiliense* is quite useful for the analysis of this book because it shows that the argument of total separation of the independence movements in Brazil and Hispanic America should be put in relative terms. There were connections between them; a manifestation of this was the republican movement of independence that took place in Pernambuco and northern Brazil in 1817. Certainly, we are not arguing that this separatist movement was the result of the events in Caracas or Buenos Aires. In reality, factors such as financial and tax burden imposed on the northern provinces is a fundamental cause to explain the tentative of independence, but the echoes of what was going in Latin America were being noticed.

The connections between the Pernambucan revolution of 1817 and the revolutions in Hispanic America took place different levels. The independent newspapers such as El *Correo del Orinoco* in Angostura (at that moment the capital of Venezuela), *Gazeta de Buenos Aires* and *Censor* in Buenos Aires reported the event in northeastern Brazil. It very well documented the debate between El *Correo del Orinoco* that backed the rebels in Pernambuco and their plan to create a republic and O *Correio Brasiliense* that strongly rejected that idea.[19] Once again, these debates show that the dialogue between the Luso and Spanish territories in America was important in those days.

The influence in political terms was crucial. When Pernambuco started its revolution, the Hispanic American countries had eight years of revolutionary experience that served, to a certain extent, as one of the models to be considered, or in Pimenta' words, it has become a space of experience. As done in Caracas or Buenos Aires, the Pernambucan leaders firstly established a Junta, a local government to substitute the imperial power. Afterward, a Constitution was approved to establish the political structure of the new state that would be republican and federalist, as in most of the Spanish territories. A crucial aspect in which the Pernambucan federalism met the Hispanic America experience was in the way to understand sovereignty. As explained beforehand, when the initial independence movements were triggered in Caracas and Buenos Aires the argument presented by their leaders was that as the unity of the Kingdom had been broken, sovereignty should be reversed to the provinces that had the right to establish a new political unity. That was exactly the same argument defended by the commanders of the Pernambucan revolution.

Both the events in Caracas and Buenos Aires influenced on those of Pernambuco. This province and the other located in the North East of Brazil have important link with the ports located in the Atlantic shore of the continent, included those in the River Plate. Thus, the Father Pedro de Souza Tenorio, one of the leaders in Pernambuco, stated that the rebels were quite attentive to what is happening in the River Plate and the whole Hispanic America.[20] One aspect of interest was the debate between federalist and unitarian that began to be developed in the River Plate. In the case of Venezuela, Bolívar was quite skeptic with the federal idea but strongly supported the republic as form of political organization. Despite his later proposals of a life-long Presidency and a provisional dictatorship, Bolívar did not favor monarchy and was committed to a constitutional government based on a social pact.

In consequence, the revolution of Pernambuco evidences that narratives and practices of the Hispanic American revolutions such as federalism, constitutionalism and, to a certain extent, republicanism, were incorporated in the Brazilian political process. Certainly, the Pernambucan revolution was eventually defeated and the federalist project furthered in that movement has been to a large extent neglected in the historiography of independence just as a result of, "anarchic impulses and anti-patriotic and individualist ambitions similar to those that affected in those same year to the Spanish America."[21] However, in the framework of constitutional movement that began in Portugal in 1821, the establishment of Juntas was generalized, following the example given in Hispanic America since 1808 and in Pernambuco in 1817.

SIMÓN BOLÍVAR AND BRAZIL

Despite the connections and interactions that existed between Hispanic America and Brazil, the leaders of the independence movement did not seem to realize the political process that was being developed because of the installation of the Portuguese crown in Rio de Janeiro. This is at least curious, because as we examined in the previous section of this chapter, both members of the Brazilian government and journalist reported and discussed the events in the Spanish territories that fought for their independence. Obviously, this situation varies from region to region in the vast domain Spain had in America. Leaders in the River Plate were quite aware and well informed about the events in Brazil but this is not surprising because a conflict with the empire about the Cisplatine Province existed almost since the occupation of this territory by Portuguese forces. However, this was not the case of the movements in northern South America and the Andes. A paradigmatic case of this was the complex relation of Bolívar with Brazil. The case of Bolivar deserves to be analyzed for diverse reasons. Firstly, Bolivar is without doubts a paramount figure in the independence movement of Hispanic America that only was devoted to creating new nation-states but also the regional unity. In this sense, it is not an exaggeration to describe him as one the founders of the idea of regional unity. Nonetheless, Bolivar excluded Brazil from his regional project, as analyzed further below. Secondly, this exclusion of Brazil has been used as an argument to those who promote the path of separation by arguing that from the early years of independence Brazil had been excluded the regional politics system in America. Finally, the relation of Bolívar with Brazil has not been properly explored in the literature on the international politics of the region in the early years after independence was achieved. This is valid either for Brazil or the rest of Latin American countries, where the view of an anti-Brazilian Bolivar is still hegemonic.

A critical issue when analyzing Bolivar's ideas on Brazil and the way he was perceived in that country is to consider that those ideas and perceptions were changing throughout the diverse phases of the fight for independence. Concerning Bolívar's views on Brazil, it is easy to observe diverse periods going from an initial silence or maybe ignorance on the events in that country. Afterwards, Bolivar did not acknowledge properly the particularity of Brazil after its independence in 1822, and this was his position until 1825, when he began to have more anti-Brazilian view.[22] At a later stage, Bolivar recognized Brazil as legitimate member of the concert of nations in the Americas. In the case of the Brazilian elite perceptions, these also moved from an initial sympathy and recognition as the leader of the independence movement, particularly by Costa and his *Correio Brasiliense*. After the revolution in Pernambuco and further instability in northern Brazil caused by federalist and republican forces, Bolivar became to be seen in a more critical way and as an intellectual and political influence of that movement. Finally, after the victory in Ayacucho and the incident in Chiquitos (analyzed below) there was a recognition of Bolivar as a leading figure in South America. Thus, the analysis of "Bolívar and Brazil" that does not consider the changing ideas and perceptions that appeared, evolved and disappeared in these periods could lead to misleading conclusions.

Two sources are significantly important to evaluate this issue. On the one hand, Bolívar was a prolific writer that during his whole life, and particularly during the independence years, developed an impressive epistolary exchange with political and military leaders in Hispanic America and Europe. The letters of the *Libertador* have been an invaluable source in the analysis of his political beliefs, his projects for his country and for Hispanic America, and certainly, of his views about Brazil. In the case of the Brazilian views on Bolivar, sources such as *Correio Brasiliense* and the *Gazeta of Rio de Ja*neiro provide us information on the way as the Venezuelan leader and his political plans and military actions were perceived in Brazil.

Bolívar was involved in the independence movements since its very beginning. He even was sent to the United Kingdom in 1810 to negotiate the British support to the new Junta that had been established on April 19, 1810. After the Cartagena Manifesto (1813) and the so-called Admirable Campaign in 1813, Bolivar became the leader of the Venezuelan independence movement but the defeat of the Venezuelan troops before the Spanish Caudillo José Tomas Boves in 1814 led him to return to New Granada and later to go into exile in Jamaica. The expeditionary campaign of Pablo Morillo conquered Bogotá, and Hispanic America seemed doomed to fail. In all this turbulent period, there was almost no reference to Brazil in Bolivar's letters.

An example of this lack of knowledge on Brazil is presented in the Jamaica Letter, a document published in 1815 during his exile in the British territory. As the Brazilian diplomat Néstor dos Santos Lima has argued, when Bolívar wrote this letter, important political events had been taken place in what was still Portuguese territory. Brazil began its way to independence after the transfer of the Portuguese Crown to Rio in 1808 when the Brazilian ports were opened to international trade and the metropolitan monopoly to trade was broken. The process continued in 1815, when United Kingdom of Portugal, Brazil and Algarve was set up. However, Bolívar seemed to be quite busy with the problems of the independence of the Spanish territories as to pay little attention to those events in Brazil. When he analyzed the state of what he called *América Meridional* (South America), no mention to Brazil was done. Lima argues that instead of an omission, what happened was that he had a lack of knowledge of the situation in that country. In reality, Bolivar pointed out in a letter the problems derived of lack of information, as one of the difficulties in the analysis of the problems of the American inhabitants. In Bolívar's words: "I have thought much about the situation of the Americans and their hopes for the future. I take a keen interest in what happens there, but

I lack much information related to their current circumstances and regarding their aspirations."[23] Based on this statement, it is valid to argue, as Lima does, that the lack of information between Brazil and the Great Colombia, mostly separated by the Amazonian forest, allows explaining the lack of consideration of Brazil by Bolivar in the Jamaica Letter.[24] In consequence, it is easy to believe that much of the information Bolivar had on Brazil "was incomplete, simplistic and even incorrect."[25]

However, as shown in the previous section (of this chapter), connections existed between the events in Hispanic America and Brazil, extensively reported in the *Correio Brasiliense*. The journal was published and distributed in London, so the problems of communication that existed between Brazil and Venezuela and New Granada were of no problem for Bolívar to obtain it. The existence of Correio Brasiliense put in relative terms the argument that the initial ignorance of Bolivar regarding Brazil was caused by lack of information. It seems more appropriate to think that between 1810 and the Pernambucan revolution, Bolivar was just too busy with the political and military events in Venezuela and New Granada as to pay attention to a country where no signal of aspirations for independence existed. Furthermore, despite its monarchic political structure, Brazil was not perceived as a risk for the independence of Hispanic American countries. The restoration of Ferdinand VII in Spain in 1814, the defeat of the Napoleonic troops in Portugal and the creation of United Kingdom of Portugal, Brazil and Algarve in 1815 and particularly the establishment of the Holy Alliance also in 1815 modified Bolivar's and other Hispanic America leaders' views vis-à-vis the Brazil.

The reports on Bolívar in the Brazilian newspaper *Correio Brasiliense* and *Gazeta de Rio* were also quite superficial in the period 1810–1817. However, as analyzed above, the *Correio Braziliense* reported in quite favorable way the events in Caracas and Buenos Aires in 1810 and also strongly criticized the restoration military actions of Spain after 1814. Nevertheless, there were no comments on Bolívar, except a mention of his travel to the United Kingdom in 2010 after the establishment of the Junta of Caracas. However, this positive view changed after the revolution in Pernambuco and the alleged influence the Hispanic American republicanism and constitutionalism had on it. However, Bolivar himself was used as an example to justify the way the revolution was suppressed.[26] O *Correio Brasiliense* compared the repression of the Pernambucan movement to Simon Bolívar's subjection of General Piar in 1817.[27] In other words, although the Pernambucan revolution movement is thought influenced by ideas like those defended by Bolívar in Hispanic America, the Venezuelan leader was not perceived in negative way or as responsible of those events.

After 1817, Bolívar succeeded in leading a military campaign to recover Venezuela, consolidate his power in New Granada and later organize new military actions in Peru and Upper Peru (current Bolivia). In those years, Brazil was living times of turmoil due to the persistent republican separatist movement in northeastern Brazil as well as the emergence of a political movement in Portugal claiming the return of João VI to Europe. After the return of the Emperor to Lisbon, a movement of Independence was consolidated that led to *Grito de Ipiranga* (Cry of Ipiranga), the Declaration of Independence by Dom Pedro I on September 7, 1822. Thus, Bolivar and other Hispanic American leaders as well as Dom Pedro I and his Brazilian collaborators were quite busy in their own political affairs as to pay special attention to other issues. As a result, the mutual unawareness remained. An example of this was manifested in a letter send by Bolívar to Francisco de Paula Santander, President of Colombia, on December 25, 1822. In that letter, Bolívar states: "the ambitious Portugal with its immense colony: Brazil," but when that letter was written 4 months and 18 days have passed since Brazil has declared its independence.[28]

After the Declaration of the Brazilian independence and the establishment of a monarchy unawareness was complemented by mistrust. The regional context was complex both for Brazil and Hispanic American countries. For these latter, independence was almost achieved after the battles of Boyacá (Colombia) in 1819 and Carabobo (Venezuela) in 1821 that had consolidated the independence of those two countries. The campaign in Peru and Upper Peru was also successful and battle of Ayacucho in December 1824 meant the definitive defeat of the Spanish project to restore the political power of Hispanic America. Despite those failures, it seemed that the Spanish authorities did not give up to their plans of restoration and in that context, the Holy Alliance, a coalition of European monarchical power created in 1815, seemed to be the mechanism to further such as re-conquest of the Hispanic American territories.

Brazil was a monarchy and the Braganza family was linked to the other European royal families. As a result, new suspicious emerged about the government established in Rio de Janeiro. Lima argues that Bolívar was not able to perceive the particularities of the Brazilian independence process and based on preconceptions considered the emperor just as an instrument of the European powers. Dom Pedro I has kinship ties with some European monarchy families. His mother Carlota Joaquina was sister of Ferdinand VII, the Spanish King against with whom Bolivar was fighting. His first wife, Leopoldine of Hapsburg was daughter of Francis I, emperor of Austria.[29] In particular, the idea of including part of the Basin of Plata, the Cisplatine Province, as part of the United Kingdom of Portugal, Brazil and Algarves, raised concerns in Bolivar.

After the Spanish defeat in the Battle of Ayacucho, Bolívar's views on Brazil became increasingly pessimistic. The perception of an imminent military action of the Holy Alliance in Hispanic America and the possible participation of Brazil as an ally in that action led Bolivar to adopt a critical position regarding this country. In a letter dated January 20, 1825, Bolivar wrote to Sucre: "Additionally, by the news that comes from Europe and Brazil, we know that the Holy Alliance is trying to help the Brazilian emperor to subjugate Spanish America by force, in order to consecrate the principle of legitimacy and to destroy the revolution."[30] In another letter to Santander dated February 9, 1825, Bolívar expressed in a quite straightforward way his view of the Brazil at that moment: "The Brazilian Emperor and the Holy Alliance are one and the same. And if we, the sovereign peoples, do not create another similar force, we are lost. No matter how much I talk on this issue, I could not say enough about it."[31]

This negative perception was put to a test in the so-called Chiquitos incident that took place in March 1825, in a moment when the potential of conflict was high. Chiquitos was a small town located close to the border of the Western Brazilian territory of Mato Grosso, close to Upper Peru. On March 28, the Governor of the Province Sebastián Ramos asked for the protection of the imperial authorities at Mato Grosso. The request was approved and Araujo e Silva, the commander of the Brazilian forces in Mato Grosso, crossed the border and annexed Chiquitos. On April 30, the Vila Rica's Local Government Board informed to the crown in Rio de Janeiro on the annexation of Chiquitos.[32] If we consider Bolívar's views on Brazil, in particular, his idea of a possible connection of this country with a restoration project of the Holy Alliance, the events in Chiquitos were not a minor issue. The potential of conflict in the Brazilian-Upper Peruvian border was quite high at that moment but neither Bolívar nor Dom Pedro I was aware of that. Bolivar knew about the events of Chiquitos before Dom Pedro I but his reaction was extremely cautious. He doubted that the affair had been planned by the Brazilian emperor, and advised prudence because if a military action against Brazil were advanced, that could become a reason for the Holy alliance to intervene.[33] Dom Pedro I and the imperial court in Rio de Janeiro knew about the incident in Chiquitos in August, five months after the decision of the Vila Rica government to annex the Upper Peruvian territory. In a communiqué of the Minister of Foreign Affairs of Brazil, dated August 6, 1825 the emperor disavowed the annexation of Chiquitos and ordered the immediate return of the Brazilian troops that were beyond the Brazilian limits. The communiqué also stressed that if the emperor had been previously consulted, he would have never approved those actions in Mato Grosso.[34]

The incident of Chiquitos was eventually a local issue that had no regional implications. The cautious behavior of both Bolívar and Dom Pedro I helped to avoid a potential conflict that would have certain impact on the fragile geopolitical stability of the region. Both Bolívar and Dom Pedro I proceeded carefully on this problem and their cautious attitude averted a larger conflict that would have certainly an impact on the fragile geopolitical stability in the region. The potential of conflict was high because Brazil was in war with the United Provinces of the River Plate after the attempt of the definitive annexation of the Cisplatine Province by Brazil in 1824. It should be remembered that Buenos Aires had tried to convince Bolivar to join the forces of the River Plate in the war against Brazil. The United Provinces of the River Plate sent two delegates to Potosi, where Bolivar was stationed, to discuss on the possible involvement of the Bolivarian Army in the Cisplatine War. The so-called Alvear-Díaz Velez Mission led by the Argentinean diplomats Carlos Maria de Alvear and José Miguel Díaz Velez aimed at convincing Bolivar to lead a Hispanic American alliance of Colombia, Peru, Upper Peru and the United Provinces of the River Plate to persuade Dom Pedro I to bring the Cisplatine Province back to Buenos Aires. It is beyond the goal of this chapter to examine in detail the "Alvear-Diaz Velez Mission,"[35] but some reflections should be made on it because this event is associated to the development of the Bolívar's perceptions and strategy about Brazil.

Alvear and Díaz Velez met Bolivar firstly in Potosi on October 8 and 27, 1825 and then in Chuquisaca on December 6. The original proposal of the Argentinean delegates was to subscribe a treaty between the nations ruled by Bolívar (Colombia and Peru), Upper Peru and the United Provinces of the River Plate. The main objective of that treaty was to request Dom Pedro I to withdraw his military forces of the Eastern Province (as the Cisplatine Province was called in Buenos Aires) and give up to any territorial claim in South America. If Brazil rejected to sign a treaty to establish the limits with its neighboring countries, the use of force will be allowed. In other words, the immediate goal was not war but diplomatic actions. For this reason, Alvear proposed to send a Commission to Rio de Janeiro to present complains about the invasion of Chiquitos and the Eastern Province. If after those diplomatic actions, the Brazilian troops were not withdrawn, a military to defend the territorial integrity should be deployed.[36]

Bolivar was not quite enthusiastic about those proposals. As his main concern was the threat of the Holy Alliance, Bolivar feared that a joint military action against Brazil could foster a similar reaction by the European Powers to defend Brazil. Similarly, Bolivar wanted to know the possible reaction of the British Empire to a joint action against Brazil. Beyond these hesitations, events in Colombia and Peru forced Bolívar to leave Upper Peru. A crucial factor in all this process was the role played by the British government in persuading Bolivar of the inconvenience of a military action in the River Plate. Bolívar wrote a letter to George Canning in March 1826 asking about the conflict between Rio de Janeiro and Buenos Aires. In quite diplomatic terms, Canning asked Bolívar to recommend to the belligerents to cease hostilities and thanked him for having refrained from any action that would have prevented the achievement of a peace agreement. Canning also recommended efforts to prevent the conflict that was spread to other countries of the region. Certainly, we are not arguing that Bolivar made his decisions based on a British coercion or diplomatic pressure. In reality, Bolívar's main concern was the possible military actions of the Holy Alliance to defend Brazil and afterwards restore monarchy in Hispanic America. In his view, the United Kingdom was probably the only existing power able to stop the plan, if existed, of the Holy Alliance. For that reason, Bolívar welcomed Canning's suggestions and confirmed, so his initial reluctance to engage in the River Plate conflicts.

After the crisis in Chiquitos and the decision of not being involved in the war of the River Plate, Bolívar began gradually to modify his perception about Brazil. It was like that: a gradual process. The reason was the threat of the Holy Alliance and his perception that Brazil was a potential ally of the European concert in restoring the Spanish power in America. This view shows that Bolivar was not certainly following some the political events both in Brazil and Europe. Of course, this was to some extent normal in period when Bolivar was involved in military and political activities in Colombia, Peru and Upper Peru and when, despite the efforts of journals such as *Correio Brasiliense* or *Correo del Orinoco*, the circulation of information was not as fast as to allow the leaders in Brazil and Hispanic to be updated on all the events in the continent. And this was the case of the relations of Brazil with the Holly Alliance.

Obviously, the familiar links between Dom Pedro I and the European royal families raised suspicions in the Spanish American leaders like Bolivar. However, conversely to what Bolivar thought, the Declaration of Independence of Brazil was not immediately welcomed by the Holy Alliance and the new country was not recognized but after diplomatic efforts of Dom Pedro I with the support of Great Britain. In particular, the Austrian Minister of Foreign Affairs, Metternich, criticized some aspects of the Brazilian independence process. Strongly committed to the principle of legitimacy, Metternich doubted whether the Brazilian independence was compatible with the principle of legitimacy. It was questioned the modality of constitutional monarchy adopted in Brazil. Moreover, the origin of title granted to Dom Pedro I was also questioned. Certainly, Metternich understood that the so-called Brazilian question could not be solved by a return to the colonization or a subjection to the condition of 1815 or even 1809.[37] However, the major concern was that if the principle of legitimacy had been respected when declaring independence. In Metternich' s words: "from the very beginning your government has cherished the most perilous ideas (...) the manner in which you later announce your independence and the sovereign title of your Regent was a frontal attack upon the principle of legitimacy."[38] Later, in a dispatch dated May 12, 1824, Metternich stated that Austria had declined to mediate between "a legitimate monarch and his placed at the head of an insurrection".[39] This situation began to be modified after the recognition of Brazil as independent state by João VI on May 13, 1825. Some months later, in December 1825, Metternich formally recognized Brazil as independent state.[40]

In other words, Brazil was fighting for being recognized by the Holy Alliance when Bolívar was expressing in his letters the concerns about the Brazilian monarchy as a possible instrument of the European conservative powers. It should be also remembered that in those years Brazil was already involved in the Cisplatine War as to foresee a military action against the rest of Hispanic American countries.

In that context, the idea of Brazil as enemy of Hispanic America republics was certainly based on an insufficient information of the political process that was taking place in that country. There were many voices in the Brazilian political system that openly favored the Hispanic American independence. Conversely to what many people thought or spread in those years, the Brazilian expert Arnaldo Vieira de Mello wrote in 1963 that the sympathy of imperial crown was, at least in public, for the revolutionaries that, despite of being republicans, fought against the same forces that did not accept to recognize independence. Mello argued that columns in the *Diario Fulminense*, a public journal managed by the imperial government, showed this support to the Hispanic American forces as well as some pamphlets published by José da Silva Lisboa, Visconde de Caiurú.[41] An example of this support was manifested in an article published by *Diario Fluminense* on March 4, 1825 devoted to inform about the battle of Ayacucho: "The tough conflict of Spanish American independence fighters with the realist, and the cause of justice and reason won; yes, Bolívar, that immortal promoter of the independence of Spanish America succeeded in ultimately expelling of the America territory the Viceroy of Peru."[42] The journal uses the case of Ayacucho and the defeat of Spain in Hispanic America as an argument in the conflict the Brazil had with Portugal regarding the recognition of its independence: "May this just be an example for Portugal of not being persistent [in rejecting to recognize Brazilian independence]."[43]

All these facts show that the idea of Brazil as a sort of satellite of the Holy Alliance was at least disputable. Factors such as the way as the Brazilian Emperor dealt with the incident in Chiquitos, the epistolary exchange with Canning beforehand mentioned as well as the warning of Francisco de Paula Santander, the Colombian vice president, who had a positive view of Brazil, led Bolívar to modify his view of Brazil and its place and role in South American regional politics.

A first tenet of this new approach was the recognition of Brazil as a different political entity than Portugal. Thus, in a letter to the Argentinean José Gregorio Funes dated July 1, 1826 Bolívar referred to the inhabitants of the

Luso-American country as Brazilians instead of Portuguese[44], as he had done in most of his previous communications. Because of the crisis over the Banda Oriental or Cisplatine Province, it was also clear for Bolívar that Brazil was a South American political actor with its own geopolitical views and interest. This was quite clear after the end of the war in the River Plate, in a letter dated November 14, 1827, Bolívar wrote: "It is said that Brazil ended its war with Buenos Aires. Concerning Colombia, I can assure you that I never had any hostile view, regarding the Emperor; conversely, I tried to keep the friendliest relations with that Court where currently lives one of our agents. What I say is that I want to have a similar harmony and, as long as I rule this government, nothing will be done against Brazil."[45]

By 1828, Bolívar had modified his perception about Brazil and Dom Pedro I. The understanding of Brazil as Constitutional monarchy that intended to be more like the British government than to the continental monarchies as well as the disappearance of the threat of the Holy Alliance allowed Bolívar to recognize that Brazil was a country with which Colombia should have friendly relations. This eventually took place in 1830, when Bolívar met in Bogotá, Louis Sousa Díaz, an Envoy Extraordinary and Ministry Plenipotentiary of Dom Pedro I. In a letter dated March 30, 1830, Bolívar showed his new views on Brazil, a country that is described in the following terms: "The Empire of Brazil, recently created by your illustrious monarch, is one of the most powerful guarantees received by the American republics in the course of their independence. Since your sovereign has set a fine example by voluntarily submitting to the most liberal constitution, he has become worthy of the applause and admiration of the world."[46]

This analysis of Bolívar's perceptions is important to demystify the view of a separation almost unsurmountable between his ideas of the American continent and Brazil. Our analysis shows that certainly in the 1810s and even in the first half of the 1820s Bolívar to some extent ignored the complex events of the emerging Brazilian political process. Only in this context is valid the argument that such an ignorance led to a denial of Brazil as political reality in South America, something the countries of the River Plate realized decades before. However, after 1824, the lack of knowledge about Brazil became in fear when this country began to be perceived as a threat and potential ally of the Holy Alliance. However, the situation was slightly different because Brazil was fighting to be recognized as an independent country by the Holy Alliance in the years Bolivar believed that the European concert could use the Brazilian territory to advance a military action. Moreover, even if Bolívar could be perceived as a potential threat to the Brazilian monarchy due to his republican ideas, his military successes were well known in the official journal of the country.

However, at the heart of this debate is the question of the mutual perception between Brazil and the region that later will be called Latin America promoted by those that favored the path of separation. To a certain extent, the Brazilian national identity project in the nineteenth century was based on the idea that Brazil was more closely related to Europe than to America. Its monarchy linked to the European royal families and the fact that the most important Brazilian political, cultural and economic poles were in the Atlantic shore looking to Europe and separated of the neighbors by the Amazonia forest allowed the construction of a project of constructing an identity in which the Hispanic American countries were the "other." The political and economic instability that characterized the Hispanic American republics after 1830 contributed to the consolidation of an identity project that fostered the path of separation. This was particularly significant in the case of the countries located in the River Plate Basin, with which the communication was easier than with the rest of South America but with which the geopolitical rivalries had existed even before independence. For those in Hispanic American countries that furthered the path of separation the problem of Brazil was not identity or monarchy but the perception that Rio de Janeiro had an imperialist vocation in South America.

In consequence, it is fair to recognize that these different identity views and geopolitical contrasting projects nurtured the path of separation in the 19th century. This notwithstanding, does not mean that interactions have not existed beyond the interventionism in the River Plate or the later war in Paraguay in the 1860s. An interesting case of these interactions is the way the Brazilian government perceived and dealt with the so-called Co-federal cycle, namely, those diverse initiatives that started in Panamá in 1826 and aimed to create an American Confederation. The mechanism to achieve that goal was the convening of International American Congresses.

BRAZIL AND THE SUYMMITRY IN THE AMERICAN CONTINENT DURING THE 19TH CENTURY

In the Letter of Jamaica, Simón Bolívar proposed in 1815 for the first time the organization of an International Congress to join the emerging Hispanic American nations into a continental confederation to defend their interests, face the external challenges and promote peace. In Bolivar's words:

> How beautiful it would be if the Isthmus of Panama could be for us what Corinth was for the Greeks! I hope that someday we will have the good fortune to install there an august congress of the representatives of these republics, kingdoms, and empires for the purpose of considering and discussing the important

issues of peace and war with the nations of the rest of the world. Such a corpora-
tion might conceivably emerge at some felicitous moment in our regeneration;
any other thought is as impractical as the praiseworthy delirium of the Abbé de
Saint-Pierre, who proposed assembling a European congress to decide the fate
and interests of those nations.[47]

Bolívar was not the only Hispanic American leaders that encouraged a continental congress. José Cecilio del Valle[48] and Bernardo de Monteagudo[49] in
Upper Peru and the River Plate also advocated for the creation of a confederation among the new independent states. This notwithstanding, Bolívar
was without doubt the leader of what was will later be called the Hispanic
America summitry[50], Pan-American Movement[51] or a Confederative Cycle[52]
that began with the convening of the Congress of Panamá in 1826 and was
extended throughout the 19th century. The cornerstone of those initiatives
was the idea that the American continent was a singular and autonomous part
of the international system different from Europe, at that moment the center
of the world political system. Based on that premises, the new independent
states furthered diverse confederal initiatives that were certainly part of the
first movement of regional integration and cooperation in Latin America.
    The role of the Brazilian Empire in this movement of integration in the
19th century is a topic of debate in the literature on the issue. In general
terms is admitted that the government in Rio de Janeiro was never actually committed to those initiatives of regional integration and cooperation
promoted by the Hispanic American nations from 1826 to the second Congress of Lima in 1865. This is an argument often presented to evidence the
predominance of the path of separation. Certainly, there is no doubt that the
Brazilian involvement in the movement of continental integration in the 19th
century was limited. However, the flip-flopping Brazilian behavior vis-à-vis
the recurrent invitation to join the American Congresses organized since the
convening of the Congress of Panamá was more an expression of realpolitik,
than a manifestation of a natural aversion to the idea of creating a regional
space in the American continent. This is a crucial issue because Brazil was
not the only country that opted for excluding from the initiatives of regional
integration and cooperation. Argentina, Uruguay and Paraguay consistently
rejected the invitation to participate in the Hispanic American congresses and
certain governments of Colombia, Chile or Venezuela were in some moments
skeptical about the regional movement. Thus, even if one considers the
widely accepted view that Brazil just was not interested in the 19th-century
summitry, one has also to make clear that was not a Brazilian exclusivity.
However, even that argument can be contested, because one thing is not
participating based on geopolitical perceptions and another quite different
thing is not being interested. The extensive diplomatic correspondence allows

arguing that Brazil actually paid attention to the regional initiatives promoted by the Hispanic American countries to the point that in diverse occasions seriously considered to participate but the changing geopolitical reality led eventually to the exclusion.

Thus, it is valid to argue that supporters of the path of integration fought in the 19th century to incorporate Brazil in the regional integration movement, even if forces of the path of separation were stronger. The problem was that behind these two positions was the identity debate of the Brazilian society (o probably more properly of the Brazilian elites) about its condition of a country ruled by a European monarchy dynasty but located in South America. In consequence, the question was if Brazil should privilege its relations with the European monarchic countries (with whom the Brazilian elites alleged to have closer links) or with the Hispanic American republics. This dichotomy Europe vs. America existed until well into the 19th century.

In this context, it is important to remember what Nelson Werneck Sodré pointed out in his *Formação Histórica do Brasil* when remembering that one major mistakes made by the Brazilian historians have been the omission of the "relation between what happens in Brazil and what happens in neighboring areas."[53] This mistake can be certainly perceived in the literature on the history of the Brazilian foreign policy. However, experts such as Amado Luiz Cervo and Clodoaldo Bueno, Paulo Roberto de Almeida and Luis Claudio Villafañe Santos have included this regional dimension in their studies. Coming back to the Brazilian participation in the 19th summitries, these experts recognize the existence of a "pro-American" trend in the Brazilian society since the early years of independence.

Thus, Cervo and Bueno argue that United States led the Monroe Doctrine and Bolívar's proposal of Hispanic American unity coexisted with a not very well-known Brazilian Americanism. According to these pundits, this Americanism was precise and pragmatics and emerged in two specific moments and due to concrete motivations in the Brazilian Parliament, as a reaction against the so-called unequal treaties subscribed with some European countries,[54]

Such ideas, as José Carlos Brandi Aleixo points out, were already present in 1819, when there were arguments by high-level Brazilian leaders in favor of an "American League," with neighbors of south and north of the continent.[55] In the case of bilateral initiatives toward the Buenos Aires government, it appears to be a continuation to the line of actions from the end of João VI's government. For example, in the proposal the last chancellor of the Portuguese monarch in Brazil, Silvestre Pinheiro Ferreira, for a Treaty of Confederation and Mutual Guarantee of Independence. According to Brandi Aleixo, Pinheiro Ferreira's objective was to assure the re-composition of the Spanish-Lusitanian family, with the aim to secure their independence and unite to confront external powers.

The Brazilian-born José Bonifácio de Andrada e Silva moved to Portugal during his youth and became professor of geology at Coimbra University; later, he also worked as inspector-general of the Portuguese mines and was also appointed as perpetual secretary of the Sciences Academy of Lisbon. During the French invasion to Portugal, he was active in the opposition forces for which he was arrested and sent to France. After his return to Brazil in 1819, he was appointed as the first minister of Foreign Affairs of the new Brazilian Empire, by Dom Pedro I. As chancellor, a key area of his attention was to secure the international recognition of the new states. Another priority was the situation at the River Plate region and the issue of the Cisplatine province.[56]

The role of Bonifácio in the establishment of some premises of the Brazilian foreign policy like, for example, the promotion of national political autonomy and the South American integration was widely recognized. Those objectives have been part of the so-called Andrada Doctrine that is based upon two premises: the integration with South American countries and the defense of autonomy.[57] With Bonifácio, the new independent Brazilian empire took its first steps toward a proposal of cooperative relation with the River Plate region. Bonifácio intended to use the economic interest of European nations in the Brazilian market, particularly, Great Britain and France, as the United States, as tool for bargaining in defense of Brazilian interest. The British priorities were related to a continuation of the economic advantages acquired in prior treaties with Portugal, but there were already voices in Brazil complaining about the disadvantage position for Brazilian manufacturing sector and other kind of advantages given to the British, as well as the problem with British demands on abolition of slavery and restrictions to slave trade. Brazil did also want to maintain control of the Amazona River and the paths toward interior South America. To make his position clear, Bonifácio opposed an initiative to contract a loan in London, seeking internal emission of bonds.[58]

In relation to Buenos Aires, Bonifácio sent a representative of the government with instructions to propose the creation of a Confederation with the River Plate Provinces, and at the same time, he also proposed a cooperation and defense treaty to the United States; all cooperation-oriented initiatives have been regarded as forbearing the famous "Monroe Doctrine," from 1823.[59] In the instructions given to Antônio Manuel Correa da Câmara appointed as agent of the Brazilian crown in Buenos Aires, dated May 30, 1882, Bonifácio stated:

After having skillfully persuaded (the Buenos Aires government) that the interests of this Kingdom are the same as those of the other States of this Hemisphere, and demonstrated the destinies they share with us, your Lordship shall promise on behalf of his Royal Highness the solemn acknowledgement of their political independence, and shall explain the invaluable benefits that would result from a Confederation or an offensive and defensive Treaty with Brazil, in order to oppose, with all Spanish American Governments, the astute plots of European policy.[60]

Bonifácio favored a project of "continental solidarity," for trade promotion and mutual defense, in the River Plate Basin and the rest of the American continent.[61] The goal of cooperation was also explicitly stated in a conversation between Manuel Corrêa da Câmara, the Brazilian representative in Buenos Ares, and Manuel José Garcia, the Argentinean minister, where the former argued that "only a perfect and sincere union of the American states would give this part of the world [...] the force it needs."[62]

A second element of the Andrada Doctrine was the commitment to defending a strengthening national autonomy. Bonifácio aimed that Brazil became a "strong and independent nation that would be listened and respected by the other nations."[63] Some authors have described this as an anti-imperialist goal that rejected the attempts of the Holy Alliance countries to ignore the independence of the new states in Hispanic America and Brazil.[64] Thus, Bonifácio believed that Brazil was a country that had an independent role to play in the international system. He argued, for example, that Brazil would welcome any foreign interest in helping to the development of the country but those foreigners should not claim for a special treatment different from that given to the Brazilian nationals.[65] This nationalist and autonomist language must be understood in the political context of 1822 and 1823 in which the Brazilian independence was recognized neither by Portugal nor the Holy Alliance and also in a moment when the separatist movements in northern territories of the Empire were contesting the authority of Dom Pedro I. In that framework, Bonifácio turned to the Hispanic American nations as potential allies in the promotion of those autonomist goals. Thus, in addressing that Brazilian independence was not recognized by Portuguese, Bonifácio promoted the idea of creating a "great alliance or American Federation entirely preserving free trade."[66]

Some Brazilian experts argue that the "Andrada Doctrine" preceded the Monroe Doctrine,[67] but other experts observe some difference between both doctrines: while Monroe's furthered an alliance against the Europeans intending to subjugate its potential allies in the sphere of influence, Andrada's aimed at establishing an alliance of sovereign nations on common objectives.[68] Beyond this debate, what is clear is that Bonifácio expressed a desire of a prominent figure in the formation of Brazil that aimed a political and economic rapprochement with the rest of the countries of the American continent. The shared common liberal approach to the organization of the new states, the establishment of mechanisms of common defense and the promotion of common interest in issues as free trade are the main tenets of Bonifácio's ideas.[69] In this view, the way forward for Brazil was not through conflict with its neighbors, but in a close relation, in the framework of solidarity and cooperation. There is indeed much of true in Brandi Aleixo's argument, that the idea of American unity represents a "constant in the foreign policy of Brazil, before and after independence."[70]

Nonetheless, it is valid to argue that Bonifácio believed in a cooperation and integration in diversity. He was a convinced monarchist and has a quite critical approach to the republicanism widespread in the Hispanic American republics. Certainly, Bonifácio defended a liberal and constitutional monarchy, different from the absolutist monarchies that Bolívar and other Hispanic American leaders rejected. He also was aware that Brazil was surrounded by young republics the leaders of which believed that America should expel royalty but that also feared the strength of being born with Dom Pedro I at head.[71] However, Bonifácio shared the view of part of the Brazilian elite of Hispanic American countries as unstable due to the choice of a republican order, but at the same time, he recognized the struggle of the Hispanic Americans to achieve their political independence. This was an example for Brazil and he pointed out: "Brazil wants to be free, and have the example in all the young states that surround it".[72]

Hipólito Costa, the founder of *Correio Brasiliense*, also supported the idea of closer economic and political relations with the rest of Hispanic America, especially with the South American neighbors. In the context of the struggle for Brazil being recognized as an independent state, Costa proposed in 1823 the promotion of offensive and defensive alliances with the rest of the American states to create an unconquered barrier to any European pretension of retake the former colonies.[73] Francisco Carneiro do Campo also favored a rapprochement with the Hispanic American countries. Campo was the rapporteur of the *Relatório da Repartição dos Negócios Estrangeiros*, a document elaborated after the abdication of Dom Pedro I in 1831. One must remember that the abdication of Dom Pedro I was described as a "glorious revolution that nationalized Brazil."[74] This idea of nationalization implied in terms of foreign policy that the new government aimed at modifying that followed during the Kingdom of Dom Pedro I, particularly concerning the signing of equal trade agreements. In this sense, the Relatório, although accepted that relations with Europe should be maintained, also pointed out that it was convenient to establish and deepen relations with the neighbors that in the future "must link much closely the political system of the association of the American hemisphere" because the different countries of that continent will be stronger together, because divide only could be "small, weak, disrespected as long as they remained divided."[75]

Certainly, these initiatives, expression of the path of integration, coexisted with others based on the path of separation as, for example, the mission of the Count of Santo Amaro to Europe in 1829 that sought to convince British and other European countries on the need of a plan to transform all the Hispanic American republics in monarchies. A crucial element of this plan was to avoid that the republics succeeded in creating a confederation.[76] This notwithstanding, the plan eventually proposed that all the monarchies created if the plan prospered should join Brazil in a great alliance of South American countries. In other words, even in this plan the idea of union existed, even if a union under Brazilian hegemony.

In other words, the idea of Brazil as part of the American continent and its participation in regional projects led to further cooperation and integration with Hispanic American countries. Even the Brazilian Parliament was critical to excessive European bias Dom Pedro I had given to his foreign policy. It was considered that relations with the American countries would be easier and more efficient than those exiting with Europe. "Relations with young American states would be less burdensome and would bring more benefits to Brazil."[77]

In consequence, it seems at least weird that Brazil eventually decided not to participate in the American summitry that started with the Congress of Panamá in 1826. As extensively analyzed, Brazil did not participate in the Congress of Panamá. In fact, Bolívar, in his periods of lack of knowledge on the Brazilian events and later of criticism to the Brazilian empire, did not invite Brazil. He also opposed to invite the United States and Haiti because he thought that that country belonged to a different cultural space. In Bolivar words: "The Americans from the North and those from Haiti, [are not invite to Panamá] simply because they are foreigners, are too heterogeneous in character to fit in. Therefore, I will never agree to invite them to take part in our American system."[78] However, the case of Brazil was different. As previously analyzed in this chapter, Bolívar perceived the Brazilian monarchy as potential political enemy (or, if it is preferred, as a potential ally of the Holy Alliance's plans of restoration). In particular, the Brazilian political regime, different from the republicanism prevailing in the continent, was the reason behind Bolivar's skepticism vis-à-vis Brazil. There was no identity issue in play, namely, Bolivar did not consider Brazil as foreigner or "other" in terms of identity. As Bushnell argues: "the omission [to invite Brazil] was not on grounds of cultural-historical heterogeneity but rather because of the independent Brazilian Empire's diplomatic and dynastic ties with continental European powers hostile to the Spanish American cause."[79]

However, the way as the incident of Chiquitos was resolved as well as the negative of Bolívar to mingle with the conflict in the Eastern or Cisplatine province, as also explained above, modified Bolívar's perception on

Brazil. Moreover, the Colombian vice president Francisco de Paula Santander decided to invite Brazil. It is frequently argued that this invitation was against Bolívar will that remained adamantly opposed to the Brazilian participation. Nevertheless, it is not known a single letter in which Bolivar canceled the order given by Santander and excluded Brazil from the Congress. It should be at least to considering this, especially when taking into account that Bolívar was quite prolific in writing to friends and surrogates about the political events of those years.

The fact was that the Colombian ambassador in London, José Manuel Hurtado conveyed the invitation to the Brazilian representative in the British capital José Rodrigues Gameiro Pessoa. Gameiro's reply was that the definitive answer to the invitation will be given once the Emperor responded. The issue was discussed in the Brazilian political circles. Some pundits thought that Brazil should participate because it could mean a gaining of influence in South America. Hipólito da Costa, for example, after discussing the project of an American League with the Colombian ambassador in London, counseled the imperial government in 1823 that the participation in the Congress or even its eventual convening in Rio de Janeiro could have geopolitical benefits for Brazil. Costa stated: "if the gathering of the envoy of all those powers is held in Rio de Janeiro, that will be no doubt the beginning of the supremacy that the Empire of Brazil in the future will exercise in all South America (…) that Congress in Rio de Janeiro will have the same preponderance that the Congress of Vienna had in Europe".[80] Domingo Costa Barros, Brazilian ambassador in Paris, argued in a similar way to Costa. For him, Brazil should participate in the Congress as a way to check the excess of the republicans. He asserted: "I can see the Empire taking part in the American cause."[81] Gameiro also advocated for the participation and believed the Brazilian representative in the Congress should serve as representative." He even proposed that "the city of [Belem de] Para, being the most central point of America and the closest to Europe, it that there that the future American congresses should be installed."[82]

After the failure of the Congress of Panamá, the Hispanic American summitry was promoted firstly by Mexico, particularly its foreign minister Lucas Alamán. It should be recalled that in Panamá was decided to continue the regional negotiations in Tacubaya on the outskirts of Mexico City. [83] This meeting also failed but throughout the 1830s, Alamán fostered several diplomatic efforts and sent emissaries, to Central America and Colombia and the rest of South America to promote what he called a "Family Pact." [84] Peru and Chile also made diplomatic arrangements between 1839 and 1845 to convene a new International American Summit.

However, the plans of Ecuadorian General Juan José Flores led to the convening of the Congress of Lima in 1847. Flores' project to restore a Spanish monarchy in Ecuador was of particular concern for Peru, due to its contiguity with that country that made the Peruvian territory a potential target of attack. The fears increased because of the involvement of the General Andrés Santacruz in the project of restoration. As a result, Peru retook the project to convene a new summit of the American States. The Peruvian Foreign Minister Jose Gregorio Paz Soldan sent in 1846 a diplomatic note to the governments of Ecuador, Bolivia, Chile, New Granada, Argentina, Uruguay, Venezuela, Brazil, Central America, Mexico, and the United States inviting them to form an alliance to repel aggressions that threatened the American nations. The Summit was held in Lima between December 1847 and March 1848, but only Bolivia, Chile, Ecuador, New Granada and Peru participated. Once the threats of invasion by Flores disappeared, the regional momentum weakened.

However, what did not decrease in the region was the persistent external aggression. In the case of Central America and the Caribbean US filibuster William Walker invaded northern México and later Nicaragua, where became President *de facto*. In response, the South American countries began a new political mobilization to organize a new American Summit. One of the first steps in this direction was taken by the Venezuelan Minister of Foreign Affairs Jacinto Gutierrez who in 1857 sent a circular to the South American countries that met in Panamá to discuss Walker's actions in Central America[85] At the same time, the Minister of Foreign Affairs of Peru contacted the Chilean government to negotiate a defense treaty. Ecuador joined this process, resulting in the signing on September 15, 1856 of the so-called Continental Treaty, subscribed by the three countries mentioned, under the assumption that the other American States would subsequently be invited to join it. Moreover, on the initiative of the Peruvian Minister Juan de Osma in Washington and the Guatemalan Minister Antonio José de Irisarri, the diplomatic representatives of Latin American countries were convened to a meeting at the Peruvian embassy in the US capital.[86] As a result of this meeting, representatives of New Granada, Guatemala, El Salvador, Peru, Mexico and Venezuela signed on November 6, 1856 a treaty of alliance called *sub spe ratis*, namely, an agreement that would be subject to future ratification.

The last American Summit was held in Lima in 1864 as a reaction to the European interventionism in Mexico, the Caribbean and South America. The United States was out of this new interventionism because the country was in civil war between the slavery-holding south and the industrial north. Some regional events triggered the movement of regional unity. One of them was the French invasion of Mexico in 1862 that led to several Peruvian diplomatic actions to establish a defensive alliance to reject foreign intervention in that country.[87] However, the conflict with Spain over the Chinchas Islands, a territory rich in guano and very important for the Peruvian economy, triggered the regional action. Because of the conflict, the Spanish navy blockaded the

Port of Callao, what was perceived as serious threats to the South American countries. It must be remembered that the independence of Peru had not yet been recognized by Spain at that time. Accordingly, the Peruvian government, faced with the threat of Spanish action, initiated several diplomatic efforts that ended with a formal invitation to Bolivia, Brazil, Chile, Colombia, Ecuador and Venezuela to a new International American Congress. Argentina and Central American countries were invited later. The Congress was held between November 1864 and March 1865. Colombia, Chile, Bolivia, Ecuador, Peru, El Salvador and Venezuela attended the Congress, while Domingo Faustino Sarmiento represented *ad referendum* to Argentina. The result was the signing of a Treaty of Union and Defensive Alliance and Conservation Treaty of Peace between the Allied Nations. Its aim was to ensure the independence, sovereignty and territorial integrity of Latin American nations and the peaceful settlement of conflicts between them. However, these treaties suffered the same fate as those signed in Panamá, Lima and Santiago were never ratified

What was the Brazilian role in this summitry movement? The literature on the issue highlights the fact that due to the mistrust vis-à-vis the Hispanic American republicans Brazil was not interested in participating in diplomatic actions that aimed to confront the European power, with which the Brazilian crown alleged to have special relations. Thus, for example, it is criticized that the empire did not react to the French interventionism in the 1830s in Mexico, Buenos Aires, Montevideo and in Brazil itself (in Amapa). If to those French actions we add the conflict of Texas led by US settlers that eventually caused the separation of that part of Mexico, it was clear to understand the Mexican and Peruvian initiatives to convene a new Congress. From the Brazilian view, the argument is that as the country was Lusitanian and monarchic space and there were not too many incentives to build up an alliance with the Hispanic neighbors and to participate in regional conferences. The issue of "otherness" is also implicit in this matter in the sense that both Brazilian and Hispanic American perceived themselves as "others" what placed limits to cooperation and led to mistrust in the case of the Hispanic American republics and a kind of lack of interest in the case of the Brazilian Empire concerning the creation of regional institutions.

However, recent publication of the correspondence of Brazilian diplomats in South American countries in the 19th century shows that the convener countries did not exclude the possibility of the participation of Brazil in the Congresses and also demonstrates that the Brazilian government was following up the events around the projected Congresses. Thus, after diplomatic demarches done by the Brazilian representative in Lima, the empire was eventually invited by Cañedo to the first Congress of Lima.[88] Between 1839 and 1845, Peru and Chile made diplomatic efforts to convene that Congress and there was an exchange of letters with the diplomatic representatives of

Brazil about the participation of that country. Like in the case of the Congress of Panamá, it was even raised the possibility that the Congress was held in Rio de Janeiro.[89] Subsequently, Brazil was invited to the Congress of Lima. Chile was particularly interested in the presence of the Brazilian Empire in the projected Congress. In a communication sent on October 1840 by Miguel Montt to Miguel Maria Lisboa, Brazilian Minister and Secretary of State for Foreign Affairs, is stressed the importance of the Brazilian participation:

> From the first steps taken by Mexico to make reality the idea of a General Congress of the New American States, the Government of Chile was persuaded that the Empire of Brazil, located in our continent, exposed to the same threats as the republics that emerged of the ruins of the Spanish domination, and animated by similar interests, was naturally called to take part in a meeting intended to strengthen mutual peace, and defend the common rights of New States.[90]

On the Brazilian side, although in some officials there was a kind of skepticism about the possibility that such congresses were convened, if this was to happen, the Brazilian participation was considered desirable. Thus, when the realization of a new congress in 1840 was discussed, Aureliano De Souza Oliviera Coutinho sent a communication to the Charge d'Affaires of the Empire in Chile, in which asserts:

> In accordance with previous dispatches of this Office, it is agreed that you, Sir, make feel in due course the extent to which the Imperial Government would like to see make a reality the great idea of a Congress or the American Diet, where different American States through their representatives be devoted to maintain their rights, establish common principles that regulated in certain issues of international and maritime law and guarantee to each other their forms of government and reciprocal limits.[91]

In a subsequent communication states:

> Being essentially American the interests of the Empire, beyond different formulas of government that could influence to avoid being part in the League that is proposed; the Imperial Government would consider as a violation of their dignity and an affront undeserved by the neighboring Nations, if that is not contemplated [the invitation] as it should, moreover, it is very well known the efforts made by Brazilians for achieving that project [the Congress], that if it is done properly, could produce incalculable results, not only by neutralizing the continuous wars and promoting civilization, but removing in America the heavy tutelage of the European powers that have so abused of their forces, taking advantage of our divisions.[92]

Thus, a possible summit of Hispanic American leaders without Brazil was, in Santos' words, "alarmed the Brazilian diplomats in the neighboring republics."[93] For example, the Brazilian Chargé d'Affairs in Santiago believed that a more proactive strategy should be developed in order to force the invitation to the Empire.[94] If warned that if the Congress was held could be "so dangerous for the Empire, if excluded, or so beneficial for America and for Brazil, if participated".[95] Certainly, those who more strongly advocated for the Brazilian participation in the Congress were the diplomats in the Hispanic American countries, while in the Court of Rio de Janeiro the main interest of participating was to avoid the formation of an anti-Brazilian alliance.[96] However, for the purposes of this book, this debate inside the imperial government ratified the existence of followers of the path of integration in the early Brazilian diplomacy. Two of these figures are Miguel María Lisboa and Duarte Ponte Ribeiro. Lisboa was the Brazilian Chargé d'Affairs in Santiago, when the negotiation to convene the first Congress of Lima was being developed and in diverse documents recommended to the Court in Rio about the convenience to participate in an American League. He even thought that Brazil could have a beneficial influence on the continent by being part of an International American Congress.[97]

When the so-called Continental Treaty was signed in 1858, the Brazilian representative in Santiago was invited but rejected the invitation for not having instructions from Rio de Janeiro. Afterwards, in an official document, the treaty was considered "impolitic and unfeasible," the reasons why Brazil would not adhere to it.[98] Concerning the Treaty *Sub spe ratis* signed in Washington, Brazil did not participate by alleging that as the meeting aimed to find mechanism to deal with the aggressions to the Central American countries, this was not an issue of Brazilian interest. In consequence, the Brazil's interest on the 1850s summitries substantially diminished compare to the Congress of Panamá and the Congress of Lima. This was also more less the case of the second Congress of Lima in 1865. Brazil did not participate by arguing the beginning of war against Paraguay and its reluctance of being part of a League against Spain, because it must be remembered that the main reason behind the Congress was the Hispanic South America war triggered by the invasion of Chinchas Islands.

In the negative of participating in the American Congresses the identity (the Lusitanian character of Brazil versus Hispanic neighbors) was the issue of discussion, but in the end the vision of Brazil as a member of the regional community and its potential influence on geopolitical developments, even without being Hispanic, prevailed. When in the 1860s, the term Latin America began to replace Hispanic America, the purported difference or "otherness" between Brazil and its neighbors in South America as an argument to exclude the regional movement, begins to lose strength, which it then confirmed with the end of the monarchy and the adoption of the republican form of government in 1889. It is true that initially the term Latin America was just a substitute for Hispanic America, but since the beginning of the 20th century, Manuel Ugarte included Brazil in his notion of Latin America99 at the same time as, in Brazil, Manoel Bomfim (in his book A America Latina: Males de Origem, published in 1905) also saw his country as part of the region. Even Rodo used the name Latin America, with Brazil belonging to a community with its neighbors[100]. In other words, Brazil ceased to be a benchmark of "otherness" because he was not considered strange. This was obvious to countries like Argentina, Uruguay or Paraguay, in whose geopolitical dynamics and economic exchanges Brazil was present from the beginning of its independent life. These aspects are examined in the following chapter.

NOTES

1. João Paulo G. Pimenta, "Las independencias cruzadas de Brasil e Hispanoamérica: el problema de las sincronías y diacronías," in Thibaud, Clément, Entin, Gabriel, Gómez, Alejandro and Morelli, Federica, L'Atlantique révolutionnaire. Une perspective Ibero-Américaine (Becherel: Les Perséides), 289.

2. Ibid., 290.

3. João Paulo G. Pimenta, Brasil y las Revoluciones de Hispanoamérica (1809–1822) (Bogotá: Universidad de Externado de Colombia, 2006), 350.

4. Coutinho quoted in Pimenta, Brasil y las Revoluciones de Hispanoamérica, 350.

5. John Lynch, Latin America between Colony and Nation. Selected essays (Houndmills: Macmillan Press, 2001), 116.

6. A Gazeta de Rio de Janeiro began to be published in 1808, when the Official Print House or Imprenta Regia was established.

7. Gazeta de Rio de Janeiro, extra no 1, February 22, 1810, quoted in Pimenta, João Paulo G., "Las independencias cruzadas de Brasil e Hispanoamérica: el problema de las sincronías y diacronías," 293.

8. O Correio Brasiliense was published monthly in London but was widely distributed in Brazil, the United States and the Hispanic American territories

9. A detailed analysis of the way as O Correio Brasiliense reported the events in the Hispanic American territories is done by João Paulo G. Pimenta in Tempos e espaços das independências: a inserção do Brasil no mundo ocidental (c.1780–c.1830) Tese de Livre Docência (São Paulo: Universidade de São Paulo – Faculdade de Filosofia, Letras e Ciências Humanas, 2012).

10. João Paulo G. Pimenta, "Las independencias cruzadas de," 294.

11. The oficial and original name in Spanish is "Plano de Operaciones que el gobierno provicional de las Provincias Unidas del Rio da la Plata debe poner en práctica para consolidar la grande obra de nuestra libertad e independencia," in English

"Operational Plan that the Provisional Government of the Province of the River Plate Should Implement in Order to Consolidate the Great Work of Our Liberty and Independence."

12. Mariano Moreno, "Plan de Operaciones," in *Plan de Operaciones, Mariano Moreno*, Prologo Esteban de Gorri. Estudios críticos Noberto Piñero y Paul Groussac. Investigación bibliográfica Mario Tesler (Buenos Aires: Biblioteca Nacional, 2007), 267–342.

13. See Pablo Chami, *Gloria y fracaso del Plan de Operaciones ¿Quién escribió el plan atribuido a Mariano Moreno?* (Buenos Aires: Prometeo, 2012); Carlos S. A. Segreti, *El Plan atribuido a Mariano Moreno* (Córdoba: Centro de Estudios Históricos, 1996).

14. In English: Harangue to the American Brazilians, on behalf of America, by their brothers the inhabitants of the vast provinces of the River Plate.

15. *Falla aos Americanos Brazilianos, em nome d'America por seus irmãos aos habitantes das vastas Províncias do Rio da Prata*, available in https://archive.org/details/fallaaosamerican00unkn (accessed: July 20, 2016).

16. João Paulo G. Pimenta, *Spaces of Experience and Historiographical Narratives in the Birth of Independent Brazil, Paper presented at the International Congress of Historical Sciences*, University of South Wales, Sydney, Australia, July 3–9, 2005, 4.

17. Floriano Guwzynski Junior, "Hipólito Da Costa e as independências na América Espanhola: O caso venezuelano," *Oficina do Historiador,* vol. 2, no.1 (2010), 81–82.

18. Ibid., 92.

19. Ana Claudia Fernandes, "A revolução de Pernambuco nas páginas do Correio Braziliense e do Correo del Orinoco: linguagens, conceitos e projetos políticos em tempos de independência (1817–1820)," *Almanack Braziliense*, no. 9, (2009), 144–153.

20. Mello, Evaldo Cabral de, *A outra independência. O federalismo pernambucano de 1817 a 182* (São Paulo: Editora 34, 2014), 143–32.

21. Ibid., 14.

22. Néstor dos Santos Lima, *A imagem do Brasil nas cartas de Bolívar* (Brasilia: Verano Editora, 2001), 23.

23. Simón Bolívar, "The Jamaica Letter: Response from a South American to a Gentleman from This Island," in David Bushnell (editor), *El Libertador: Writings of Simón Bolívar* (Oxford: Oxford University Press, 2003), 17.

24. Néstor dos Santos Lima, *A imagen do Brasil*, 26.

25. José Carlos Brandi Aleixo, "Visão e atuação internacional de Simón Bolívar," *Revista de informação legislativa*, vol. 20, no. 80 (1983), 46.

26. Jane Herrick, "The Reluctant Revolutionist: A Study of the Political Ideas of Hipólito da Costa (1774–182)," *The Americas*, vol. 7, no. 2, (1950), 178–179.

27. Manuel Piar was one the leaders of the Venezuelan independence movement but he did not follow in diverse occasion instructions of Bolivar. He was eventually judged by a military court and executed in Angostura in 1817.

28. Néstor dos Santos Lima, *A imagen do Brasil*, 28.

29. José Carlos Brandi Aleixo, *Visão e atuação,* 46.

30. Bolívar quoted in Lima, *A imagem do Brasil*, 30.

31. Bolívar a Santander, Lima a 9 de febrero de 1825, *Archivo Santander*, vol. 12, 245.

32. Argeu Guimarães, *Bolívar e o Brasil* (Paris, Edição do "Livre Libre," 1930), 137–138; Néstor dos Santos Lima, *A imagem do Brasil*, 33.

33. Seckinger, Ron L., "The Chiquitos Affair: An Aborted Crisis in Brazilian-Bolivian Relations," *Luso-Brazilian Review*, vol. 11, no. 1 (1974), 27.

34. Arnaldo Vieira de Mello, *Bolívar, O Brasil e os nossos vizinhos do Prata (Da questão de Chiquitos á Guerra Cisplastina)* (Rio de Janeiro: Gráfica Olimpica Editora, 1963), 83.

35. See Ernesto Restelli, (compilador) *La gestión diplomática del General Alvear en el Alto Perú (Misión Alvear Díaz Vélez)* (Buenos Aires: Documentos del Archivo del Ministerio de Relaciones Exteriores y Culto, 1927); Uriel Nazareno Bronco, "La política en Buenos Aires y Simón Bolívar en tiempos de construcción estatal suramericana: la opción bolivariana en el conflicto por la soberanía en la Banda Oriental (1824–1828)," *Temas de Historia Argentina y Americana*, no. 19 (2011), 15–46. A Brazilian view to the issue is found in Arnaldo Vieira de Mello, *Bolívar, O Brasil e os nossos vizinhos do Prata (Da questão de Chiquitos á Guerra Cisplastina)*, 183–216.

36. Uriel Nazareno Bronco, "La política en Buenos Aires y Simón Bolívar en tiempos de construcción estatal suramericana: la operación bolivariana en el conflicto por la soberanía en la Banda Oriental (1824–1828)," 34.

37. Manfred Kossock, *Historia de la Santa Alianza y la emancipación de América Latina* (México: Editorial Cartago, 1983), 249–250.

38. Metternich quoted in William Spence Robertson, "Metternich's attitude toward revolutions in Latin America," *Hispanic American Historical Review*, vol. 21, no. 4 (1941), 551.

39. Ibid., quoted in William Spence Robertson, "Metternich's attitude toward," 552.

40. William Spence Robertson, "Metternich's attitude toward," 556.

41. Arnaldo Vieira de Mello, Bolívar, *O Brasil e os nossos vizinhos do Prata (Da questão de Chiquitos á Guerra Cisplastina)*, 77.

42. Ibid., 78.

43. Ibid.

44. Néstor dos Santos Lima, *A imagem do Brasil*, 41.

45. Simón Bolívar quoted in Néstor dos Santos Lima, *A imagem do Brasil*, 49.

46. Ibid., Reply to Louis Souza Díaz, Envoy Extraordinary and Minister Plenipotentiary of His Majesty the Emperor of Brazil. Bogotá, March 30, 1830, in UNESCO, *Simón Bolívar: The Hope of the Universe* (Paris: United Nations Educational, Scientific and Cultural Organization, 1983), 305.

47. Ibid., *The Jamaica Letter: Response from a South American to a Gentleman from This Island,* in Bushnell, David (editor), *El Libertador: Writings of Simón Bolívar* (Oxford: Oxford University Press, 2003), 28.

48. José Cecilio Del Valle, "Proyecto de Confederación Americana. 1822. Soñaba el Abad de San Pedro: Y yo también se soñar," Del Valle; José Cecilio, *Obra Escogida*, Caracas, Biblioteca Ayacucho, 1982.

49. Bernardo De Monteagudo, "Ensayo sobre la necesidad de una Federación General entre los Estados hispanoamericanos y Plan de su organización," in Bernardo de Monteagudo, *Escritos Políticos*, Buenos Aires, EMECE, 2009.

50. José Briceño Ruiz, "Los congresos hispanoamericanos en el siglo XIX: identidad, amenazas externas e intereses en la construcción del regionalismo," *Revista de Relaciones Internacionales de la UNAM*, no. 118 (2014), 131–170.

51. Alonso Aguilar, *Pan-Americanism from Monroe to the Present* (New York: Monthly Review Press, 1968).

52. German A. De la Reza, *El Ciclo Confederativo. Historia de la integración latinoamericana en el siglo XX* (Lima: Universidad Nacional Mayor de San Marcos, 2012).

53. Nelson Werneck Sodré, *Formação Histórica do Brasil* (São Paulo: Editora Brasiliense, 1973), 156.

54. Amado Luiz Cervo and Clodoaldo Bueno, *História da Política Exterior do Brasil* (Brasilia: Editora UNB – Instituto Brasileiro de Relações Internacionais, 2002), 42.

55. José Carlos Brandi Aleixo, "O Brasil e o Congresso Afictiônico do Panamá," *Revista Brasileira de Política Internacional*, vol. 43, no. 2 (2000), 174.

56. Flávio Mendes de Oliveira Castro, *Dois séculos de história da organização do Itamaraty, 1808–2008* (Brasília: Fundação Alexandre de Gusmão, 2009), 22.

57. Rolando Carmona, "Bonifácio, Gênese do pensamento nacional," *World Tensions*, vol. 9, no.16 (2013), 211.

58. João Alfredo dos Anjos, *José Bonifácio, Primeiro Chanceler do Brasil* (Brasília: Fundação Alexandre de Gusmão, 2007), 92.

59. Ibid., 91.

60. José Bonifacio a Correa da Câmara, Rio, May 30, 1822, in Jorge Caldeira (ed.), *José Bonifácio Andrada e Silva* (São Paulo: Editorial 34, 2002), 148.

61. Germán A. De la Reza, *El Ciclo Confederativo. Historia de la Integración Latinoamericana en el siglo XIX*, 78.

62. Dos Anjos, João Alfredo, "José Bonifácio: o patriarca da diplomacia brasileira," 102.

63. Francisco de Asses Barbosa, "José Bonifácio e a política internacional," *Revista do Instituto Histórico e Geográfico Brasileiro*, vol. 260 (1963), 259.

64. Rolando Carmona, "Bonifácio, gênese do pensamento nacional," 211.

65. Ibid., 212.

66. Barbosa, Francisco de Asses, "José Bonifácio e a política internacional," 261.

67. Therezinha de Castro, *Jose Bonifácio e a unidade nacional* (Rio de janeiro: Distribuidora Record, 1972), 102.

68. Rolando Carmona, Bonifácio, gênese do pensamento nacional, 211.

69. Amado Luiz Cervo and Clodoaldo Bueno, *História da Política Exterior do Brasil*, 42.

70. José Carlos Brandi Aleixo, "O Brasil e o Congresso," 175.

71. José Bonifácio Andrada e Silva, "A dissolução da Assembleia foi mais que um crime, foi um erro palmar," in José Bonifácio Andrada e Silva, *Projectos para o Brasil*, edited by Miriam Dolhnikoff (São Paulo: Editora Schwarcz Ltda, 2005), 217.

72. , "Os Brasileiros querem ter liberdade," in Andrada e Silva, José Bonifácio, *Projectos para o Brasil*, edited by Miriam Dolhnikoff (São Pulo: Editora Schwarcz Ltda, 2005), 202.

73. Francisco de Asses Barbosa, "José Bonifacio e a política internacional," 270.

Distant But Not Absent

57

74. Luis Claudio Villafañe Gomes Santos, *O Brasil entre a América e a Europa: O Império e o Interamericanismo (do Congresso de Panamá ao Congresso de Washington)* (São Paulo: Editora UNESP, 2004), 72.

75. Relatório quoted in Luis Claudio Villafañe Gomes Santos Santos, *O Brasil entre a América e a Europa*, 72.

76. Edmundo Heredia, *Confederaciones y Relaciones Internacionales* (Buenos Aires: Grupo Editor Latinoamericano, 2000).

77. Santos, Luis Claudio Villafañe Gomes, *O Imperio e as República do Pacifico: as relações do Brasil com Chile, Bolívia, Peru, Equador e Colômbia – 1822–1889* (Curitiba: Editora UFPR: 2002), 18.

78. Bolívar, Simón, *Letter to General Francisco de Paula Santander: The Brazilian Empire, Upper Peru, North Americans, and Other Problems*, Arequipa, May 30, 1825, in Bushnell, David (editor), *El Libertador: Writings of Simón Bolívar*, 147.

79. Bushnell, David (editor), *El Libertador: Writings of Simón Bolívar* (Oxford: Oxford University Press, 2003), XLIV.

80. Costa, quoted in Ron Seckinger, *The Brazilian Monarchy and the South American Republics, 1822–1831: Diplomacy and State-Building* (Baton Rouge: Louisiana State University Press, 1984), 41.

81. Costa Barros, quoted in Ron Seckinger, *The Brazilian Monarchy*, 141.

82. Gameiro, quoted in Ron Seckinger, *The Brazilian Monarchy,* 41.

83. German A De la Reza, "El traslado del Congreso anfictiónico de Panamá al poblado de Tacubaya (1826–1828)," *Revista Brasileira de Política Internacional*, vol. 49, no. 1 (2006), 68–94.

84. Josefina Zoraida Vázquez, "El Pacto de Familia. Intentos mexicanos para la integración hispanoamericana: 1830–1847," *Revista de Indias*, vol. LX, no. 193 (1991), 545–570.

85. Ricaurte Soler, *Idea y cuestión nacional latinoamericanas de la independencia a la emergencia del imperialismo*, 3 ed. (México: Siglo XXI editor, 1987) 165.

86. Andrés, Townsend, "Patria Grande, pueblo, parlamento e integración," in Hugo Vallenas (ed.) *Andrés Townsend. Libertad e integración en América Latina, Textos Esenciales* (Lima: Fondo Editorial del Congreso, 2004), 228–229.

87. Robert W. Frazer, "Latin-American Projects to aid Mexico during the French intervention," *The Hispanic American Historical Review*, vol. XXVIII, no 3, (1948), 377–388; De la Reza German, "La Asamblea Hispanoamericana de 1864–1865, último eslabón de Anfictionía," *Estudios de Historia Moderna y Contemporánea de México*, no. 39 (2010), 71–91.

88. Luis Claudio Villafañe Gomes Santos, *O Brasil entre a América e a Europa*, 86.

89. Cópia da nota de 27/07/1841, do Sr. Miguel Maria Lisboa ao Sr. Ramón Luis Irarrázaval, *Cadernos do CHDD*, vol. 1, no. 2 (2003), 155.

90. Nota de 16/10/1840, do Sr. Manuel Montt ao Sr. Miguel Maria Lisboa, *Cadernos do CHDD*, vol. 1, no. 2 (2003), 140.

91. Despacho de 05/10/1840, do Sr. Aureliano de Souza e Oliveira Coutinho ao Sr. Miguel Maria Lisboa, Encarregado de Negócios do Império do Brasil no Chile, *Cadernos do CHDD*, vol. 1, no. 2 (2003), 277.

92. Despacho de 23/02/1841, do Sr. Aureliano de Souza e Oliveira Coutinho ao Sr. Miguel Maria Lisboa, Encarregado de Negócios do Império do Brasil no Chile, vol. 1, no. 2 (2003), 281.

93. Luis Claudio Villafañe Gomes Santos, *O Brasil entre a América e a Europa*, 87.

94. Ibid., 87.

95. LIB em Santiago, Oficio Reservado no. 3, de 10 de Julho de 1839, quoted in Luis Claudio Villafañe Gomes Santos, *O Brasil entre a América e a Europa: O Império e o Interamericanismo (do Congresso de Panamá ao Congresso de Washington)*, 87–88.

96. Luis Claudio Villafañe Gomes Santos, *O Brasil entre a América e a Europa*, 90.

97. Ibid., *O Imperio e as República do Pacifico*, 60.

98. LIB em Santiago de Chile, Oficio no. 7, de 16 de novembro de 1856, quoted in Santos, Luis Claudio Villafañe Gomes, *O Brasil entre a América e a Europa*, 93.

99. See Ugarte Manuel, *El porvenir d América Española* (Valencia: Prometeo Sociedad Editorial, 1910), 71.

100. José Enrique Rodó, "Iberoamérica," in José Enrique Rodó, *Obras completas* (Madrid: Aguilar, 1967), 689–690.

Chapter 3

Brazil and the Making of Latin America

This chapter takes it beginning during the late 19th century, when the concept of Latin America took its first steps across the region, as well as in Brazil. There is a general agreement among scholars in that period is marked by a consolidation of Brazilian nationhood and state borders. The success in both dimensions has also been attributed to the influence of Brazil's legendary diplomat and Minister of Foreign Affairs, José Maria da Silva Paranhos Junior, more known as the Barão do Rio Branco (1845–1912). It is indeed remarkable how diplomats have formed and become national symbols in Brazil, starting with Alexandre de Gusmão, followed by José Bonifácio and Rio Branco. There are of course differences among them, but we will also explore some lines of continuity.

In reference to Rio Branco and his time, the emergence of a new national conception as well as foreign policy doctrine is said to follow the idea of "Brazil as an island." Along this line, pundits point out that it was not until the government of Kubitschek that regional integration projects began to be viewed in a more positive way. Yet, as many hold, it was actually not until the late 1970s and mid-1980s that the process started, and took off by the early 1990s, with the conformation of the Common Market of the South (MERCOSUR).[1] Until this time, and largely following the idea of "Island" attributed to Rio Branco's legacy, it is argued that Brazil was considered as "different from all the others of Latin America, which was then the stage of endless political turmoil."[2]

As will be addressed in this chapter, the ideas of Brazilian "isolationism" must be taken with care. First, these were not as hegemonic as some might believe. As in the past, there were visions and proposals of Brazilian convergence with the region, not only in terms of state policies but also in the search of a common nationhood. The concept "convergence" is used here as an umbrella for different kind of initiatives, to a greater or lesser extent, closer to the "path of integration." Agreements and treaties among states, or proto-states, as was the case of most during the early post-colonial period, were made in the framework of more ambitious goals of union. In the case of Brazil, the projects of Carlota Joaquina and Dom João VI, analyzed in chapter 1, are two examples. Even if some of the agreements were taken separately, such as the Treaty of Confederation and Mutual Guarantee of Independence with the United Provinces of the River Plate, there were powerful interests seeing these as part of a more ambitious process of convergence. Of course, not all actors, many times the most influential ones, did regard bilateral initiatives as part of a convergence, but as separated initiatives fostering particular goals. This leads us to the second issue addressed in this chapter. Along the line of this book, the outcomes need to be analyzed with a historic perspective, considering the contextual complexities of each period. We share, for example, the view that Rio Branco represented a new identity, goals and lines of action for a national, Brazilian, foreign policy. Yet, we question the use of the "isolationist" concept, sustaining a general Brazilian "national" position, that some trace until our days.

Our point on this is that this "isolationist" path was actually formed in connection with forces pushing for integration and convergence. Two elements to be highlighted here are that there is a connection in ideas of convergence with origin in the colonial period, and these have been relevant to the conformation of the idea of modern Brazil. Even if they might not succeed, they did not disappear, but survived within what a kind of "isolationist" nationalism.

ORDER AND ANARCHY

After the failure of creating a kingdom of South America or a union with the United Provinces of the River Plate, as the other countries of the region, Brazil continued its path of constructing an own nation-state. A difference between Brazil and most of the other countries of the region (with the exception of Chile) was that Brazil managed to avoid territorial break-ups. This does not mean that there were no serious secessionist attempts or other kind of revolutions and upheavals. In fact, there were plenty of them. Nonetheless, the Brazilian elites cultivated a view of their country as an oasis of "imperial" stability in a turbulent environment of "anarchic" and "violent" Spanish-speaking neighbors. A source of such vision was the prolonged and conflictive process of constructing a state in the River Plate region, where the Argentinean *caudillos* were regarded by Brazilian elites as a stereotype of primitivism and barbarism.

Indeed, the conformation of new states, and what Darcy Ribeiro called "germinal civilizations,"[3] was problematic across the former Spanish America. The ephemeral experience of an Empire of Mexico ended in 1823, and broke up with the Central American region. Central America was in turn confronted with internal conflicts of its own, leading to latter dissolution of the United Provinces of Central America in 1840. In general, with the dead of Bolivar in 1830, the forces pushing for convergence lost momentum, leading to what Felipe Herrera called the "fragmented nation."[4] Another example of this fragmentation was the dismantling of the post-colonial state Gran Colombia (1819–1831) that included, for example, the territories of present-day Colombia, Venezuela, Ecuador and Panamá. In the case of the United Provinces of the River Plate, the fragmentation started with the loose of territories such as Paraguay in 1811, Upper Peru (that became Bolivia in 1825), the Banda Oriental in 1828 and the Malvinas Islands in 1833. It almost ended with a definitive division of the Argentinean Republic in two states, The Argentinean Confederation and the State of Buenos Aires, between 1853 and 1860.

In the framework of such conflictive panorama, Brazil was perceived as an oasis of unity, a picture that was particularly spread by the Brazilian elites themselves. Yet, this "unity" was not natural, but required harsh and violent repression. After the creation of the Empire of Brazil in 1822, there were several attempts of independence and revolutions such as the aim of creating a republic in northern Brazil, the Confederation of the Equator (1824), in current Pernambuco, Ceará and Paraíba; the secessionist and republican *Revolução Farroupilha* in the state Rio Grande do Sul (1835–1845), or the social Malê (1835) and Cabanagem (1835–1840) revolts.[5] The list is long, and continues into the 20th century.

Toward the second half of the 19th century, the image of Brazil as an island of "order and progress" was more difficult to sustain, at least in relation to the image of progress and modernity—with the maintenance of the retrograde and increasingly internationally condemned institution of slavery. After the Slavery Abolition Act in 1833, the British were a major force in the global fight against slavery. By the later part of the 19th century, the same was true for all Spanish-speaking republics and the United States, after the end of its civil war in 1865. An important milestone in the promotion of internal changes in Brazil was the Paraguay War, between 1865 and 1870. This war meant a return toward a joint military action with the Argentineans, after The Platine War (1851–1852),[6] at that moment in alliance with the Argentinean Federalists against Buenos Aires (see chapter 1).

In the Paraguay War the alliance was with the recently united Argentinean Republic and its common army, and included the Oriental Republic of Uruguay (that had also newly consolidated its unity after a civil war) in an external military intervention that was larger and more long-lasting character than any one before. The Paraguay War, also known as the War of the Triple Alliance[7], was also different from other points of view. It was a war against one of the most stable and long-lasting South American states since independence, and it was a war among states—not with or against *caudillos*. Another issue of this war was the strong representation of Afro-American soldiers in all the three allied armies, which pushed forward a questioning of the slavery issue in Brazil—the only country where it remained. As Ori Preuss correctly pointed out, the Paraguayan War (1865–1870)

> (…) not only heightened sensitivities about slavery and race, but also had other, more visible effects on Brazilians' perceptions of their neighbors and themselves. To begin with, the protracted armed struggle exposed the inefficiency and backwardness of Emperor Dom Pedro II's Empire, thus undermining the status of the monarchy as a source of pride. Second, joining forces with the recently established Eurocentric liberal government of Argentina…produced cracks in the alleged Brazilian monopoly on civilization in Latin America.[8]

Finally, the Paraguay War did also imply a shift in the South American power balance. One of the most important issues here was how it contributed to the final pacification and unification of the Argentina, which was rapidly transformed into one of the most prosperous countries of South America and the world. Between 1870 and 1890 Argentina had an average export growth of 6.7 percent and an export purchasing power of 6.7 percent, compared to 2.5 and 3.8 for the case of Brazil.[9] Moreover, in the case of Brazil, the post-war period made increasingly evident the great social, ethnic and political cleavages that were already inherent in Brazil's complex social and economic structure. This took place along a major structural change in the national economy. Traditional power groups based in the northern part of the country and historically linked to sugar cane exports, the empire and slavery, loosed strength vis-à-vis new exports sectors with different social and geographic structures—principally oriented toward the coffee sector. In this shifting context, internal conflicts, backward institutions and lack of national cohesion started to openly challenge the dominant images of unity, order and progress.

The mirror to the neighbors, particularly Argentina but also Uruguay and Chile, played an important part in this process. Former apprehensions about Argentinean expansionism or the view of Spanish America as anarchic and tyrannical by nature gave way to new views. The linkage between this and the Paraguay War can be observed in the words of Francisco Otaviano de Almeida Rosa, the Brazilian Plenipotentiary minister for Triple Alliance Matters in Argentina and Uruguay, who held that "joining forces would help the two races, the Argentine and the Brazilian, to overcome their mutual hatred and...constitute the basis for reconciliation and friendship."[10]

OPENING DOORS FOR "CONVERGENCE"

The role of the Paraguay War in a renewed rapprochement between Brazil and its southern neighbors is not only generally neglected by current research, but it is also disconnected with the pre-war period. As we have shown earlier, it was not the first example of common undertakings, or of visions of unity. Yet, in this case it contributed to a deepening of crisis in Brazilian society and institutions, leading to the replacement, in 1889, of the monarchic system with the so-called First Republic, where the country was given the name of United States of Brazil by the 1891 Constitution.

The use of the name United States was not casual, but reflected the overall change of power relations among states in the American continent. One of the symbolic events of this shift was the First International Conference of American States, held in Washington, D.C. from January 20 to April 27, 1890. After initiative from the United States, almost all states of the continent gathered in Washington to discuss about initiatives of building a Pan-American community, which included a customs union, a common currency and other advanced proposals of regional integration. Perhaps some of the most advanced ever, to have been discussed by the chiefs of state of this continent. Much of these came from the United States, but there were also some from the Latin American side, such as the institutionalization of regional rules for mediation and conflict solution.[11] This international event was also the first of to be attended by Brazil, as a republican state. There is no place here to analyze this conference in depth, enough is to say that although most of the proposals presented there failed, the United States managed to set itself at the center of the continental relations. One reason to bring this to our analysis is that, at this moment, it meant to highlight advanced ideas of regional integration, but also to promote a new national-continental identity: Pan-Americanism. For the case of Brazil, it meant a way of forging a new and modern Brazilian identity as part of a broader American identity based on common values and political forms that unified the whole continent.

However, even if the name Pan-Americanism was new, this was not necessarily the case of the "American" continental projection and identity. As pointed out earlier, it had been used since the early 19th century, in the United States as well as in Spanish and Luso-American countries. José Bonifácio had been regarded as one of the first to advance ideas of America as a system of states. Moreover, in national terms, "Americanos," as a national-continental identification, was probably the most widespread regional identity well into the 20th century. Pan-Americanism could be regarded as an offspring of that, with great influence in Brazilian foreign policy, which after 1889, again, became more oriented toward regional integration issues.

The Brazilian government's positive position on a Pan-American customs union might have been one the clearest commitments in this direction, but there was more. Some scholars hold that since Rio Branco, Brazilian foreign policy has been guided by a Pan-American ideal, where what is good for the United States is good for Brazil.[12] Our point is that this view is misleading. As we analyze in next part, the rise of "Pan-Americanism" took place hand in hand with the emergence of a counter-identity: Latin Americanism. Even if it had its origins among Spanish-speaking Americans,[13] it did also influence Brazilian ideas, identities and policies. In what respect to the influence on foreign policy, Ori Preuss has made a great contribution for the understanding of this issue, through the identification of three Brazilian foreign policy visions by late years of the 19th century: 1) Pan-American, 2) Latin American and 3) the "Brazilian island."[14] What is most innovating in this is not the well-known first and third dimensions, but the seldom acknowledged (for this period of time) second one: the Latin American, and its influence on the other.

THE EMERGENCE OF "LATIN AMERICA"

The Paraguay War and latter political shift toward Republic in 1889 contributed to a change in the narrative of "separation" with the region. An important part of this process was the rapprochement with Argentina. It is important here to underline the concept "rapprochement." In this case, it meant a re-establishment of cordial relations, or at least serious intentions of achieving them, but also opening the door for those political and economic groups intending to go beyond only "cordial relations." There is more to be made on the identification of these forces. This position came from commanding heights of the state and part of the economic elites. It did also stem from influential intellectuals, pursuing ideas with similarities to those we have outlined from colonial times and the period of independence. One can also see here links to the Pan-Iberian unionism and the prior searching for integration between Spain and Portugal, also in America. The Treaty of Madrid, and the role of Alexandre de Gusmão, has been upheld as an example of that "spirit."

By the end of the 19th century, the rapprochement, alliance and even more ambitious ideas for union had no longer any link to a common kingdom. These were also losing their Iberian attachment, albeit it did, to some extent, remain through the important cultural concept "Latin" that was now increasingly used in connection with the geographic concept of "America."

It could be said that the increasing alignment to the region marked the very birth of the new Brazilian republic, on December 7, 1889, when the new President Deodoro da Fonseca (1889–1991) "decreed that the following day would be dedicated to honoring the Argentine Republic with official ceremonies and demonstrations of friendship."[15] In this new line of action, the Argentine threat was no longer associated with barbarism, but with progress, of which the abolition of slavery was a symbol. Showing the linkage of this issue and the vision toward the neighbors, da Fonseca held that "the day of abolition, Brazil was reborn as a civilized nation, leaving behind not only its barbarous past as a slave-owning society, but also its traditional rivalries with Spanish America."[16] The Paraguayan War continued to be a living memory also around twenty years later, during the Argentinean president's, Julio Roca (1880–1886; 1898–1904), visit to Rio de Janeiro in 1899, where a delegation of the war veterans participated in the reception of the Argentinean president.[17]

Another issue fostering the rapprochement was the peaceful resolution of boundary disputes between Brazil and Argentina around the Misiones-Palmas region (known as the *questão das Missões*), through the arbitration of the US president Stephen Grover Cleveland, in 1895. Several meetings were held among high-ranking officials to negotiate a settlement on this territorial issue, in each country, as well as in Montevideo, Uruguay. The peaceful solution of this thorny theme was greatly celebrated in both countries, particularly in Brazil that was favored by the Cleveland mediation. Taking this good spirit to a new level, the rapprochement was followed by the mutual visits of Presidents Roca to Brazil, in 1899, and Manoel Ferraz de Campo Salles to Argentina, in 1900. These encounters were not only social gatherings. There was here an opening toward new security-oriented conceptions, with the goal of expanding toward a common regional outlook.

The divergence between pro- and anti-convergence forces was also present in Argentina, with President Bartolomé Mitre (1862–1868) as closer to the first position, while President Domingo Faustino Sarmiento (1868–1874) and influential intellectuals and politicians such as Juan B. Alberdi were more representative of the latter.[18] Roca's government was favorable to an alignment with Brazil, as well as it implied a change in the former view of the Argentinean state about its territory. Roca favored a territorial widening and had a "continental" scope in terms of its foreign policy. "Continental" in this case did not necessarily meant conflict with the neighbors, but rather of shared hegemony. One example was the intention to include Chile in a growing awareness of a common interest as the basis for southern peace and security. Here is one of the origins in the notion of an Argentine-Brazilian-Chilean (ABC) alliance, which embodied feelings, values and perceptions that were part of the two presidential visits. But it also reflected intensifying anxieties over external aggression, which promoted the emergence of a separated Latin

American identity. One of the people that played a key role in advanced ideas of unity was the first Minister of Foreign Affairs of the Brazilian republic, Quintino Bocaiuva (1889–1891). As Lidia Besouchet explained, his proposals of alliance with Argentina had strong ideological foundations, with the strong support of Mitre, who argued that the treaties of both countries were "inspirer of American peace."[19]

This leads us to a third issue contributing to a new regional outlook, which is related to foreign—non-Latin American—powers; fundamentally, but not only, the United States. The "giant of the north," as the United States was usually called, had already showed its imperialist face in the mid-19th century, with the takeover of large part of Mexico's territory. That line of action was continued at the Spanish-American War, in 1898, with the intervention of Cuba and Puerto Rico, something that caused strong reactions in the Latin parts of the American continent. Some key names in voicing anti-imperialist, and anti-"Yankee" views, were Spanish-speaking intellectuals and politicians such as José Martí (1853–1895), José Enrique Rodó (1872–1917) and Manuel Ugarte (1875–1951), all authors that were also read in Brazil.

There is no place here to review the history of the concept Latin America,[20] we can though briefly say that these people were part of a movement that formulated new forms of "we" and "them" in the continent. The Cuban, José Martí, was, for example, a strong anti-imperialist voice in the 1889 Washington Conference, using the concept of "our America" to differentiate "Anglo" and "Latin" Americans. He was one of the sources of influence of the Uruguayan Rodó, whose most influential work emerged as a reaction to the intervention of the United States in the Caribbean, with the aim to identify values and ideas that would sustain a "Latin" alternative to "Anglo" American utilitarianism and imperialism. However, Marti never used the concept "Latin America," and Rodó referred fundamentally to *Hispanic America*, Ibero America and later on *Magna Patria*; one of Rodo's contributions was the incorporation of Brazil in his ideals of cultural and national community.[21] As Robert Patrick Newcombe explains, in Rodó, the "commonality of language, even if overstated by foreigners, is responsible for the deep fellow feeling that is key to his *americanista* vision" and a "symbol of tribal identity."[22] However, making a more decisive step toward the incorporation of Brazil was the Argentinean intellectual and political activist Manuel Ugarte, who clearly regarded Brazil as part of the "Latin American" nationhood. In his view, Brazil's destiny as a nation was inseparable from the rest of the continent.[23]

The evolution of such ideas was not alien to Brazilian intellectuals and policy makers, where there also was a growing us-versus-them feeling toward the United States and other foreign powers. As Preuss shows in his study of this period, the influential intellectual and diplomat, Rui Barbosa

(1849–1923), did, for example, describe the Monroe Doctrine "as an expression of US hegemony over 'the two Americas'" pointing out that the threats of that time were rather "located in this continent rather in the old." Another influential intellectual and diplomat (Brazilian ambassador in the United States), to speak in this terms was Joaquim Nabuco (1849–1910), who argued that "nobody can say that Brazilian policy and diplomacy today can continue to be the same as before," and suggesting new forms of response to North American imperialism.[24] Moreover, in his book *Balmaceda*, Nabuco outlined a positive opinion of Chile and new views vis-á-vis Buenos Aires, influenced by a period of strong Argentinean economic prosperity steps of approximation, such as the visits of Roca to Rio and Manoel Ferraz de Campo Salles to Buenos Aires. From the Argentinean point of view, this change reflected concerns for increasing US leverage in the region as well as its commercial competition. Argentina was, in fact, one of the staunchest opponents to the US initiatives in the Washington Conference of 1889.

One of the clearest voices around this issue was the Brazilian Eduardo Prado, which Ugarte himself pointed out as one precursors of Latin America.[25] Prado was a monarchist political writer, from one of Brazil's wealthiest and most influential families. During the 1880s, he traveled to Montevideo, Buenos Aires, Valparaíso and Santiago, and he, during the 1890s, published his influential book, *A ilusão Americana*. In earlier articles, most likely due to the observations of his travels, he advocated a period of increasing contact with the reality of Spanish-speaking countries, as well as a growing awareness of their achievements.[26] That attraction was probably fostered by an increasing criticism to the US imperialism in the region, as well as Prado's adamant rejection of any US involvement with the Latin American nations. Along this line, *A Ilusão Americana* pointed out the negative political, economic and moral influence of the United States, over Brazil and the rest of the continent as well. An interesting issue with Prado was that he, in this book, often recurs to the concept Latin America to designate the "we" of the Spanish- and Luso-speaking countries of the American continent.[27]

Prado's book could be regarded not only as a predecessor of Ugarte but also of Rodo's famous book, *el Ariel*, that was published in the early 1900s. In fact, although Rodo's book is regarded as pivotal in the construction of a Latin American identity, differently to Prado, he does not use the concept of Latin America to identify a "we" among the Latin countries of the American continent. The important here are the shifts that were occurring in Brazil, where the idea of "island" was increasingly changed toward that of Brazil as part of a continent; not only in geographic but also in national, security and philosophical terms. According to people such as Prado, Brazil was also confronted with similar challenges to its neighbors, where the United States and other foreign imperialisms were regarded as a bigger menace than internal rivalries; the role of "Latinity," the universal character of the "Hispanic" legacy and of course, Catholicism were all strong pillars of this view."[28]

It is though important to remark that the concept of Latin America was still not widely used at this time, neither in Brazil nor in the rest of the region. In fact, between 1879 and 1883, Bolivia and Peru where still fighting against Chile in the War of the Pacific. What was emerging, after the bloody wars of the Andes and the Paraguay War at the Southern Cone, could be described as a proto-Latin American nationalism, which was expressed particularly in the field of literature and by visionary political essays. By the late 19th century, this concept began to leave the closer intellectual groups, to enter into more political and technical levels. The need of finding new form of gathering "Latin" countries emerged in the form of Latin America, but also as "South America," in both cases joining Brazil with the Spanish-speaking countries.

In respect to Brazil, one might though identify two positions about these growing positive views toward the neighbor countries. One of them contained a positive view around Latin America, with proposals for further integration, including the exploration of common national identity. Besides Pardo's initial writings, one of those that came closer to the pro-"Latin American'" view was the diplomat and scholar, Manuel de Oliveira Lima (1865–1928), who also served as Brazil's minister to Venezuela. Rejecting the enthusiastic Pan-American "Monroist" position, Oliveira Lima was mostly concerned with the confrontation of imperialism, which demanded unity to balance the "giant of the North." As Maria Theresa Diniz Forster explained, in Oliveira Lima's view, the suspicions among Latin American countries should be overcome by mutual understanding, where a key issue was the union of Brazil and Argentina due to their common bonds as civilization and race.[29] It is, however, important to point out that the divisions among the above-mentioned positions, and the people identified with them, were not clear-cut, since the author and political actors often shifted their positions depending to the agenda and personal experiences. This unionist stand toward Argentina is also the one that we have pointed out among relevant political leaders, in both countries.

In relation to the other position, the "Latin" or "South" American identities were generally not regarded as contradictory with the "Pan-American" or "American" dimensions. Nabuco, for example, was one of those who held that Brazil's continental insertion could take place without breaking with the United States. In his view, Latin America was not able to make "a great material leap forward in the foreseeable future, nor did he believe in its power to defend itself. Fearful of foreign aggression, he thought the South should throw in its lot with the North, emphasizing shared continental values." This position is perhaps what is most associated with Brazilian foreign policy and the mainstream view of national elites. In fact, Prado himself is pointed out finally coming closer to this line, when he openly condemned those who participated in building a "false and artificial solidarity with Brazil's neighbors." According to Preuss, he ended up advocating for Brazil's difference with *other* Americans, Spanish and English and that Brazil's main historical mission was to achieve hegemony in South America's Atlantic rim.[30]

Both Nabuco and Lima had a close intellectual exchange with Rio Branco that since 1902 acquired a key position at the commanding heights of the state, as Minister of Foreign Affairs (1902–1912). He favored what Preuss defined as the "Luso-American" way, a kind of middle position seeking good relations with the neighbors in the framework of a broader Pan-American convergence. Rio Branco did not reject or suppress the debate about this issue, which was also conducted by important intellectuals and diplomats from within Itamaraty, as the Brazilian Ministry of Foreign Affairs was called. In fact, he managed to make a synthesizing of cultural and diplomatic elements from different paths, into a long-lasting national project.

AN "ISLAND" WITH "CONTINENTAL" PROJECTION

Rio Branco's foreign policy was characterized by the maintenance of special relation with Europe, closer links with the United States and a rapprochement with the Brazil's Latin American neighbors. This later aspect implied a clear delimitation of borders with most of the countries of the region, but also initiatives promoting increasing regional cooperation, principally along the ABC framework. The aim of achieving a closer collaboration with the neighbors was, however, balanced within the framework of the Pan-American integration project. It is though important to remind that the adoption and commitment to an "American" system and even of a broader (Pan)-American identity was neither an invention of Rio Branco nor intellectuals of these days. It was not either an invention of US foreign policy. As we pointed out before, at least for the case of Brazil, this dimension was already present, both during the time of Dom João VI and, particularly, in the latter proposals by the José Bonifácio. As Alvaro Lins pointed out, what Rio Branco did was to unite in the national foreign policy elements of Brazil's monarchic and republican periods.[31]

Sustaining the view of Rio Branco as "isolationist," many see him as representative of an old Luso-Spanish cleavage. Nonetheless, much of his line of action was not isolationist but the building and strengthening areas of connection with the region. In that sense, he was perhaps also influenced by "Latin Americanist" views, such as those promoted by people like Manoel de Oliveira Lima, José Veríssimo and Manoel Bonfim; who was a forbearer in the linkage of Latin Americanism and socialist ideas.[32] Thus, the middle position conditioned a closer alignment to the United States, with a deepening of rapprochement with Argentina and other Latin American countries. About this, one could say that Rio Branco continued the line of former Chancellor, Quintino Bocaiuva, who was both champion of Brazilian-Argentine rapprochement as well as an old admirer of the United States.[33] This "admiration" was maintained in time, parallel to the growing power of the United States, in the region and the world. A milestone in the search of amity with the United States was the Third Pan-American Conference, which took place between July 23 and August 27, 1906, in Rio de Janeiro, where the United States was upheld as a continental leader. This, however, did not meant to be subservient and Prado's "alert" remained at the Brazilian commanding heights, as well as the pro-regional "Latin" position. In fact, the Brazilian government elites where increasingly concerned with the goals of achieving regional leadership. The question is if that would be made through the search for hegemony as "island," or by a shared hegemony in the framework of "integration" and "union."

Those who hold the view about Brazil as following the United States, and closed to the region, should explain all other, parallel initiatives that were made. To be sure, there were not only intellectual debates about regional identities, isolated from practice. Besides the mentioned presidential visits and initiatives, there were also new forms of encounters that are interesting for the issued that were treated as well as their composition. One example is the first South American Congress of International Private Law, in Montevideo (1888–1889) that discussed highly relevant issues such as the solution of disputes among countries and a South American legal code of private and international rights.[34] Another was the Latin American scientific conferences, held in Buenos Aires (1898) and Rio de Janeiro (1905).[35] Some years later, in 1908, the first Congress of Latin American Students was held in Montevideo, 1908, where José Enrique Rodó was invited as key note speaker.[36] Not all of these initiatives were led by the government, but, taking into account the view of many leading officials, it is difficult to see this as separated. In our view, these should be regarded as part of the aim in conforming and defining a regional space that would include Brazil.

THE SEARCH OF REGIONAL LEADERSHIP

There is no doubt that the Barão of Rio Branco set the basis for what was to be the outline of Brazilian foreign policy. There might be, however, different interpretations about what this outline is about, as well as in what ways it has influenced the national foreign policy until our days.

In relation to Latin America, one of the issues associated with Rio Branco was the ABC treaty. As pointed out before, the ABC framework was an earlier dimension of South American rapprochement, which took a more real form in the project of a "Pact of Cordial Intelligence" between Argentina, Brazil and Chile, advanced by Rio Branco in 1909. This project turned into a Pact of Non-aggression, Consultation and Arbitrage, signed by the ministers of foreign affairs of these countries, on 25 May 1915, although it was afterward only ratified by Brazil.

It might be generally agreed that the goal of the pact was to facilitate the peaceful solution of international controversies, but there are different interpretations on the meaning, driving forces and scope of the so-called ABC pact. According to Luiz Alberto Moniz Bandeira, the ABC was motivated by a kind of anti-imperialist resistance, aiming to mark distance from the United States. This position is rejected by other, stressing that Rio Branco sought a form of "collective," "shared" or "dual hegemony" over the South American sub-system at the same time as he sought a closer alignment with the United States.[37] Along this line, it has been mentioned that his Pan-Americanism aimed to "multilateralization of the Monroe Doctrine."[38] In our view, even if Rio Branco might have pursued what Bethell called an "Americanization" of Brazilian foreign policy,[39] it did not imply the acceptance of a subservient position. Moreover, an exaggerated emphasize of pro-US inclinations in Brazilian foreign policy together with an overdimension of the "rivalries" with the Latin American countries might also lead to misleading conclusions.

Even though some see the Brazilian-Argentinean rivalry as *natural* and *conflictive*, and the ABC as a way of "isolating Argentina"[40]there are reasons to think that the strategy was more farsighted than that. Particularly, if one, as Carlos Eduardo Vidigal correctly does, highlight that parts of the pact can be linked to the foreign policy of the empire and the affirmation of Brazilian interests in South America.[41] As mentioned before, these interests had, since before independence, a "continental" (South American) scope, where a closer relation with Argentina was (at least recurrently) a strategic guideline. The issue here was not of "isolating" Argentina but to conform a common space of cooperation, where there were forces aiming for deeper forms of integration. The reason for this was geopolitical: on the one hand, it aimed to foster a "continental" projection that required of close regional partners, on the other hand, it put limit to foreign and much stronger powers.

During the early 20th century there were new reasons for that, since the increasingly powerful role of the United States in regional and global geopolitics pushed forward the need for friendly relations and the imperative of marking own areas of influence. The case of the takeover of Panamá by the United States, in 1903, from Colombia, a South American country, was an example of an imperialist aggression toward a South American state, at the border of Brazil. But the US interest in South America did not end at the periphery of the continent. It was later on directed to the South American heartland, to the Amazonian Acre region belonging to Bolivia, about which there was even a book written by the US president Ted Roosevelt.[42] According to Prado, the US interest in the Amazon region was already present by the mid-19th century, when it was held that the three most needed commodities by the United States were "coffee, sugar and robber." It was also here where Prado warned for the intentions of forming filibuster groups with intention to take over the Amazon region, with the same methods used against Mexico and Central American countries.[43] This interest appeared to continue by the late 19th century, with the creation of a private company called Bolivian Syndicate and its promotion of plans for the creation of an independent state in the Acre region. At stake, here was the increasing role of rubber for the burgeoning US car industry.[44]

Eduardo Prado's "alert" was being heard at the Brazilian government, which led Rio Branco to search new forms of peaceful negotiation with the Bolivian government, to extend national (Brazilian and Bolivian) sovereignty over that territory. There were, however, different views on how to do that, leading to a confrontation with Rui Barbosa who favored the use of force if Bolivia did not agree on Brazilian territorial demands. Rio Branco sought to avoid armed conflicts at all cost, not only in Bolivia but with all South American countries. In fact, one of his most remarkable achievements was to have solved Brazil's territorial negotiations with the neighbor countries, without armed conflicts; adding approximately 342.000 square miles of territory, an area greater in size than France.[45] It is probably correct, as Carlos Henrique Cardim holds, that Rio Branco was afraid of negative consequences that such conflict with the neighbor countries would have for Brazil's diplomatic room of maneuver, at that particular moment and for the future.[46]

We should not either forget that the takeover of Panamá was preceded by the military attack, in 1902, by the Great Britain, the German Empire and the Kingdom of Italy, on the Venezuelan city, Puerto Cabello, in reclaim for a debt payment. The response of the United States to this was to announce the Corollary Roosevelt to the Monroe Doctrine aiming, as earlier, to keep European powers out of the Americas. Yet, in this case, there was an extension of US influence assuming the role of international "police power," with a self-authorized right of intervention in the internal affairs of other Western Hemisphere states.[47] Rio Branco had a non-conflicting reaction to both the Panamá intervention and the Roosevelt corollary. Yet, he marked an interesting precedent that Brazil would only recognize the new Panamánian republic, in common agreement with Argentina and Chile, since these nations "should act, simultaneously, strengthened by a unity of points of view and proceedings."[48] This could be regarded as a continuation of the ABC line of action from his predecessors and another step toward the Pact of Cordial Intelligence, from 1909. At the same time as Rio Branco sought to maintain good relations and take as much advantage as possible of the US-regional project, he marked the need of consolidating an own South American space.

It is indeed a matter of interpretation, if that was aimed to exert Brazilian hegemony, or, as suggested by Mota Ardenberg, in the search of a shared influence, with Argentina and Chile.[49] Our long-term perspective leads us along Ardenberg's line of thinking. The search of peaceful relations in the region was a fundamental point of departure in Rio Branco's foreign policy because he knew that despite Brazil's enormous potential, it could not confront non-regional powers without the support of the neighbors.[50] Aware of all limitations of Brazil, he needed both to avoid conflicts with the great powers and an alliance of the neighbors against Brazil. In other words, paraphrasing Juan Carlos Puig, one could say that Rio Branco's search of autonomy needed to *marcher sur le fil du rasoir.*[51]

Beyond the domain of the national state level, it is also important to acknowledge Brazilian contacts with the Spanish-speaking countries, which existed at sub-national levels. We already outlined in chapter 1 the widespread contacts that existed across imperial territories. The catholic missions were a part of this, but there was also a flow of transnational cultural, social and economic relations, across state borders. One post-colonial example was the Revolution of the *Farrapos* in 1835 and the renewed conflicts in 1893, in the so-called Revolution of the *Maragatos* (1893–1894). These were clearly separatist revolutions, with an important intervention on the separatist side, by *montoneros* from Uruguay and Argentina. These, mostly *gaúchos*, were generally close to Federalist forces, led by local *caudillos* with strong popular attachment, voicing strong rejection toward elites and imperialism.[52] But there were more ideas here than those across borders, since there were also military assistance, with caudillos and their *gaúchos* supporting each other.[53] The attempts of building a republic of *gaúchos* failed, yet, the popular attachment, the anti-imperialist stand and the feeling of brotherhood across borders were maintained. It is certainly not a coincidence that is was by *gaúchos* (as people with origin in Rio Grande do Sul call themselves) that future proposals of alignment with the neighbors would come.

The *Farropas* revolution failed to achieve its separatist goals, but that was not the case concerning the line along the "path of integration" of the state. There was a peak of this in 1912, when the Argentinean president Roque Sáenz Peña (1910–1914) visited Brazil, and held that *todo nos une, nada nos separa.*[54] Rio Branco died shortly after that, and the countries were again increasingly separated by the return to power of forces promoting the "path of separation." But, that would change again soon. In sum, Rio Branco's legacy implied a friendly approach toward the United States, but always the "alert" to its big power tendencies. It also searched for the upholding of a Brazilian distinctiveness, not as "island," but as part of a continent. The "geopolitics of peace" that Vidigal refers to[55] is, in our view, linked to a geopolitical conception of the South American territory, where the balance to the non-regional great powers could only be maintained in alliance with the neighbor countries. There was no place here anymore, to Brazilian imperialistic experiments.

TURNING BACK TO THE REGION

During the 1920s, there were deep economic and structural changes causing shift in regional and global frameworks of economic and political relations. At the international economic level, we refer here to the deep economic crisis of the world economy, causing a deep break in Great Britain's role as a financial and commercial node of the international economy. This was particularly problematic for Latin America, and the Southern Cone countries that have had, historically, deepen dependence and advantages of its relation with the British economy. That was particularly true for Argentina, Uruguay or Chile, and also for Brazil. Other countries of Latin America, such as Mexico and Central America, had already been increasingly incorporated in the US economic sphere. Yet, as the global economic crisis continued to deepen, nobody could escape.

The deep contraction in the export of traditional Brazilian export commodities, as coffee, together with the latter import limitations due to the European war, led to an economic crisis. This was worse than the one in 1889, but similar in the sense that it caused strong changes in power relations, across productive sectors and geographic regions. The forces formerly sustaining the so-called old republic were now severely weakened and confronting the challenge of new social groups. Most of this discontent converged in support of a new popular leader from Rio Grande do Sul, Getulio Vargas, who came to power in 1930, after a revolution against the dominant oligarchic regime.

Vargas sought to transform the country, with the goal set on a structural reform of the economy. Brazil had been enormously dependent of the export of primary goods, with a decentralized structure, lack of control of its own territory and resources, and weak national finances to promote development-oriented policies. The latter issue implied new form of policies fostering industrialization, in order to overcome foreign dependency on this sector as well the double export bias, in primary goods and too few foreign markets.

Not only Brazilians but also the rest of the Latin American countries were affected by this negative context, with Argentina and Chile among some of the hardest hit by the crisis. In the case of the former, it became painfully clear by the Roca-Runciman Treaty, in 1933, where Argentina had to accept a reduction of prices for its primary goods export to Great Britain as well as reduction of tariffs for British industrial imports to Argentina, in order to maintain its exports to the British market.[56] In the case of Brazil, the ugly face of the new world system was experienced through the enormous asymmetry of 6 percent in the price of import goods, and the 25 percent decline of export goods, leading to an approximate decline in 30 percent of terms of trade. Things were not much better by the late 1930s. Despite an increase in volume of Brazilian coffee exports, the prices of coffee would fall around 25 percent.[57]

This kind of issues led to a renewed attention toward the region, in political, economic, but also concerning identity (nationhood)-related issues. One example was the new relation with Mexico, partly also as an effect of the Mexican revolution in 1910, that set the country on a new line of relation with the region. This stressed, for example, the common links, based on a common Hispanic-American and Ibero-American identity. There was here a clear policy, from the Mexican side, to promote the integration of Brazil into the "Latin" cultural space, aiming to strengthen regional alliances to compensate its vulnerability toward the United States. For this reason, Mexico sent to Brazil, in a special mission, its Minister of Education, José Vasconcelos. He pursued a more visible presence of Mexico in the southern part of the continent, promoting ideas of integration in relation to defense, economic and cultural-related issues. Later on, during the 1930s, Mexico did also send as ambassador, one of its most renowned intellectuals, Alfonso Reyes.[58]

This kind of intellectual exchanges did not go unnoticed in Brazil. In fact, there was also here a new generation of scholars and intellectuals, promoting broader transnational identities, in the line of those mentioned above. One of this was the anthropologist Gilberto Freyre that found a special attraction to Spanish literature and philosophers, such as Miguel Unamuno and Ortega y Gasset.[59] Moreover, as Flora Sussekind points out, his work took place in a direct dialogue with Bonfim "as evidenced by the many references to *O Brasil na América* (1929), *O Brasil na história* (1930) and *A América Latina* that can be found in *Casa grade e Senzala* (the Masters and the Slaves, 1933)."[60]

Parallel to this, a whole new kind of ideas emerged in the area of geopolitics, promoted during the 1930s, by the geographer Everardo Backheuser. He pointed out the imperious need for the consolidation of national territory, giving a central role to centralization and a stronger role to the state. The focus of Backheuser was also beyond national frontiers, speaking of a South American "continental projection," beyond the traditional focus on the River Plate Basin. Along this line, the Brazilian projection as a growing power had as its core *lebensraum*, not Latin America, but the South American continent. With that scope, the national outlook had to move, according to Backheuser, to the heartland of South America that was the Amazonian region and particularly the territory around Bolivia.[61]

Backheuser strategic insights were of great importance in Brazil. It laid out
the ground for the construction of what later became a Brazilian geopolitical
school, with large influence in policy makers. Yet, even if the analytical framework was different, its main strategic lines are a continuation from prior ideas.
That can be seen in one of the most influential studies in geopolitics, where
Mario Travasso's outlines the "continental projection" of Brazil. Much of this
has main point of departure what he calls the "march to the west,"[62] which is
the same as the *drang nach westen* to which J. Pandia Calógeras referred in his
earlier work (see chapter 1)[63]; in fact, Pandia Calógeras even writes the preface
of Travasso's book. To be sure, this *drang nach westen* of "continental" scope
was not only a matter of intellectuals. There was here a continuity from the
days of the empire, in relation to strong belief in centralization, national unity
and territory, which marked the Vargas administration, where these issues
were made part of the education program at the military academy, and of new
state entities (by the late 1930s) such as the *Instituto Brasileiro de Geografia
e Estatística* (IBGE) or the *Conselho Nacional de Geografia*.[64]

This period saw the emergence of a kind of "geographic ideology"[65]
through which the Brazilian state promoted a policy of national territorial
control and occupation, particularly at its frontiers and the vast Amazonian
region. One example of this engagement was the intervention to mediate in
the border conflict between Colombia and Peru around the so-called Leticia
issue, during the late 1920s. Brazil was here a key actor at the Treaty of
Salomón-Lozano, reaching a peaceful solution of this conflict, in 1934. Brazil
played also an active role in efforts to mediate in the Chaco War, between
Bolivia and Paraguay (1932–1935).[66] For some, this regional outlook implied
the construction of an area of Brazilian hegemony, not of integration, something that sustained continuity in the hypothesis, and action, of rivalry with
Argentina. Nevertheless, this was not the line of Vargas government. For this
reason, in 1935, Vargas' ambassador to Washington and later his Minister of
Foreign Affairs, Oswaldo Aranha, held that "nothing explains our [Brazilian]
support toward the United States on its issues in Central America, without an
attitude of reciprocal support for Brazil in South America."[67] Nothing very
different here to Rio Branco's position, nor to the one, earlier on, in its cautious relations toward the British Empire. Without entering into conflict with
influential great powers, the intention here was to transform South America
into an autonomous region. At least in the case of Vargas, it was understood
that this could not be made by Brazil alone. Again, we see here a confrontation with those searching for Brazilian hegemony, with those pursuing shared
hegemony. This meant an alignment with Argentina that in the case of Vargas
had much higher ambitions than prior initiatives in this direction.

An interesting and scarcely mentioned example was the contacts to establish a
progressive liberalization scheme, with the outspoken goal of creating a custom

union that in time would also be opened to the other countries of the region.[68] The first initiatives for this were made in bilateral discussions of new trade initiatives to deal with wartime emergencies. But this revived, as Edgar J. Dosman, pointed out, the "long-standing dream of the formation of a common market in the River Plate Basin, anchored by Brazil and Argentina but including Uruguay, Paraguay, and if possible Chile, which would bury their rivalry and together create a South American bloc in the world economy.[69]

As Dosman further tells, in private meetings with the Argentinean president, Minister of finance, Federico Pinedo and Raúl Prebisch (at that moment President of the Argentinean Central Bank), Vargas "underlined his support for building a large regional market." All this would be confirmed in a River Plate Basin Conference Conference to be held in January 1941 that also aimed to set up a secretariat in Buenos Aires with an explicit support of Pan-Americanism. Another officer with great influence was the Argentinean Minister of Foreign Affairs and former ambassador in Brazil, Julio Argentino Pascual Roca, son of the former president Julio A. Roca.

Even if caution was made to explicitly assure alliance to Pan-Americanism this convergence was not regarded with much enthusiasm by the United States. Both Roca and Pinedo lost their positions and Aranha finally refused to attend the conference, which was to be held in Montevideo on 27 January.[70] More research is needed around this episode, but it appears that Argentina and Brazil were still attached to different economic and power spaces; Brazil to the United States and Argentina (still during this period) to Great Britain. Both countries intended to maximize the opportunities for national development by exploiting the rivalries among the different great powers, including approximations toward Germany. It is probably not a coincidence that around the time of this negotiation with Argentina, Brazil assured, on April 1941, the support of United States president Franklin Delano Roosevelt (1933–1945), for the construction of the steel mill complex, *Companhia Siderúrgica Nacional* (CSN), at Volta Redonda. This was central for the Brazilian project of national industrialization, which was at the key of Vargas' strategy. But it implied an open participation of Brazil in the war efforts in Europe, and probably did also contribute to the freeze of integration initiatives with Argentina, that at that moment was confronted with the United States due to its neutrality policy. However, circumstantial political issues did not mean a distancing of Vargas' government from the neighbor countries.

NOTES

1. Jeffry Cason, "On the Road to Southern Cone Economic Integration," *Journal of Latin American Studies and World Affairs*, vol. 42, no. 1 (2000), 23–42; Karl Katlenthaler and Frank O. Mora, "Explaining Latin American Economic Integration:

The Case of Mercosur," *Review of International Political Economy*, no. 9 (2002), 72–97.

2. Clodoaldo Bueno, Tullo Vigevani and Haroldo Ramanzini Júnior, "Latin American Integration: a Brazilian View," in Andrés Rivarola Puntigliano and José Briceño Ruiz (eds.), *Resilience of Regionalism in Latin America and the Caribbean: Development and Autonomy*, (London: Palgrave Macmillan, 2013), 209.

3. Darcy Riberio, *O Povo Brasileiro* (São Paulo: Companhia das Letras, 2006), 59.

4. Felipe Herrera, *America Latina Integrada* (Buenos Aires: Losada S.A., 1964).

5. See, Leslie Bethell, *Brazil. Empire and Republic, 1822–1930* (Cambridge: Cambridge University Press, 1993 [1989]).

6. Fought between an alliance between the Argentine Confederation, the Empire of Brazil, Uruguay and the Argentine provinces of Entre Ríos and Corrientes, against the Governor of Buenos Aires, Juan Manuel de Rosas.

7. This was due to the alliance between the Argentine Republic, the Empire of Brazil and the Oriental Republic of Uruguay.

8. Ori Preuss, *Bridging the Island: Brazilians' Views of Spanish America and Themselves, 1865–1912* (Madrid: Iberoamericana – Vervuert, 2011), 37–8.

9. Victor Bulmer-Thomas, *The Economic History of Latin America since Independence*, Second edition (Cambridge: Cambridge University Press, 2003), 64.

10. Ori Preuss, *Bridging the Island, 1865–1912*, 83.

11. Fredrik Johannesson, *Det Panamerikanska Problemet 1826–1920. En Studie i Modern Politik* (Norrköping: Norrköpings Tidningars Aktiebolags Tryckeri, 1922); Leandro Morgenfeld, *Vecinos en Conflicto. Argentina y Estados Unidos en las Conferencias Panamericanas (1880–1955)* (Buenos Aires: Ediciones Continente, 2011).

12. Alain Rouquié, *América Latina. Introducción al Extremo Occidente* (Mexico D.F: Siglo Veintiuno Editores, 1997), 411.

13. Arturo Ardao, *Nuestra América Latina. Temas Latinoamericanos 1* (Montevideo: Ediciones de la Banda Oriental, 1986).

14. Ori Preuss, *Bridging the Island*, 164.

15. Ibid., 98.

16. Ibid., 58.

17. Ibid., 148.

18. José Paradiso, *Um Lugar no Mundo. A Argentina e a Busca de Indentidade Internacional* (Rio de Janeiro: Civilização Brasileira, 2005), 53.

19. Lidia Besouchet, *Rio-Branco e as Relações Entre Brasil e a República Argentina* (Rio de Janeiro: Ministério das *Relações* Exteriores, 1949), 46.

20. See, Miguel Rojas Mix, *Los Cien Nombres de América* (Barcelona: Lumen, 1992).

21. Arturo Ardao, *La Inteligencia Latinoamericana* (Montevideo: Universidad de la República, 1996), pp. 53. See also, José Enrique Rodó, "Ibero-America," in *Obras Competas de José Enrique Rodo*, (ed.) Alberto José Vaccaro (Buenos Aires: Ediciones Antonio Zamora, 1948).

22. Robert Patrick Newcombe, "José Enrique Rodó: 'Iberoamérica,' the Magna Patria, and the question of Brazil." *Hispania*, 93, no. 3 (2010): 368–379, 372, 376.

23. Miguel Ángel Barrios. *El Latinoamericanismo en el Pensamiento Político de Manuel Ugarte* (Buenos Aires: Editorial Biblos, 2007); Manuel Ugarte, *El Destino de un Continente* (Buenos Aires: Ediciones de la Patria Grande, 1962 [1923]).

24. Ori Preuss, *Bridging the Island*, 133.

25. Manuel Ugarte, *El Destino de un Continente*, 145.

26. Ori Preuss, *Bridging the Island*, 44.

27. Eduardo Prado, *A Ilusão Americana* (Brasília: Senado Federal, Conselho Editorial, Edições do Senado Federal, vol. 11, 2003).

28. See for example, Eduardo Prado, *A Ilusão Americana*, 81.

29. Maria Theresa Diniz Forster, *Oliveira Lima e as Relações Exteriores do Brasil: O Legado de um Pionero e sua Relevância Atual Para a Diplomacia Brasileira* (Brasilia: Fundação Alexandre de Gusmão, 2011), 118.

30. Ori Preuss, *Bridging the Island*, 93.

31. Alvaro Lins, *Rio-Branco (O Barão do Rio-Branco) 1845–1912*, vol. 2 (Rio de Janeiro: Livraria José Olympio Editora, 1945), 392.

32. Flora Süssekind, "Shifting Frontiers – Manuel Bonfim and A América Latina: An Introduction," *Journal of Latin American Cultural Studies: Travesía*, vol. 11, no. 1 (2002), 65–76, 75.

33. Ori Preuss, *Bridging the Island*, 127.

34. Fredrik Johannesson, *Det Panamerikanska Problemet*, 39–40.

35. INTAL, "Historia Latinoamericana. Congresos Científicos Latinoamericanos," *Integración Latinoamericana*, vol. 2, no. 14 (1977): 95–96.

36. Alberto Methol Ferré, "Del Arielismo al Mercosur," in Leopoldo Zea and Hernán Taboada (eds.), *Arielismo y Globalización* (México D.F: Instituto Panamericano de Geografía e Historia, 2002), 33.

37. Guilherme Frazão Conduru, "O Subsistema Americano, Rio Branco e o ABC," *Revista Brasileira de Política Internacional*, vol. 41, no. 2 (1998), 74.

38. Ibid., 77–78.

39. Leslie Bethell, "Brazil and Latin America", *Journal of Latin American Studies* 42, (2010): 457–485, 465.

40. Carlos Eduardo Vidigal, "Rio Branco, Los Tratados de ABC y la Construcción de la Potencia Cordial," in Maria Ignacia Matus Matus and Gilberto Aranda Bustamante, *A 100 Años del ABC: Desafíos y Proyecciones en el Marco de la Integración Regional* (Santiago: CESIM-IEI, 2016), 43, 51.

41. Ibid., 49.

42. Theodore Roosevelt, *Through the Brazilian Wilderness* (New York: Charles Scribner's Sons, 1914).

43. Eduardo Prado, *A Ilusão Americana*, 69.

44. Luiz Alberto Moniz Bandeira, *Conflicto e Integração na América do Sul. Brasil, Argentina e Estados Unidos. Da Tríple Aliança ao Mercosul* (Rio de Janeiro: Editora Revan, 2003), 73–5.

45. E. Bradford Burns, *A History of Brazil* (New York: Columbia University Press, 1970), 323.

46. Carlos Henrique Cardim, "O Barao do Rio Branco e Rui Barbosa," in Carlos Henrique Cardim & João Almino (eds.), *Rio Branco a América do Sul e a Modernização do Brasil* (Rio de Janeiro: EMC – Edições, 2002), 188.

47. Mark Eric Williams, *Understanding U.S.-Latin American Relations. Theory and History* (New York: Routledge, 2012), 102.

48. Luiz Alberto Moniz Bandeira, *Conflicto e Integração* 101.

49. R. M. Ardenberg, "Rio Branco e a Emergência do Ambiente Científico no Brasil," in Carlos Henrique Cardim and João Almino (eds.), *Rio Branco a América do Sul e a Modernização do Brasil* (Rio de Janeiro: EMC – Edições, 2002), 363.

50. Guilherme Frazão Conduru, "O Subsistema Americano," 65.

51. Juan Carlos Puig, *Doctrinas Internacionales y Autonomía Latinoamericana* (Caracas: Universidad Simón Bolívar, 1980), 153.

52. Arthur Ferreira Filho, *Historia Geral do Rio Grande do Sul* (Porto Alegre: Editora Globo, 1978).

53. Ibid., 174–5.

54. "Everything unite us, nothing separate us," quoted in L. M. Moreno Quintana, *El Sistema Internacional Americano* (Buenos Aires: Facultad de Derecho y Ciencias Sociales, 1925), 475.

55. Carlos Eduardo Vidigal, "Rio Branco, Los Tratados," 49.

56. The treaty was signed by the Argentinean vice president Julio Argentino Roca (son) and the British trade representative, Walter Runciman.

57. Boris Fausto, *O Brasil Republicano. Economía e Cultura (1930–1964). História Geral da Civilização Brasileira*, vol. 4 (São Paulo: Difel, 1984), 17, 24.

58. Regina Aída Crespo, "Cultura e política: José Vasconcelos e Alfonso Reyes no Brasil (1922–1938)," *Revista Brasileira de História*, São Paulo, vol. 23, no. 45 (2003), 187–208.

59. Elide Rugai Bastos, *Gilberto Freyre e o Pensamiento Hispânico. Entre Dom Quixote e Alonso el Bueno* (Bauru: EDUSC/ANPOCS, 2003), 156.

60. Flora Süssekind, "Shifting Frontiers – Manuel Bonfim," 70.

61. Everardo Backheuser, *Curso de Geopolítica Geral e do Brasil* (Rio de Janeiro: Gráfica Laemmert Limitada, 1948).

62. Mario Travassos, *Projeção Continental do Brasil* (São Paulo: Companhia Editora Nacional, 1947), 243.

63. J. Pandiá Calógeras, *A Política Exterior do Imperio*, vol. 1 (Brasília: Senado Federal, 1998), 155, 159.

64. Wanderley Messias da Costa, *Geografía Política e Geopolítica* (São Paulo: Editora Universidad de São Paulo), 186–7.

65. Antonio Carlos Robert Moraes, *Geografia Histórica do Brasil* (São Paulo: Anna Blume, 2009), 124.

66. Amado Luiz Cervo & Cloaldo Bueno, *Historia da Politica Exterior do Brasil*, 240–244.

67. Luiz Alberto Moniz Bandeira. "O Brasil e a América do Sul," in Henrique de Oliveira Altemani and Antônio Carlos Lessa (eds.). *Relacões Inernacionais do Brasil. Temas e Agendas*, vol. 1 (São Paulo: Editora Saraiva, 2006), 272.

68. Mario Rapoport and Eduardo Madrid, *Argentina- Brasil. De Rivales a Aliados* (Buenos Aires: Capital Intelectual, 2011), 268.

69. Edgar J. Dosman, *The Life and Times of Raúl Prebisch, 1901–1986* (Montreal: McGill-Queen's University Press, 2008), 126.

70. Ibid., 133.

Chapter 4

"Setting the Path for Integration"

Developmentalism, Nationalism and Integration

This chapter is devoted to Brazilian relations with other Latin American countries since the mid- 20th century, to the preamble of deeper integration with Argentina, by the mid-1980s. A starting point of this chapter is about the change of course toward the region, during the Vargas administration, in relation to Brazil's insertion to the region. One aspect of this was a closer alignment with Argentina and the government of Juan Domingo Perón (1946–1955). Another was the position of Vargas's government to support the creation and permanence of the CEPAL—that became one of the most important promotors of Latin American regional integration. Vargas was successful in this issue, but not concerning a deeper alliance with Argentina. He faced strong reactions from anti-integrationist groups in Brazil, who used the Argentinean issue as a way of conducting a hostile campaign against the government; at the end, leading to Vargas suicide. Yet, his positive position on rapprochement with Argentina and the Latin American countries was not forgotten. It was in part followed by the posterior government of Kubitschek, during the brief government of Jânio da Silva Quadros (1961–1961) and, particularly, by Vargas's former Minster of Labor (and Kubitschek's vice president), João Goulart (1961–1964). Even if there was a break of integration-oriented initiatives after the military coup in 1964, this chapter outlines a gradual return of integration-oriented initiatives since the government of Artur da Costa e Silva (1967–1969).

VARGAS AND "LATIN AMERICA"

By the late 1940s, Vargas had lost his former supporter and ally, Franklin Delano Roosevelt, and the new US authorities set a lower priority for Latin

American countries, including Brazil. Having sided with the allies, or not, the post-war situation for the Latin American countries, including Brazil, was problematic. There was a search for markets to their export goods as well as credit to finance the maintenance and growth of the industrializa-tion process that had been going on during the prior decades. Particularly in relation to the industrial sector that took great advantage of the import sub-stitution that received a boost during the world wars. In the case of Brazil, Vargas government had been able to find advantageous deals and sources of financing through what Gerson Moura called a policy of "pragmatic equi-distance," referring fundamentally to Brazil's dealings with Germany and the United States.[1] Yet, in our view, the analysis of this external framework as proposed by Moura, dealing with Brazil's relation to different great pow-ers, cannot give a proper understanding of its foreign policy, without fully taking into account the regional dimension. In the case of Vargas, and in different ways his followers mentioned above, the "pragmatic equidistance" did also involve the region. This is one of the issues that this chapter intends to address. Our point is that the region mattered to such an extent that the proper word to label the government's foreign policy strategy was not "prag-matic equidistance," but "autonomy." As we see it, there might have been "pragmatism" at the beginning, but by the 1950s, pragmatism had evolved into an ideological package with two main components: autonomy and national-developmentalism.

One of the issues that marked the emergence of a Latin American dimension in Brazilian government policies and foreign policy thinking was the creation of CEPAL, in 1948, with headquarters in Santiago de Chile. It is important to note that this happened while the United States promoted the re-invention of Pan-Americanism through a new continental initiative, in the creation of the Organization of American States (OAS), also in 1948. This entity was an institutional continuation of the Pan-American Union, created during the late 19th century. Yet, the OAS had much less ambitious than its predecessors, born in the far-sighted integrationist proposals of the Washington conference of 1889. There were much of values, norms and security-oriented issues in the OAS, but not much related to trade and sources of development financing, which was what the Latin Americans were mostly interested of.

This time, the initiative to think in terms of regional integration was of the Latin Americans, and that is one reason for their search to create other entities through which they could promote their own priorities. We speak about entities, in plural, since there was more than CEPAL during these years. One example was the Guatemalan leadership in promoting (with the assistance of CEPAL) the creation of a Central American Common Mar-ket. Another initiative was made at Latin American regional level. Again, Guatemala was a key player as the country hosting the first Conference of

Latin American Universities, in 1949. Something that led to the creation of the Unión de Universidades de América Latina (UDUAL).[2]

CEPAL was part and driving force of this Latin American integrationist wave. Originally proposed by Latin American diplomats at the UN's Economic and Social Council (ECOSOC), its mandate was to make advanced studies on Latin America's economic and social structures, to analyze the problems for development and make strategies to overcome them. Although this entity was incorporated within the UN's organizational umbrella and its general secretary would be named by the UN's general secretary, the ownership was of the Latin American governments, with observers from outside. There were many novelties here. One was this regional ownership. Although there was much influence from experts around the world (particularly from the UN system), CEPAL grouped a body of high-level Latin American experts and scholars that would be led by another Latin American: the Argentinean economist, Raúl Prebisch.[3] Another novelty was the official recognition about the "development" issue and the need, and demand, for common regional strategies to overcome underdevelopment and a "peripheral" position in the world system.

Beyond all this, we would like to remark the fact that one of the dimensions chosen by governments to promote integration, at different levels, was the "Latin American." The creation of CEPAL was the first time that an international entity, partly owned by the states, used the word "Latin America" in its official name. This showed the increasing legitimacy of the concept "Latin America," which now started to gain widespread acceptance, although it had not yet really become of popular use. Another remarkable thing was that Brazil participated in all this, not as an odd guest, but as a leading country. In fact, although this is often overlooked, Brazil took the role as main promoter. Even if the original initiative to create CEPAL came from a Chilean diplomat, and other Latin American representatives at the UN's ECOSOC,[4] it was Vargas who played a key role in assuring CEPAL's survival. The birth of CEPAL was a highly controversial issue. It was promoted by the Latin American governments, but it was resisted by the United States that wanted to give priority to the OAS. It was also rejected by the Soviet Union that was afraid of more pro-market entities at the United Nations, by countries that were closer to the United States.

Due to the insistence of Latin American governments and other, such as France, there was an open door to create CEPAL in 1948, but its continuity had to be ratified in 1951, after a report from ECOSOC. At that moment, according to Gert Rosenthal, the United States had set a strong offensive to incorporate CEPAL to the OAS.[5] By that time, the Soviet Union had changed position, and favored the maintenance of CEPAL. The big hurdle was to confront the US government. That was not an easy task after the war when there was "a major advance in the influence of the US in Latin America."[6] Brazil was, however, not a driving force during the creation process of CEPAL, which coincided with the government of Eurico Gaspar Dutra (1946–1951). At this moment, the major interest in supporting the creation of CEPAL was in the promotion of industrial re-equipment and to deal jointly with the global prices of primary goods. [7] Yet, the official position was to have a low profile and avoid confrontation with the United States.

There was a new context in 1951, but also, with Vargas presidency, a more active Brazilian government concerning regional integration. According to a Brazilian key actor at CEPAL, Celso Furtado, there was a general agreement among the Latin Americans to maintain CEPAL, something that had particularly strong support among the Central Americans. Yet, there was a need of a leader behind which all could group in order to confront the United States. While countries such as Mexico and Argentina hesitated and were not willing to step up, it was Vargas' Brazil who openly led the Latin American countries in their position to maintain the commission—with success. In Furtado's opinion, what determined this Brazilian resolution was that "Vargas's had a clear perception in that a country such as Brazil needed to broaden its spaces of international action, which was what was at stake here."[8] This meant a major step toward the region concerning the Brazilian foreign and economic policy. But there was more, this also marked an identity shift, in a new and, until CEPAL, unprecedented official attachment to a regional identity—in common with the Spanish-speaking countries.

Until then, the only official commitment to a regional identity was linked to "America," which meant a belonging to the same system as United States and other Latin countries of the continent. By the early 1950s, without abandoning the strong linkage with the United States and Pan-Americanism, Vargas led Brazil a step closer along the "path of integration," which was also going to be one of the most important issues promoted by CEPAL. Going back to Furtado again, it can be argued that to broaden Brazil's international room of maneuver, Vargas was interested in maintaining the autonomy of CEPAL and to that purpose fostered ideas of union among Latin Americans.[9]

VARGAS AND PERÓN

Toward the mid of the 20th century, Vargas' development-oriented project was presenting good results, but the Brazilian economy was, as always, highly vulnerable to the ups and downs of the international market due to its great dependence on primary goods exports, concentrated in few commodities and few markets—besides a chronic dependence on foreign investments and loans. This was, again, a highly problematic issue by the early 1950s, when Vargas returned to government for a second period (1951–1954)—after winning open democratic elections. At this time, also coinciding in power with the presidency of Juan Domingo Peron, in Argentina (1946–1955), that was an outspoken promoter of Latin American autonomy and integration. This issue, as such, was not a novelty. What was new with Perón was that he was, as president and through one of the most powerful states of the region, heralded Latin Americanism and integration as national ideologies and objectives.

With CEPAL, Perón and other forces across the region, the "path of integration" was beginning a new and expansive wave, this time adopting an attractive regional identity, through the concept of "Latin America." Despite all being said and written about the "natural rivalry" between Brazil and Argentina, there is much evidence in that Vargas' closer line of action toward the region, also included Argentina. Something of strategic importance in order to create a common regional space to foster Brazilian industrialization and autonomy.

A more immediate background to this was the initiative of the early 1940s to an agreement with Argentina, which we analyzed in chapter 3. And, if we look a bit further back in time, we find the ABC pact. In these cases, the motivations were oriented to either security, as in the case of the ABC, or trade, as in the 1940s where the states negotiated advanced integration-oriented proposals such as a customs union. Yet, during the early 1950s there was a new qualitative change, which was particularly interesting in the case of Brazil. Embracing the Latin American dimension implied a major shift in "national" alignments, since the adoption of Pan-Americanism as part of the countries international identification. In this sense, the official acceptance of the concept of "Latin America" could be regarded as a new step toward the path of integration.

The issue was not only discursive, since Vargas also nominated people in key positions that were positive toward this advanced form of involvement with the Spanish-speaking countries. One of these was Brazil's new ambassador in Buenos Aires, a *caudillo* from Rio Grande do Sul, João Batista Lusardo. With roots in the revolutionary movement during the 1930s, Batista Lusardo maintained a tight relation with Argentina and Uruguay (where he also served as ambassador). In his view, the peoples of this region were of the same nation, and Brazil should continue its traditional policy of understanding with the peoples of America, among whom a particular role would be given to the River Plate Basin countries.[10]

When Perón launched the proposal for a new ABC pact, in 1951, Batista Lusardo was one of the most enthusiastic supporters, since he saw great possibilities for Brazil and the region. Perón was indeed a driving force behind the second ABC, but the origins of the initiative are more complex. As we argued before, the idea of cooperation among the ABC countries already existed during the late 19th century. Later on, in 1929, the Chilean president Carlos Ibañez del Campo (1927–1931 y 1952–1958) had proposed a Southern Union, and there were here visions concerned with the promotion of monetary union, customs union and other kind of advanced objectives.[11] Concerning the economic dimension, much of that was inspired in the work of the Argentinean economist, Alejandro Bunge, which by the early 20th century had written about a Customs Union of the South, which included Brazil.[12] All this should not be delinked from other movements in line with the path of integration, such as the 1941 proposal of a custom union, where the broadening toward inclusion of Chile and other South American countries was considered.

Thus, the new geopolitical framework advanced by Peron did not come out of the blue. In fact, as Carlos Piñeiro Iñíguez suggests, besides the above-mentioned antecedents and ideas, Perón's national and regional development and geopolitical project was highly inspired in the experience with the neighbors. But Vargas' *Estado Novo* was probably one of the most relevant sources of inspiration, where Argentinean military strategists, such as José María Sarobe, had acquired ideas and contacts that later would have strong influence on Perón.[13] However, the new ABC proposal was very different from the earlier one, in that this had no link to the Pan-American framework. It followed, in some way, the above-mentioned opposition between CEPAL and OAS, since it had autonomist ambitions in respect to external powers.

There was, though, one important difference here with CEPAL, that was related to the South American framework in which, at least Perón, was framing these initiatives. Perón went as far as to promote the creation of a United States of South America, with Argentina and Brazil as a key axis.[14] Perhaps, since the days of King João VI, no leading political personality had spoken so clearly of South America as a geopolitical unit, and a common state.[15] In this sense, it was Perón who was actually closer to central ideas from the Portuguese Empire, and not the Brazilians fiercely opposing Vargas's linkage with Argentina and the South American countries. This opposition could not either accept other parts of the ideas advanced in the framework of the second ABC, related to economy where Perón and other South American politicians were, in fact, ahead of CEPAL in terms of fostering integration.

Yet, like in the past, these kinds of advanced integrationist initiatives did also face strong resistance and there is a debate concerning the extent to which Vargas actually shared the visions of Perón. It is clear, however, that Vargas had sent signals of approximation, such as the nomination of Batista Lusardo.[16] Moreover, if we have in mind Vargas' earlier initiatives and the people he choosed to maintain the links with Argentina, it is likely that there were intentions of a deeper union with Argentina.[17] Yet, as Rio Branco,

Vargas had to *marcher sur le fil du rasoir,* not only because the internal opposition in Brazil but also due to the strong hostility of the United States toward Peron's government. As argued by Moniz Bandeira, the negative correlation of forces forced Vargas to be reserved on this point.[18] The sensibility in Brazil around this issue can be seen in how it became the center of opposition's campaign against Vargas' government, and at the later military/ civilian conspiracy that led to his suicide in 1954. There are different opinions on the role of the United States in this, but it is clear that the positive view on state involvement in the national development projects of Peron and Vargas and the ideas around import substitution-oriented measures to foster intra-regional trade (with stronger state support) were not in line with the position of the United States that "private capital could and should shape Latin American development.[19]

Vargas's death led to a halt in the path of integration and a brief return to the antagonist path of separation, whose supporters accused Perón to be a "new Rosas" and a "new Hitler."[20] Yet, the room of maneuver of Vargas's opponents was limited by the powerful popular reaction that his suicide generated, where the masses went out to the streets against those identified as perpetrators of his death and as supporters of an anti-popular coup. Anti-imperialism, particularly against the United States, was a strong feeling here, together with a strong wave of popular nationalism. This strong reaction and the projection of Vargas' political image possibly laid the bases for the continuance of Varguismo, through the electoral victory of Kubitschek in 1956. With Kubitschek "developmentalism" became a national ideology with strong attachment to popular movements, but also to sectors of the army and the private sector, especially at the industry. This "developmentalist" ideology did also mean a strategy of maintaining a closer relation with the neighbors, to large extent, in line with Vargas' continentalist approach.

If one should describe continentalist thinking in few words, it would be the unity on a territory of continental dimension. Again, this outlook, with great pervasiveness in parts of Brazilian political, intellectual and economic elites, was not an invention of Rio Branco or Vargas, but had deep roots since the time of the Portuguese Empire. What Vargas did was to continue along that tradition but using the new models associated to modern states, as those outlined by Everardo Backheuser and Mario Travassos (see chapter 3). We are aware in that there are different interpretations on this. Of course, there are different interpretations on what this "tradition" was about. The outlook of the "Brazilian island" was part of this, but also the "continentalist" outlook, searching to consolidate a shared space to guarantee peace, autonomy and in the minds of some, the search for "union." Even if Vargas failed to achieve his objective, his long political struggle and ultimate sacrifice managed to create the basis for the geopolitics of development and integration with a "continental" outlook. Without leaving the Latin American framework, South America increasingly emerged, or rather re-emerged, as the core regional framework of Brazilian regionalism. For those continuing along Vargas' path the issue was clear, Brazil was neither an island nor a continent. The continent was South America, and the control of this territory had to be shared. That was the view of the Treaty of Madrid, of the first ABC and in the later search of a Brazilian-Argentinean axis. This time, also in search of a common ground within the Latin American region.

DEVELOPMENTALISM AND REGIONAL INTEGRATION

Jucelino Kubitschek had many achievements during his period of government, but what probably will be remembered as one of the most remarkable is the moving the countries' capital from Rio de Janeiro, to a totally new-built city, named Brasilia. There is much to say about this, not the least the great economic impact it had. What concerns us here is the geopolitical dimension. The initiative to move the capital cannot be separated to "continentalist" outlook mentioned before, in line with ideas that had also been advanced by Backheuser and Travassos. It did, indeed, aimed to reach a factual centralization and occupation of the national territory, but there was also a "continental projection." Brasilia pointed toward the Amazon region and from there to the South American heartland.

Shifting the capital to central Brazil was part of the *drang nach westen* to consolidate the heartland of the continent. We mentioned, in chapter 1, how this vision took form during the Portuguese Empire. Its goal was not just to control the Amazon, nor the silver mines of Alto Peru (current Bolivia), it was also to reach the long-desired pathway to the Andes and from there to the Pacific Ocean. As was also explained in chapter 1, this was one of the reasons for the foundation of Colonia de Sacramento, back in the 18th century as well as for the earlier expansion toward the Amazonas region, within the framework of the Iberian Union. With Vargas and Kubitschek, this "continental outlook" was invigorated, but not with imperialism or hostile hegemony, but through increased regional cooperation.

During Kubitschek's government, the industrialization efforts promoted by Vargas continued and were starting to deliver. By the late 1950s, the Brazilian industrial sector was growing at record levels, yet, limited by a narrow domestic economy, it was in badly need of export markets. In spite of a cooler attitude toward CEPAL at the beginning of his mandate, Kubitschek's government finally adopted a more friendly and proactive position in support of CEPAL's initiatives in relation to integration and industrialization.

One example was the Meeting of Experts on Iron and Steel in São Paulo, in October 1956, where, as Edgar J. Dosman pointed out, "the Brazilian private sector registered in force, the first time it had rallied so evidently behind ECLA."[21] There were political, ideological but also structural elements, behind the direction of Kubitschek's policy orientation. The two world wars transformed industrialism into a priority, in the bigger countries, Argentina, Brazil and Mexico, but also in smaller ones such as Chile and Uruguay. Thus, a feature of the post-war period was an accelerating industrial growth. As pointed out by Rosemary Thorp, by the 1950s, for the first time "manufactured goods were being traded within Latin America: Brazilian, Argentine, and Mexican textile exports to other Latin American countries, for example, rose from almost nothing in 1939 to 20 percent of total exports by 1945."[22]

None of these meant, however, that Brazil had the intention of seeking conflict with the United States, or of rejecting the continental, American, dimension. On the contrary, the line of balancing the interest of the great powers, the United States in particular, was maintained by Kubitschek. He actually intended to give new life to Pan-Americanism, seeking, to attract the United States to his initiative of a Pan-American Operation (OPA in Spanish and Portuguese),[23] with the goal of creating a kind of Marshall Plan for Latin America. One objective here was also to substitute bilateralism, for the construction of multilateral platforms from Brazilian development and foreign policy initiatives are conducted.[24]

By the early 1960s there was, in fact, an opening in the United States for initiatives from Latin America, as well as a more positive outlook at its integration initiatives. The United States did even accept, as first president of the newly created Inter-American Development Bank (1959), the Chilean economist, Felipe Herrera—former minister of Ibañez del Campo and an adamant promoter of Latin American integration and nationalism. There was actually an unprecedented collaboration between the US government and Latin American experts and leading politicians. Kubitschek was part of this, and one of those who inspired and collaborated with the original project leading to the Alliance of Progress.[25] This collaboration was supported by US president John F. Kennedy (1961–1963), who pointed out that the goal of the Alliance was to promote social justice, growth and political stability

Yet, there was nothing even close to a kind "Marshall Plan" here, and the US government became, instead, fundamentally concerned with security issues along its own priorities. The United States rejection of the OPA and other forms of economic support for Latin American development–oriented proposals led Brazil toward a more active engagement in regional alternatives, through the Latin American dimension. Brazilian policymakers and private sector companies started now to converge around the need to promote the creation of a Latin American trade agreement, with other countries of the region and the CEPAL. There was though an important debate concerning the ambitions of this agreement. From the side of CEPAL and other actors in this process (governments, experts and intellectuals), the goal should be to establish a common market, along similar lines as those discussed in prior proposals and visions of integration; remember that Prebisch had been part of the 1941 negotiations with Brazil. At the late 1950s, there was also a new model for this kind of entities, which was the European Economic Communities (EEC), created in 1957. Nevertheless, this more ambitious integrationist position failed to get the upper hand in Latin America, at that moment.

The result was the creation of LAFTA, in 1961, which was more like another newly created European institution, from 1960, the European Free Trade Association (EFTA). The word "free market," in LAFTA, indicates that the scope was for a less ambitious type of integration than original proposals of common market. It was politically and economically difficult to go all the way, many countries did not either want to confront the United States, which was, in relation to integration, only positive to the idea of free market–oriented process.[26] Yet, even if the defenders of more ambitious forms of integration were disappointed with the outcome of the process leading to LAFTA, this entity marked a new phase in the historical process of Latin America regional integration.

LAFTA was the first intergovernmental economic regional integration organization, to survive from its cradle, and it was the second international organization with Latin America in its title. Differently to CEPAL, LAFTA was fully owned by Latin American countries, but similarly to CEPAL Brazil played a major role in its creation and sustenance. For Brazil, this meant a clear step in the continuity of Vargas' line of action. It is though important to make clear that its membership did not really cover the whole Latin American region, since the Central American countries went their own way, with a more ambitious project of creating a Central American Common Market (CACM). Nonetheless, almost all South American countries were part of this, and Mexico, something that gave legitimacy to the "Latin American" scope of LAFTA. There was though nothing of the *gaucho*, regional spirit in Kubitschek, which might have existed in Vargas. What predominated here was an accentuation of a national and regional economic process that was stimulated by Vargas and Kubitschek's developmentalism.

From the perspective of Brazil, the industrial sector, or the aim to consolidate it, was a driving force of the path of integration, and it did after the end of Kubitschek's mandate. It continued, in an even more ambitious way, by the following "Varguista" governments of Jânio da Silva Quadros (1961) and Vargas' former Minister of Labor, João Goulart (1961–1964). The latter was, like Vargas, from Rio Grande do Sul, and played a pivotal role during Vargas' government. Moreover, when the anti-Peronist campaign in Brazil forced Vargas to remove Batista Lusardo, he chose Goulart as his contact toward

Peron and Argentina. The "path of integration" was not only continued but led to more ambitious forms in the governments that followed Kubitschek. Developmentalism also acquired a foreign policy doctrine, called the *Doctrina da Política Externa Independente* (PEI), where one of the key promoters was the diplomat and minister of Foreign Relations, Francisco C. de San Tiago Dantas (1961–1962). The PEI implied a new thinking in relation to Brazil's insertion to the international system, with the objective to promote its development autonomy and occupy a central role at the center of the system.[27]

According to Amado Luiz Cervo and Cloaldo Bueno, the PEI implied continuity with Vargas' second government and its tendency to mark distance from the United States foreign policy.[28] That is certainly true, and this distancing was, in fact, made a bolder way than ever before. Part of this was concerned with continuing building on the geopolitics of integration and the search of national autonomy, in tandem with the region. It is important to note that this was done without abandoning the Pan-American dimension.

This frustrating experience[29] led many Latin American countries, including Brazil, to a continued ambition toward the "path of integration." In the case of Brazil, at the economic sphere, this was made through LAFTA and CEPAL, in the political one, by defending the principles of autonomy and sovereignty in different levels. One example was by grouping among Latin American countries to oppose the United States at the OAS, in relation to its attempts to overthrow the Cuban government, after 1959. A way of doing so was Quadros' award to Ernesto Che Guevara, in 1961; granting him Brazil's highest *medal* to a foreigner.

The former identification of the Argentina-Brazil axis, as a center piece of a national development–oriented strategy, was maintained, and Quadros made decisive steps in this direction through a direct contact with the Argentinean president Arturo Frondizi (1958–1962) in the border city of Uruguayana. Both presidents explored different common development-oriented policies, which also included a convergence in terms of foreign policy. Along this line, Brazil and Argentina, for example, made a proposal to the US government to mediate in the Cuban crisis, and Frondizi even invited Guevara to a confidential meeting in Buenos Aires, 1961.[30] It is true as Cervo and Bueno explains that Quadros' foreign policy included a stronger linkage to Latin America. This was expressed through new forms of understanding with the the river Plate Basin nations, along the so-called Uruguayana treaties that could be regarded as tools for cooperation and systems of common consultation.[31] All this in the frame of what was to be known as the "Uruguayana spirit."

The government of Goulart continued along this path, attending to a new meeting with Frondizi in 1961. There was no doubt about the pro-regional line of thinking of both governments, their support for CEPAL's ideas, democracy and their Latin American scope that was showed, for

example, through a close attachment to the situation of Cuba and the Caribbean. There was also strong opposition to this line of action in both countries.
In Brazil, Goulart was scorned by the opposition, who called him "Juancito
Goulart."[32] What "Juancito" did was to take advantage of a new pro-integration and developmentalist-oriented government in Argentina (since the coup
against Peron in 1955) to promote more a new rapprochement. Frondizi had,
for sure, already supported this direction since the creation of LAFTA, during Kubitschek's mandate, but with Quadros and Goulart, the aims became
more ambitious, through the "spirit of Uruguayana," reaffirming the defense
of democracy and the promotion of development—not only to complement
their economies but also as a way of integrating their markets, to become the
central node of a greater Latin American market.[33] According to San Tiago
Dantas, the relations between Brazil and Argentina and all Latin American
countries were driven by a feeling of collaboration, common support and
affection that would led them toward working in the interest of all other
nations of the hemisphere and a constant integration in economic and cultural
fields.[34]

Nevertheless, even if the "path of integration" had reached higher levels of
ambition, since Vargas presidency, the independent foreign policy was still
confronted with limited room of maneuver, due to the correlation of forces
at each national context (in Argentina and Brazil), as well in the framework
given by the great powers. The international polarization during the Cold
War cannot be out ruled as one contributing element behind a new "domino
effect" in the fall of pro-integration-oriented Latin American presidents.
After a first wave of coup d'état or pressures for institutional change leading
to the fall of Jacobo Árbenz in Guatemala (1951–1954), Vargas (1954) or
Perón (1955), there was a second one with a coup against Frondizi (1962),
against Bolivia's president Víctor Paz Estenssoro (1960–1964) and Goulart
(1964). In the case of Brazil, this coup implied the beginning of a long period
of military government.

THE JANUS FACE OF BRAZILIAN MILITARY GOVERNMENTS

The new military regime, led by Mariscal Humberto Castelo Branco (1964–
67), was regarded with positive eyes by the United States, who also received
Brazilian military support to a new military intervention in the Caribbean:
the Dominican Republic, in 1965, in the framework of the OAS. The "path
of integration" was here substituted by a "path of alignment" with the United
States, where Brazil took the role of what has been called; "sub-imperial
power."[35] Yet, the word "imperial" did not really fit Brazil's foreign policy
designs toward its neighbors. Castelo Branco's foreign policy could actually

be regarded as a brief parenthesis in relation to the PEI, although this divergence, in some aspects, was not as radical as it is sometimes pointed out. With the subsequent *de facto* government of Marshal Artur da Costa e Silva (1967–69), the government shifted its policy toward a more developmentalist line. At that moment, the geopolitical vision was more inspired in the thinking of General Golbery do Couto e Silva (1911–87), whose influence among government elites marked important changes in respect to national geopolitical visions.

In what Samuel Pinheiro Guimarães has called a "national version of the military strategic vision,"[36] this government pursued a policy of "limited autonomy," assuming a subordinated role to the "Western" world, under the leadership of the United States and the Doctrine of National Security, within the framework of the global fight against communism. This position concerning autonomy could be regarded as a realist vision of the limited national possibilities to pursue a more autonomous line of action, such as the one advocated by the PEI. Yet, the military governments intended to maintain the central goal of national development through industrialization which led to the other face of the military government's foreign policy. The Brazilian government elites could not resist the force of gravity toward the region, that had been going on since the "geopolitics of development" established by Vargas. [37]

Hence, it is not surprising that, during the military period (including Castelo Branco's government) there were pro-integration-oriented initiatives. One example is the one made by the Castelo Branco's Minister of Planning, Roberto Campos, in 1967, to Argentina's Minister of Economy, Adalbert Krieger Vasena, during the presidency of General Juan Carlos Onganía (1966–70). Campos' proposal was to create a customs union among the two states, searching for bilateral integration. This renewed bid for a rapprochement with Argentina was made in the framework of new emphasis given toward a South America–oriented policy, taking some distance of the Latin American dimension. This has been attributed to certain fears of Brazilian business groups concerning a further approximation to Mexico and the use of this country as a beachhead by US multinationals to compete in more integrated Southern Cone markets on more favorable conditions.[38]

A custom union is an advanced form of regional integration, but, as pointed out before, this was not a new issue in Brazil's foreign policy. With this proposal, the Brazilian government showed a return to more ambitious initiatives along the "path of integration." One difference with former governments was through a clearer stance concerning the focus on the "continental" South American dimension as framework of action, along the line that had been pointed out by geopoliticians such as do Couto e Silva.[39] This implied two points of direction that were not new in Brazilian geopolitical strategies.

One was directed toward the river Plate Basin, particularly toward Argentina; and another toward the Amazonian region. Concerning the first, besides the proposal for a customs union with Argentina, the Brazilian government did also pursue an approximation among all countries of these sub-regions, which resulted in the River Plate Basin Treaty, in 1969. The objective of this treaty was to unite efforts to promote economic development and physical integration in the River Plate Basin. One of the results of this was the creation, in 1971, of the Financial Fond for the Development of the River Plate Basin Countries (FONPLATA).

Certainly, the "spirit of Uruguayana," namely, an environment favorable to deep integration between Argentina and Brazil, was affected by the Brazilian plans to build a dam in the Parana River to develop hydroelectric energy. In reality, Janio Quadros had proposed in Uruguayana to joint efforts to pool the resources of the rivers of the River Plate Basin[40]. However, the Act of Cataratas signed in 1966 by Brazil and Paraguay established a bilateral commitment to develop a hydroelectric station in the Parana River without considering Argentina. The diplomatic reaction in this latter country was negative and it was the beginning of a diplomatic impasse that was deepened in 1973, during the Emílio Garrastazú Médici' government, when the Itaipú Treaty was signed. The impasse eventually was resolved in 1979. This conflict has extensively presented in the literature as an example of the Brazilian regional ambitious and, we say, as an example of the path of separation. However, actions of cooperation and integration were developed with Argentina even in the context of such a diplomatic impasse. For example, during the government of Costa Silva was established a Brazil-Argentina Executive Commission for the Coordination of some issues in the framework of LAFTA. As mentioned above, the FONPLATA was created in 1971.

The government of Emílio Garrastazú Médici and his "Diplomacy of Prosperity" was the era of the Brazilian economic miracle and the ideology of *Brasil Grande Potência*. Médici was a close ally of the United States, but the national and international context had changed. At national level, the Brazilian major concern was the continuity of the project of national industrial development, a process that took place in a moment when the East-West conflict lost relevance due to the emergence of the North-South conflict. Certainly, Médici did not subscribe to the "thirdworldism" but he understood that the international system had changed and that "the era of U.S. dominance had been replaced by a 'new world order.'"[41] Thus, the aim was to improve the Brazilian place in the international stratification of power, which implied the consolidation of the project *Brasil Potencia*. Normally, it is highlighted that during this period Brazil was eager to wield a hegemonic power in the region, example of which were the Brazilian intervention in the coup d'état of Hugo Banzer in Bolivia in 1971 or the so-called

Operação Trinta Horas, a military intervention in Uruguay if the left-wing coalition *Frente Amplio* won the elections in 1971. Allegations have also been that the Brazilian military dictatorship collaborated in the coup d'état to Salvador Allende in 1973.[42] Similarly, Brazil would have abandoned the regional initiatives during this period and would have opted for a pragmatic bilateralism. All that is true and we are not interested in denying historical facts but it does not mean the Brazilian government was unaware on what went on in the South American neighborhood. Although in some aspects in a reprehensible way (as the interventionism in Bolivia), the Médici's government was involved in the regional political dynamics that was considered crucial for the country's political stability and the economic development strategy. This latter aspect is crucial and Médici recognized its importance in his book *Nosso Caminho*:

> The notion that development rests on the national effort, considering the regional peculiarities, it is far from meaning that the way to go must be solitary. More than ever, we need Inter American cooperation and solidarity and concerted action by Latin America, given the analogy of their basic problems. To deal with the close correlation between economic and social development and foreign trade, a joint effort, vigorous and always renewed, is indispensable to correct deformations and overcome obstacles to the pace of our development.[43]

Thus, Médici did not only intervene but also tried to promote a rapprochement with some countries with specific goals. Brazil needed not only to diversify its investments and trade partners but also guaranteed new sources of energy required for the continuation of the industrial development. Latin America was perceived as a potential provider of energy and the Brazilian government offered significant investments of that area to Colombia, in particular to explore the new coal deposit and to Bolivia, to develop a gas pipeline and a still center close to the Brazilian border.[44] It was during his government that the Itaipú Treaty was signed. He also promoted the physical integration with Uruguay and Paraguay. He made official visit to Bolivia, Paraguay, Uruguay and Venezuela (being the first Brazilian president to visit this country). The relations with Argentina were still affected by the Itaipú project but, as Tatyana Scheila Friedrichl and Guilherme Athaides Guimarães properly assert, by the period 1973–1974, the only dispute between Argentina and Brazil was that related to Itaipú but in issues such as trade, the progress was important to the point that the bilateral exchange was the most important in Latin America, a trend that will be deepened by the end of the 1970s.[45] Furthermore, high-level political contacts remained and even a Presidential Summit took place when the Argentine president Alejandro Agustín Lanusse met in 1972 his Brazilian counterpart Garrastazú Médici.

The Ernesto Geisel's government and his "Pragmatic and Ecumenic Foreign Policy" had significant implications for the relations with Latin America and particularly with the South American neighbors. One feature of this new policy was the definitive rupture of any automatic alignment with the United States, example of which were the initiatives to establish strategic partnerships with Germany (West Germany at that moment) and Japan. Another element of the new foreign policy was a major involvement in Latin America. An example of this was the support given to the Mexican-Venezuelan project of creating a Latin American Economic System (SELA). Beyond that regional dimension, Brazil signed a bilateral agreement on Science and Technology with Mexico in 1974 and a Treaty of Friendship and Cooperation with Paraguay in 1975.[46]

The other direction of Geisel's action was toward the Amazonian region, which ended with the signing of the Amazonian Cooperation Treaty (ACT), in 1978. The ACT was signed by the Republics of Bolivia, Brazil, Colombia, Ecuador, Guyana, Peru, Suriname and Venezuela. It contained accords concerning the establishment of a Committee for the Protection and Management of the Amazonian Flora and Fauna, as well as different development programs for the Amazon region as a whole.[47] Nevertheless, the idea of fostering cooperation with the Amazonian countries went back much earlier. In 1940, Getulio Vargas (the first Brazilian president that gave particular attention to the northern region) gave a speech in which he highlighted the potential for cooperation with Amazonian countries. He recognized the existence of what he called a "spirit of fraternization" and called for gathering these countries to establish the basis for an agreement among them.[48] The idea was never implemented until Geisel retook it and promoted the diplomatic actions to make it a reality.

During Geisel's government initial steps were given to find a solution to the conflict on Itaipú. Actually, after the coup d'état in March 1976, the Brazilian military regime adopted a relatively friendlier view toward Argentina. When the Minister of Foreign Affairs of this country Oscar Camilión gave support to the Brazilian nuclear plan, the doors were opened to a further cooperation on this issue between both countries. As explored more fully in the next chapter, President João Baptista Figueiredo will be responsible for deepening the bilateral relation with Argentina.

However, it is important to remark that this South American focus in Brazilian foreign policy did not mean the elimination of the Latin American dimension. Brazil did, in fact, attempt to revive and renew the LAFTA process, through a refunding of this entity into what was named the Latin American Integration Association (LAIA), in 1980. The reason for this was that Brazil had by then become the largest and most expansive industrial powerhouse of South America, and both government and private sector searched for external markets to secure its growth and consolidation. Even if it falls out of the scope of our study, we might also add here that there was even a global direction along this line of action. And part of this, even during Castello Branco, was not related to unconditional support toward the United States and its "Western" allies. We refer, for example, to a continuation of the military governments support to the defiant alliance among developing states at the United Nations Conference on Trade and Development (UNCTAD), created in 1964. Brazil supported Raúl Prebisch as general secretary of UNCTAD, who transformed this entity into a new platform for Latin American developmentalism, but also a catalyst of these ideas to other developing states.[49]

The United States was indeed influential in internal Brazilian and Latin American affairs, and there is ample evidence on its support to the 1964 coup in Brazil. Still, as shown by Carlos Gustavo Poggio Texeira, there were also many limitations to its involvement in South America, and particularly, in large countries such as Brazil. This was partly so because of the Brazilian engagement and support to other countries of the region in the fight against communism. According to Poggio Texeira, this Brazilian stand "successfully affected US-cost benefit calculations, which made the US less likely to resort to an imperial strategy in the South American subsystem."[50] What is most interesting in respect to the theme of our book is that, for this or other reasons, the Brazilian military had room of maneuver for own actions, sometimes not along the United States, and certainly favoring what Poggio Texeira calls, a "regional subsystem."

GRAPPLING WITH "NATIONHOOD"

Although the military did pursue integration-oriented economic and political initiatives, there were interesting links to regional national identities to which Brazil was associated, in different forms. If we take as parameter the speeches of Brazilian representatives at the United Nations' General Assembly between 1946 and 2006,[51] one can observe some interesting shifts. During the first decades, there was a strong association to concepts such as "Western," "Christian" or Pan-Americanism and a broader "American" outlook. The concept "Latin America" gained strength toward the end of the 1950s and continued to increase after that. It was also often used during the long military period; in 1979, for example, President, General, João Baptista Figueiredo (1979–1985) spoke about "the sister Latin American nations."[52] During this period there were also increasing references to the "sister" African states. The mentions to South America did, in fact, not appear until the late 1980s, after which these gained a predominant position.

Yet, although other regional identities were used, the main scope of the foreign policy, as for all other countries, was around a Brazilian-centered nationhood, or what Preuss identified as Rio Branco's "Luso-American" orientation. In the case of "South America" this Brazilian centeredness was somehow reinforced since this concept was mainly used as a geopolitical territorial framework. Differently to concepts such as "Western," "Pan-America" or "Latin America," South America did not contain any idea that could be associated with a particular form of nationhood or civilization.

However, these considerations and the data presented above should be taken with care since it is mostly related to whoever was at the commanding heights of the state. Yet, as it was the case of the *farroupilhas* in the 19th-century Rio Grande do Sul, there were also things happening in other parts of the Brazilian society. The pro-Hispanic and "Latin American" connections that gained more relevance since the 1950s developmentalist governments was not only a matter of governmental discourse, or political and economic initiatives, such as LAFTA or LAIA. Between 1930s and 1960s a whole new intellectual movement emerged in Brazil, made up by some of the country's leading scholars and pundits. Taking into account what has been analyzed in this and earlier chapters of our study, we can fairly say that these should not be regarded as, what Leslie Bethell called, "surprising"[53] exceptions, to the voices arguing for the "path of separation." One of these "exceptions" was the influential intellectual, Gilberto Freyre (1900–1987). Referring to the national identity, he concluded that the Brazilians needed to acquire a clearer consciousness of its Hispanic condition, in order to remark its unique and singular position as double Hispanic people—in a Pan-Hispanic world, a culture with gigantic projections toward human future.[54]

Another was the anthropologist and sociologist, Darcy Ribeiro, who, as Freyre, wrote extensively about Brazilian national culture. These two were intellectual icons of a generation, and even if they identified Brazil's Luso-American particularities, they also regarded Brazilian culture and nationality as belonging to a bigger, Hispanic and Latin American "we." In the case of Ribeiro, he referred to singular elements of the "Brazilian island"; but these were regarded as the crucible of a broader "American" and "Latin American" civilization. In his view, Brazil was a natural part of all these nationhood's, a position that, by the way, was also maintained also among foreign, well-known Brazil pundits, such as Ferdinand Braudel.[55] The list is in fact much longer and important than what the forbearers of the path of separation use to acknowledge. To mention some other names, we have for example the outstanding thinker, Paulo Freire, which regarded himself as Latin American. His book *The Pedagogy of the Oppressed* had an enormous impact across the region and is, without doubt, regarded as part of the Latin American thinking in terms of social rights.[56]

The analysis and conception of Brazil and the region was continued and deepened by other, such as the sociologist Octavio Ianni, who was deeply linked to the line of research and thinking of people such as Freyre, Sergio Buarque de Holanda, Caio Prado Júnior or Florestan Fernandez, Fernando Henrique Cardoso, Nestor Werneck Sodré, Theothonio dos Santos, Maria da Concepcao Tavares, Celso Furtado; some quoted in this book, but all highly influential in Brazil and Latin America, and part of the current thinking close to the "path of integration." Along this line, Ianni saw Brazil as part of a Latin American nationhood, which was considered a kind of "fifth frontier."[57] This concept is a metaphor for movements and imaginations across frontiers, and the constant dilemmas in the relation between state and nation. While Brazilian geopoliticians, such as those mentioned above, have studied this from a state-centered perspective, Ianni focuses on the "imagined nation," arguing that the nation is always in movement, it is "formed and reformed along history. Born and reborn, according to the movements of people, social forces, forms of labor and life, controversies and struggles." The "nation," in his view, always transfix its frontiers, or never manage to reach them.[58] For Brazil and the other countries of the region, Latin America is part of this fifth frontier, which cannot be ignored, as little as other, such as Pan-America, America or the West. Much of the ideas and positions mentioned above have been dismissed as "romantic,"[59] and this might be a correct word if attributed to "national" conceptions. Yet, we rise a caveat in seeing those promoting and adopting these "romantic" framings as separated from the reality, particularly if one means policymakers. To be sure, most of the pundits mentioned above have been, in different forms, part and active collaborators with political movement behind the democratic developmentalist governments. The military regime implied a break between sectors of this *intelligentsia* and the national state. It was also when many of these intellectuals went to exile o other Latin American countries, which actually implied both deepening in their Latin American consciousness and a deeper knowledge of the neighbor countries. That was, for sure, the case of leading social scientists such as the later on President Fernando Henrique Cardoso (1995–2003) or Celso Furtado, both active at CEPAL. This issue needs further study, but it appears as if, during the military wave of the 1960s, the "Latin American" identity took prominent steps forward. On the one hand, it remained and was even deepened as official identification of international initiatives among states, as well as in the positioning of the region toward the international community. On the other, it became "popular," as common identity of popular movements resisting the military regimes, but also promoted by the (in Latin America always strong and influential) catholic movement. In this, the "theology of liberation" was of great influence in spreading ideas but also a common "Latin American" identity, and Brazilians were strongly involved in all this.

This can also be seen in other areas of popular culture such as music or literature, where the "Latin American" identity became strongly associated with anti-authoritarianism and fight against (US) imperialism involvement across the region. All this new wave of common political objectives and identities finally incorporated many Brazilian intellectuals, cultural personalities and politicians into the "Latin American" nationhood. A prominent part of this was made by the so-called Movement of Popular Music that had as one of its leading names the famous singer-songwriter, Chico Buarque de Holanda— son of the above-mentioned historian, Sergio Buarque de Holanda.

There was of course an enormous cleavage between this group and the ruling military governments in relation to the meaning and use of the concept "Latin America." Yet, during the 1970s and 1980s, it was used by both, giving the "Latin American" national dimension a profile that was stronger than ever before, this time also expanding among social movements. Perhaps, the most advanced supra-national ideas in Brazil were outlined by Darcy Ribeiro who, by the late 1970s and early 1980s, wrote in favor of the adoption of national dimensions beyond actual frontiers, through which the Latin American peoples could find their future. This, in his view, was to be the outcome of a civilization process which was a result of the Iberian colonization. Yet, this process could not, in his view, be advanced successfully by elites, but had to be based in popular inclusion, by peaceful amalgamation, and an acceptance of the diversity existing in the *Patria Grande* (big fatherland).[60] Ribeiro touches here an important element, which also is one of the weaknesses of "fifth frontier" dimensions in Brazilian national and externally oriented policies. Beyond democratic or authoritarian, autonomist or more aligned with great powers, developmentalist or liberal, republican or monarchic, these have generally been definitions of elites. Perhaps, the "Latin American" identity during the since the 1960s managed to, some extent, break that pattern. For those intending to promote different forms of regional integration, it could be good to remember Ianni's words, that even if the present is dominated by the illusion of identity symbolized in the state, "it is the people that finally gives it the ultimate right and capacity to exert command."[61]

In what respect the "path of integration," in the early 1980s was a curious moment of reunification of this antagonist forces, leading to a renewed wave of integration. The Falkland/Malvinas War, in 1982, played an important role in this. Even if Brazil, officially, maintained a neutral position, it did in reality support Argentina. This conflict had a crucial importance since it led to a new disappointment with the Monroe Doctrine and was a confirmation of the marginal role of Argentina, and South American, with respect to the international priorities of the United States. This also meant a weakening in legitimacy and scope for the National Security Doctrine, as well as for the American/Pan-American dimension, even among those parts of the military forces that had been the backbone of its support.

The new period of democratization that, for the case of Brazil, Argentina and Uruguay, took place by the early and mid-1980s led to a new phase in Brazil-Argentinean relations, as well as for the relations between Brazil and the rest of the region. Brazil had now become a clear regional power, and was the leading force for integration in the Southern Cone, through Mercosur. But also at the Latin American levels, where Brazil was a leading country in support of the *Contadora* group, promoting a peace process in Central America, and the latter creation of the Latin American security-related organization, such as the Rio Group. It is also in this period, when the Latin American dimension is being push aside, although not eliminated, by the increasing role attributed to South America, as a central geopolitical framework for Brazil's relation with the neighbor countries.[62]

HELIO JAGUARIBE: BRAZIL AND LATIN AMERICAN REGIONALISM

We would like here to pay special attention to another key figure in the promotion of the path of integration, namely Helio Jaguaribe. One of his most outstanding features has been his large influence, both as important scholar in the analysis and proposals related to the need for closer relations between Brazil and its Latin American neighbors, but also in relation to policy-making, as one of the key names behind Brazilian strategies oriented toward the "path of integration." There are many coincidences with the integration strategies followed by different Brazilian governments and his proposals, especially after the 1980s.

The idea that Brazil should follow a gradual strategy beginning with the promotion of bilateral integration with Argentina and concluding with the whole Latin American region has been recommended by Jaguaribe since the 1950s. Coincidence or not, that has been exactly the strategy developed by the diverse Brazilian governments since the beginning of the bilateral cooperation and integration promoted by José Sarney (1985–1990).

Jaguaribe's approach to regional integration began to be developed in his years at the *Instituto Superior de Estudos Brasileiros* (ISEB)[63] in the 1950s. In those years, Jaguaribe backed Brazil regional integration with Latin America countries in general and with Argentina in particular. His early reflections on this issue took place in a moment when integration with Argentina became a matter of public debate after the General Juan Domingo Perón proposal of a new ABC treaty with Brazil and Chile. That proposal caused negative reactions and in the famous denunciation of the Minister of Foreign Affairs, João Neves, President Getulio Vargas was accused for allegedly have committed a crime of high treason by accepting the project of integration with Argentina and Chile under the leadership of Perón.

The journal *Cadernos de Nosso Tempo* sponsored by ISEB and directed Jaguaribe published an article on the issue. The authorship of that article is attributed to Jaguaribe.[64] Nonetheless, rather than analyzing the incident Peron-Vargas or Neves' allegations, the paper made an evaluation of the integration of Brazil with Latin America and with Argentina. Jaguaribe started by rejecting the two arguments raised by Neves: firstly, that Latin America integration, beginning with Argentina, Brazil and Chile would generate a division of the Americas and would affect Pan-Americanism and, secondly, that any rapprochement to Argentina will be negative for Brazil.

Regarding the argument that Latin American integration could impact Pan-Americanism and led to a division of the continent, Jaguaribe contested the assumption of the existence of real continental unity with the United States. His argument was that there were substantial economic and cultural differences between that country and its neighbors south of the Río Bravo. In this respect, Jaguaribe asserted:

> There can be no doubt, therefore, that the interests of Latin Americans do not agree or can never match entirely or even predominantly with those of the North Americans, and therefore, for Brazil, not all forms of "pan-Americanism" are convenient, being particularly harmful for us those that expose us to the Yankee pressure without any counterweight, with nothing that allows us to avoid that our integration into the US sphere of influence led us to a colonial condition of "satellite." In this sense, the argument that any division between the Americas, that is, any attempt to maintain the specificities, the economic, cultural and political differences among American countries "implies a prejudice" to "America" [the continent], is based on the reference to a mythical entity, America, which in concrete terms refers to North America.[65]

Similarly, Jaguaribe criticized the argument that any integration between Argentina and Brazil would have negative consequence for this latter country. Conversely, he thought that integration was essential for them and for South America, as he recognized in the following statement:

> It is a General Perón's demonstration of lucidity, whatever the criticisms one can make on him on other aspects and for other reasons, the fact that, not ignoring the advantages that would deriving for Brazil (...) from a closer Brazilian-Argentine relationship, he supports it by understanding that this is the only way the Latin American countries should survive to the impact of the Yankee and Soviet expansionism.[66]

After these arguments, Jaguaribe proposed a series of measures to further integration in the fields of economy, culture and politics. Among the measures, he recommended the promotion trade, the creation of a clearing house mechanism, the design of a "Latin American plan for economic development," the establishment of a Latin American system of solidarity and collective security and even the creation of a Latin American community of defense.[67]

This article is of great value to understand Jaguaribe's ideas on regional integration and cooperation, ideas that will deepen in the following decades. On the one hand, he recommended that integration had to be conceived in relative terms because independence and sovereignty of states should be respected; on the other hand, Jaguaribe warned it should be considered that many Latin American countries were still insufficiently developed and, in consequence, integration should avoid adopting rigid or uniform models. These two limitations were, in his view, "derived from the reality of the facts, are imperatives that have an impact when some people, due to romantic idealism or because of their nationalist aspirations, advocate for a total fusion of Latin America."[68]

A crucial argument in Jaguaribe's view on Latin American regionalism was that the Argentine-Brazilian integration and cooperation should be the initial stage of the process of regional unity. Specialists such as Silvina María Romano[69] have showed how this "Jaguaribean" idea was influential during the developmentalist governments of Janio Quadros (January-August 1961) and João Goulart (1961–1964). As explained in the previous chapter, a rapprochement between the two countries took place during the Quadros government, when Arturo Frondizi was president in Argentina (1958–1962). This was the Uruguayana summit explained in the previous chapter, in which an agreement that included Convention of Friendship and Consultation and a Political Declaration was signed. Romano also argues that Jaguaribe's ideas also had an impact on the independent foreign policy pursued by the government of Goulart. One of his proposals was that if Brazil wanted to achieve greater independence vis-à-vis the United States, should foster closer ties with Argentina.[70] This idea of closer relations with Argentina was backed by San Tiago Dantas, Brazilian Minister of Foreign Affairs that promoted the independent foreign policy. Dantas defended the deepening of bilateral cooperation with Buenos Aires, as argued by Jaguaribe, and even aimed to create a full Latin American free trade area.[71]

However, as it is known, after the coup d'état of 1964, the military regime commitment to Latin American integration diminished. This situation remained at least until the mid-1970s, when the Brazilian military governments promoted a nationalist discourse and showed an ambiguity in its relations with Latin American countries. Jaguaribe was critical of that ambiguity. In his view, the military government felt that "in its relations with the rest of Latin America, the country has little to gain, because they are countries of economic and technological level equal to or lower than ours, a reason it is convenient to have a pattern of relations bilateral, correct relations, but not too close."[72] The military also wanted to send a clear message to their neighbors, in the sense that closer relations could impose on Brazil responsibilities without a *quid pro quo*, in the name of regional solidarity.[73] Jaguaribe did not endorse those policies, and actually believed that although the military government had not theoretically abandoned an integrationist orientation, "the premises of regional integration were in practice abandoned."[74] Therefore, Jaguaribe criticized that the Brazilian government had managed to reconcile for some time a "theoretically integrationist foreign policy with a divergent practice with it."[75]

However, when at the end of the military regime a rapprochement with Argentina began to be developed, Jaguaribe backed those actions. Afterward, he was one of the Brazilian pundits that supported the process of bilateral integration that began in 1985 in Foz de Iguaçu. In fact, these events seemed to validate his approach to integration announced in his papers from the 1950s, where he insisted on the need for closer relations between Argentina and Brazil, a stepping stone in the construction of Latin American integration. Thus, in a paper published in 1987, Jaguaribe argued that one of the reasons to promote integration and cooperation between Argentina and Brazil was that both countries had quantitatively and qualitatively insufficient conditions to address critical national development objectives. In particular, Jaguaribe highlighted the economic, technological and managerial shortcomings that existed in Latin America and limited the strategies of economic development. He believed that regional integration and cooperation provided to Argentina and Brazil tools to achieve what he called a "critical level" needed to foster economic development.

Beyond the domestic problems, Jaguaribe also perceived international factors that encouraged bilateral cooperation, in particular the complex political and economic situation the region experienced in the 1980s. Factors such as the crisis in Central America that had become a battlefield of the Cold War and the vulnerability of the Andean region due to political instability, the proliferation of guerrilla movements and drug trafficking were issues of concern for Jaguaribe. These domestic and international factors produced what the Brazilian pundit described as "double vulnerability" of Latin American countries. These problems could be worked out by promoting a broad regional consensus to foster an alliance for cooperation and development.[76] In his view, that alliance should be carried out first by a "close cooperation" between Argentina and Brazil. He argues that such a cooperation, besides being indispensable to the national interests of both countries, was the only effective possibility of increasing the margin of viability of Latin America countries and led to a reversal of the negative trends mentioned above.[77]

These two elements (integration and cooperation to improve the viability and promote development, and Latin American regionalism beginning from an Argentina-Brazil axis) are crucial to understand Jaguaribe's view of the Brazilian relations with its neighbors. Thus, autonomy and development were two critical issues in Jaguaribe's approach to regional integration and cooperation and, once again, by chance or not, these two issues became central concerns of the Brazilian administrations after the end of the Cold War.

For Jaguaribe, due to national constraints experienced by Latin American states, regional integration is as "an aggregate dimension in the project of autonomous development."[78] Through regional integration, the Latin American countries aimed at multiplying resources and markets, improving scale of production and encouraging development.[79] For this reason, for Jaguaribe, integration was not just free trade, but also a mechanism to create institutions that allow foreign exchange savings, foster the scientific and technological training, promote joint development projects and increase the bargaining power of Latin American countries.[80]

Jaguaribe also considered that given the enormous heterogeneity of Latin America, it was unfeasible the immediate integration of all the countries of that region. At this point, the author is consistent with an argument that he had defended since the 1950s in his time at the ISEB. Consequently, he conceived regional integration in concentric circles,[81] the first of which is Argentina-Brazil. In the 1990s, when the Mercosur was created a larger circle emerged, and at the beginning of the new millennium another circle was set up with the project of the South American Community of Nations (SACN), which was transformed in 2007 in UNASUR. More recently, the establishment of the Latin American and Caribbean Community of States (CELAC) meant the setting up of a bigger circle.

In the 1990s, when the ideas of open integration policies based on economic liberalism were hegemonic, Jaguaribe analyzed the issue of the model of economic development as something associated with national viability of Latin American countries. In this regard, he objected that the countries of the region had been opted for a radical liberalism. Instead, he argues that the less developed countries should adopt a more lucid vision of their international relations and economic strategies. In his view, the adoption of radical liberalism that it does not exist even in the developed countries would have negative effects on industrial development and employment in Latin America. However, he did not propose a return to nationalist autarkic projects that have had harmful effects leading to an obsolescence and loss of competitiveness. Instead of it, Jaguaribe proposed what he called "a pragmatic liberalism" that entailed a pragmatic mixture "of basic liberalism and selective protectionism."[82]

When the process of building of a new South American regionalism began in the 1990s, firstly through the proposal of a South American Free Trade Area (SAFTA), later by the SACN and eventually with the creation of UNASUR, Jaguaribe linked these new projects to his ideas on regional and national autonomy. He insisted in considering regional integration and cooperation as mechanism to increase the margin of regional autonomy. This would have been the greatest contribution of Mercosur and UNASUR, to which Jaguaribe conceived as one of the pillars of a South American system in which "countries will have conditions for a successful autonomous development and mechanisms to generate and improve productive sectors to achieve international competitiveness."[83] However, he introduced a change in his proposals: although the author continued to consider the integration of Argentina and Brazil as the core of South American integration, the incorporation of Venezuela into the process was considered necessary. For Jaguaribe, the new ABV Triad [Argentina, Brazil, triad Venezuela] would lead to the consolidation of Mercosur and, consequently, of the SACN. This would imply the emergence of a new independent regional actor in the global scene that potentially could have an international impact.[84]

Finally, it is interesting to observe that the development of the Brazilian integration toward Latin American, after the end of military regimes, followed the path recommended by Jaguaribe. As it is analyzed in the following chapter, after the demise of LAFTA and the limited success of LAIA, a new regional momentum began in 1985 when the bilateral integration between Argentina and Brazil is triggered. The process is widened to the Southern Cone with the signing in 1991 of the Treaty of Asunción that created Mercosur. Afterward Brazil encouraged an unprecedented process that aimed to construct a South American regional bloc excluding Mexico and the Central American countries. This is not other thing than the idea of integration as concentric circles as proposed by Jaguaribe.

NOTES

1. Gerson Moura, *Autonomia na Dependência. A Política Externa Basileira de 1935 a 1942* (Rio de Janeiro: Editora Nova Fronteira, 1980), 63.

2. Arturo Ardao, *La Inteligencia Latinoamericana*, 57. See also the homepage of UDUAL, http://www.udual.org/historia.html (accessed: August 16, 2016).

3. Andrés Rivarola and Örjan Appelqvist, "Prebisch and Myrdal: Development Economics in the Core and on the Periphery," *Journal of Global History*, no. 6, (2001), 29–52.

4. Hernán Santa Cruz, "La creación de las Naciones Unidas y de la CEPAL," *Revista de la CEPAL*, no. 57, (1995), 17–32.

5. Andrés Rivarola Puntigliano, "De CEPAL a ALALC: tres vertientes del pensamiento regionalista en Latinoamérica," in José Briceño Ruiz, Andrés Rivarola Puntigliano and Angel Casas Gragea (eds.), *Integración Latinoamericana y Caribeña. Política y Economía* (Madrid: Fondo de Cultura Económica de España, 2012).

6. Rosemary Thorp, "The Latin American Economies in the 1940s," in David Rock (ed.), *Latin America in the 1940s. War and Postwar Transitions* (Berkeley: University of California Press, 1994), 16–41, 44.

7. Luiz Eduardo Fonseca de Carvalho Gonçalves, *As relações Brasil-CEPAL* (Brasília Fundação Alexandre de Gusmão, 2011), 31.

8. Celso Furtado, *A Fantasia Organizada* (Rio de Janeiro: Paz e Terra, 1985), 116; see also, Gert Rosenthal, "ECLAC: A Commitment to a Latin American Way toward Development," Berthelot, Yves (eds.), *Unity and Diversity in Development Ideas. Perspectives from the UN Regional Commissions* (Blomington, Indiana: Indiana University Press, 2004), 173.

9. Ibid., 115–16.

10. Glauco Carnerio, *Lusardo. O Ultimo Caudillho*, vol. 2. (Rio de Janeiro: Editora Nova Fronteira S.A., 1977), 325.

11. Carlos Piñeiro Iñiguez, *Perón. La Construcción de un Ideario* (Buenos Aires: Siglo XXI Editora, 2010), 546.

12. Alejandro Bunge, *Una Nueva Argentina* (Buenos Aires: Ed. Guillermo Kraft Ltd., 1940).

13. Carlos Piñeiro Iñiguez, *Perón. La Construcción*, 494.

14. Juan Domingo Perón, *Los Estados Unidos de América del Sur* (Buenos Aires: Ediciones Corregidor, 2008).

15. Gilberto Aranda Bustamante and Lucas Pavez Rosales, "El Legado del ABC: un Southfalia Suramericano para la Convergencia en la Diversidad," in Maria Ignacia Matus Matus & Gilberto Aranda Bustamante (eds.), *A 100 Años del ABC: Desafíos y Proyecciones en el Marco de la Integración Regional* (Santiago: CESIM-IEI, 2016), 23, 9–33.

16. Paulo Renan de Almeida, *Perón – Vargas – Ibáñez. Pacto ABC. Raízes do Mercosul* (Porto Alegre: Edipucrs, 1998), 124.

17. Iuri Cavlak, *A Política Externa Brasileira e a Argentina Peronista (1946–1955)* (São Paulo: AnnaBlume, 2008), 201.

18. Luiz Alberto Moniz Bandeira, *Conflicto e Integração na América do Sul. Brasil, Argentina e Estados Unidos. Da Tríplice Aliança ao Mercosul*, 257.

19. Bevan Sewell, *The US and Latin America. Eisenhower, Kennedy and Economic Diplomacy in the Cold War* (London and New York: I.B. Tauris & Co. Ltd., 2016), 37.

20. Paulo Renan de Almeida, *Perón – Vargas – Ibáñez*, 42, 164.

21. Edgard J. Dosman, *The Life and Times of Raúl Prebisch 1901–1986* (Montreal: McGill-Queen's University Press, 2008).

22. Rosemary Thorp, "The Latin American Economies in the 1940s", 47; see also David Rock, "Latin America and the United States," in David Rock (ed.), *Latin America in the 1940s. War and Post-war Transitions* (Berkeley: University of California Press, 1994), 18, 1–40.

23. Amado Luiz Cervo and Clodoaldo Bueno, *História da Política Exterior do Brasil* (Brasilia: Universidad de Brasilia, 2002), 288.

24. San Tiago Dantas, *Política Externa Independente* (Brasilia: Fundação Alexandre de Gusmão, 2011), 24.

25. L. Ronald Scheman, "The Alliance for Progress: Concept and Creativity," in L. Ronald Scheman (ed.), *The Alliance for Progress. A Retrospective* (New York: Praeger, 1988), 51, 3–63.

26. Joseph Grunwald, Miguel S. Wionczek and Martin Carnoy, *Latin American Economic Integration and U.S. Policy* (Washington, DC: The Brookings Institution, 1972).

27. Enrique de Oliveira Altemani and José Augusto Alburquerque Guilhon (ed.), *A política Externa Brasileira na visão dos seus Protagonistas* (Rio de Janeiro: Editora Lumen Juris, 2005), 53.

28. Amado Luiz Cervo and Clodoaldo Bueno, *História da Política Exterior*, 327.

29. Celso Furtado, *A Fantasia Desfeita* (Rio de Janeiro: Paz e Terra, 1989), 155.

30. Jorge G. Castañeda, *La Vida en Rojo. Una Biografía del Che Guevara* (Madrid: Alfaguara, 1997), 260.

31. Amado Luiz Cervo and Clodoaldo Bueno, *História da Política Exterior*, 331.

32. Glauco Carnerio, *Lusardo. O Ultimo Caudillho*, 403.

33. Amado Luiz Cervo and Clodoaldo Bueno, *História da Política Exterior*, 331.

34. San Tiago Dantas, *Política Externa Independente*, 24–5.

35. Vivian Trias, *Imperialismo y Geopolítica en América Latina* (Montevideo: Ediciones del Sol, 1967), 227.

36. Samuel Pinheiro Guimarães, *Desafios Brasileiros na era dos Gigantes* (Rio de Janeiro: Contraponto, 2006), 61.

37. Andrés Rivarola Puntigliano, "Geopolitics of Integration' and the Imagination of South America," *Geopolitics*, vol. 164, (2011), 846–864.

38. Roberto Campos, *A Laterna na Popa,* Memórias 2 (Petrópolis RJ: ParkGraf Editora Ltda, 2004), 749.

39. Golbery do Couto e Silva, *Geopolítica do Brasil* (Rio de Janeiro: Livraria José Olympo, 1955), 183, 189.

40. Tatyana Scheila Friedrich and Guilherme Athaides Guimarães, *"Ensaios de integração: Brasil e Argentina no século XX, pontos de aproximação e de afastamento até a formação do Mercosul,"* *Estudos Internacionais*, vol. 3, no. 1, (2015), 122.

41. Quoted in Hall Brands, "Third World Politics in an Age of Global Turmoil: The Latin American Challenge to U.S. and Western Hegemony, 1965–1975," *Diplomatic History*, vol. 32, no. 1, (2008), 110.

42. On these interventions, see: Alessandra Beber Castilho, *"O golpe de 1964 e a politica externa brasileira dentro do contexto repressivo,"* *Revista NEIBA Cadernos Argentina – Brasil*, vol. 2, no. 1, (2014), 57–68; Angelo Del Vecchio, "Política e Potência no Regime Militar Brasileiro," *Projeto História, São Paulo,* vol. 2, no. 1, (2004), 169–196; Andre Leite Araujo and Carlos Gustavo Poggio Teixeira, "A posição do Brasil no sistema diplomático da Bacia do Prata entre 1969 e 1974," *Boletim Meridiano 47*, vol. 16, no. 148, (2015), 10–17.

43. Emílio Garrastazú Médici, *Nosso Caminho* (Brasilia: Departamento de Imprensa Nacional, 1972), 41.

44. Antônio Carlos Moraes Lessa, "Instabilidade e mudanças: os condicionantes históricos da política externa brasileira sob Geisel (1974–1979)," *Revista de Informação Legislativa*, vol. 34, no. 133, (1997), 77.

45. Tatyana Scheila Friedrich and Guilherme Athaides Guimarães, Ensaios de integração, 126.

46. Filipe Almeida do Prado Mendonça and Shiguenoli Miyamoto, "A Política Externa do Governo Geisel (1974–1979)," *Século XXI*, vol. 2, no. 2, (2011), 16.

47. Luis E. Aragón, *The Amazon as a Study Object. Building Regional Capacity for Sustainable Development* (Stockholm: Stockholm University, Institute of Latin American Studies, 1994), 79.

48. Antônio Manoel Elíbio Júnior, "De Vargas e Geisel: as Estratégias da Política Externa Brasileira para a Criação do Tratado de Cooperação Amazônica - TCA (1940–1978)," *Cadernos do Tempo Presente*, no. 10, (2012), 1–10.

49. Alice H. Amsden, "Import Substitution in High-Tech Industries: Prebisch Lives in Asia!," *CEPAL Review*, no. 82, (2004): 75–89.

50. Carlos Gustavo Poggio Texeira, *Brazil, the United States, and the South American Subsystem. Regional Politics and the Absent Empire* (Lanham: Lexington Books, 2012), 103.

51. Luiz Felipe de Seixas Corrêa (ed.), *O Brasil nas Nações Unidas 1946–2006* (Brasilia: Fundação Alexandre de Gusmão, 2007).

52. Ibid., 360.

53. Leslie Bethell, "Brazil and 'Latin America,'" 483.

54. Gilberto Freyre, *O Brasileiro Entre os Outros Hispanos: Afinidades, Contrastes e Possíveis Futuros nas suas Interrelações* (Rio de Janeiro: Livraria José Olympo Editora, 1975), xiv.

55. Fernand Braudel, *The Perspectives of the World. Civilization & Capitalism, 15th–18th Century*, vol. 3 (New York: Harper & Row, Publishers, 1979).

56. Paulo Freyre, *Pedagogy of the Oppressed* (New York: Bloomsbury, 2012 [1970]); see also, Gustavo Gutiérrez, *A Theology of Liberation* (New York: Maryknoll, 1973).

57. Octavio Ianni, "A Questão Nacional na América Latina," *Estudos Avançados*, vol. 2, no. 1, (1988), 17–18.

58. Ibid., 31.

59. Clodoaldo Bueno, Tullo Vigevani and Haroldo Ramazini Júnior, "Latin American Integration. A Brazilian View," in Andrés Rivarola Puntigliano and José Briceno-Ruiz (eds.), *Resilience of Regionalism in Latin America and the Caribbean. Development and Autonomy* (Houndmills: Palgrave Macmillan, 2013), 208.

60. Darcy Ribeiro, *América Latina: a Patria Grande* (Rio de Janeiro: Fundação Darcy Ribeiro, 2012), 12, 13.

61. Octavio Ianni, "A Questão Nacional," 32.

62. Luís Cláudio Villafañe G. Santos, *A América do Sul no Discurso Diplomático Brasileiro* (Brasília: FUNAG, 2014).

63. The ISEB (the Higher Institute of Brazilian Studies in English) was a national think tank created in 1956 under the Administration of Juscelino Kubitschek. ISEB was dissolved in 1964 after the coup d'état against Goulart.

64. Thus, Alessandro Candeas in his book *A integração Brasil-Argentina. História de uma ideia na "visão do outro,"* published in Brasilia by the Foundation Alexandre de Gusmão in 2010, attributed to Jaguaribe the authorship of the article. See Candeas,

A integração Brasil-Argentina. História de uma ideia na "visão do outro" (Brasilia: FUNAG, 2010), 90.

65. Helio Jaguaribe, "A denúncia de João Neves," *Cadernos de Nosso Tempo*, no. 2, (January–February 1954), Rio de Janeiro, 89.

66. Ibid., 90.

67. Ibid., 92–94.

68. Ibid., 91.

69. Silvia María Romano, "Brasil, Argentina y la integración regional durante la década de 1960 en el marco de las relaciones con Estados Unidos," *Confines*, vol. 4, no. 8, (2008), 37.

70. Helio Jaguaribe, "A denúncia de João," 37.

71. Daniel Amicci, "La trayectoria hacia la Cumbre de Uruguayana: máxima expresión de la aproximación entre Argentina y Brasil durante el desarrollismo," *Confines*, vol. 8, no. 15, (2012), 142.

72. Helio Jaguaribe, *Brasil: crises e alternativas* (Rio de Janeiro: Zahar, 1974), 116.

73. Ibid., 116

74. Ibid., 117.

75. Ibid.

76. Ibid., 44.

77. Ibid.

78. María Elena Lorenzini. "Pensando desde el Sur: ideas, aportes y contribuciones teórico-conceptuales de Helio Jaguaribe para comprender las realidades latinoamericanas," in Alejandro Simonoff (compilador). *Los pensadores del Cono Sur. Los aportes de Jaguaribe; Methol Ferré, Puig y Tomassini a las Relaciones Internacionales*, Cuaderno de Trabajo no. 8, junio 2014 (La Plata: Instituto de Relaciones Internacionales de la Universidad Nacional de La Plata, 2014), 27.

79. Ibid., 27.

80. Hélio Jaguaribe, "A integração Argentina-Brasil," *Revista Brasileira de Política Internacional*, vol. XX, no. 117–118, (1987), 44.

81. María Elena Lorenzini, "Pensando desde el Sur," 28.

82. Helio Jaguaribe, "Significação e alcance do Mercosul," *Aportes para la Integración Latinoamericana*, Argentina, vol. II, no. 3, (1996), 19.

83. Helio Jaguaribe, "América Latina y los procesos de integración," *Cuadernos de Relaciones Internacionales, Regionalismo y Desarrollo*, Mérida, Venezuela, vol. 5, no. 9, (2010), 25.

84. Helio Jaguaribe, *O Brasil ante o século XXI*, Instituto de Estudos Avançados da Universidade de São Paulo, available at: http://200.144.188.13/iea/textos/jaguaribeseculo21.pdf (accessed: September 16, 2014), 2.

Chapter 5

Brazil and the Contemporary Path of Integration

From MERCOSUR to CELAC

The Brazilian involvement in Latin American regionalism certainly advanced with the participation of this country in LAFTA since 1960 and the Brazilian promotion of the Amazonian Cooperation Treaty in the 1970s, as explained in the previous chapter. However, it is well known that both processes stagnated.

Brazil was initially enthusiastic with LAFTA to the point that its first secretary executive was Romulo Almeida, a Brazilian economist close to Getulio Vargas and João Goulart. However, despite its initial success, LAFTA entered a period of crisis in the mid-1960s after a substantial tariff reduction that had taken place. The reluctance of some countries of advancing in the liberalization of trade as well as the perception in the small- and middle-sized countries in Latin America of an unequal distribution of costs and benefits of the integration led to a stagnation of the process that continued throughout the 1970s and eventually caused the transformation of LAFTA into LAIA in 1980. The Brazilian view of LAFTA was also modified. In fact, as beforehand mentioned, LAFTA was to a large extent a project furthered by Brazil and the countries of the South American Southern Cone as a response to what was regarded as CEPAL's too ambitious proposals on regional industrialization. This notwithstanding, after the shortcoming the process showed and particularly as result of the coup d'état in 1964 that overthrew President João Goulart, the military governments of Castelo Branco fostered a diplomatic alignment with the United States and began to consider LAFTA as a "utopic initiative."[1] The division that the region experienced after the proliferation of coup d'état in the Southern Cone created a distance between these countries and other important Latin American states such as Mexico, Venezuela, Colombia or Costa Rica that remained attached to democracy and criticized the violation of human rights by the military governments. This factor obviously affected the development of LAFTA. In the case of Brazil, it must be also considered the bias of the Brazilian foreign policy that, based on the principle of universalism or universalist realism as proposed by Amado Cervo and Clodoaldo Bueno, promoted strategic alliances with countries beyond Latin America, such as Germany or Japan. This caused that LAFTA had not a special place in the military foreign policy. This does not mean that LAFTA stopped being important for Brazil, because economic sectors showed their concerns about the crisis of the regional scheme and its impact in the Brazilian strategy of economic development.[2]

The Treaty for Amazonian Cooperation is often forgotten when examining Latin American regionalism but this is important for the analysis of this book because this was first Brazilian proposal of integration with a region distinct to the River Plate. The project was proposed in February 1977 and after certain hesitations from the neighboring countries the project was backed by Venezuela, Peru, Bolivia, Colombia, Ecuador Guyana and Surinam. The goal of the Treaty was to create a regional organization in the Amazon basin river that further the improvement of physical integration, programs of development and economic complementarity among member countries. In this sense, the Treaty was a replicate of that Brazil had signed in the late 1960s with the Plate River Basin nations.[3] Furthermore, the Treaty was promoted in a period in which the Andean Group was the most important integration scheme in Latin America and it happened to be that all the member of that regional group joined Brazil in the Amazonian Treaty. That led to conjectures on a possible convergence or rapprochement between Brazil and the Andean Pact.[4] However, the evolution of the Amazon Treaty was quite disappointed: no significant project of physical integration or plan for join economic development of the Amazonian basin was advanced and the regional scheme stagnated.

The criticism to LAFTA shortcomings took place in a moment when Brazilian relations with Latin America were experiencing a difficult period, particularly with Argentina due to conflicts under the construction of Itaipú Dam and the nuclear programs furthered in both countries. The relations with northern neighbors were also difficult because of the perception of a Brazilian expansionism, perception that existed even in the early years of democracy, when President Sarney announced the *Projeto Calha Norte* in 1985.

Nonetheless, during the government of Ernesto Geisel, initial steps were given to overcome that negative perception, with the Treaty for Amazonian Cooperation being an example of it. However, it is from the government of João Baptista Figueiredo (1979–1985) that a real rapprochement with the region is retaken after years of mistrust fostered by the military regimes. Figueiredo began a strategy of promotion of closer links with the Latin American countries. The process started with an improvement of the relations with Argentina, to include subsequently the Southern Cone countries, the rest of South America and Latin America as the final stage. The strategy was eventually implemented by the democratic governments that took office after 1983.

THE BILATERAL COOPERATION WITH ARGENTINA AND THE CREATION AND DEVELOPMENT OF MERCOSUR

It is hard to understand the trigger of the Argentine-Brazilian integration without considering the national, regional and global processes that influenced the Brazilian decision to further that process. Certainly, the transformations in the international economic structure and global politics explain the launch of regional integration in the Southern Cone in the mid-1980s and early 1990s. Factors such as the re-democratization of the region, the debt crisis and subsequent economic stagnation that began in 1982, the end of the Cold War and the process of globalization are factors mainly considered in the literature on the issue.

However, it is fair to recognize that the initial steps in the rapprochement between Argentina and Brazil took place a little before those events. Actually, from the second half of the 1970s and in the subsequent period of restoration of democracy in the early 1980s, gradual diplomatic actions fostered by last Brazilian military government aimed at improving relations with Argentina, actions that concluded in 1985 (when democracy prevailed in Brazil and Argentina) with the beginning of the bilateral cooperation between both countries.

The progressive approximation of Argentina and Brazil between 1976 and 1985 was mainly a response to an international situation more and more unfavorable to both countries, which made integration and cooperation a relevant economic policy tool. In the United States, the democratic administration of President Jimmy Carter (1977–1981) gave a turn to the US policy of supporting authoritarian governments, by adopting a speech that promoted democracy and human rights. Similarly, the US government had strengthened the policy of non-proliferation of nuclear weapons by reducing military aid and applying economic and diplomatic sanctions on countries that ignored that policy. This situation affected Argentina and Brazil. Firstly, the tolerance regarding the violations human rights carried out by the military regime under the struggle against communism in both countries came to an end and, on the other hand, Washington condemned nuclear development programs developed by Buenos Aires and Brasilia. These were initial factors that encouraged a rapprochement between the two countries, an example of which could even be found in 1975, when the United States expressed its disapproval of the agreement of transfer of nuclear energy between Germany and Brazil; the Argentine ambassador Oscar Camilión manifested his solidarity with Brazil.[5]

Economic factors were also crucial. The increase in oil prices since 1974 and its impact on energy costs forced the Brazilian government to accelerate the quest for alternative energy sources: the construction of dams in the Parana River. As explained in the previous chapter, this process began in the 1960s and the Itaipú agreement was signed in 1973. However, a continued conflict with Argentina on this issued affected the development of that project, a reason why it became crucial for Brazil to negotiate agreements to solve it.[6] By the same token, growing protectionism in the United States and the European Community in the late 1970s also led both countries to seek new regional and extra-regional markets. Brazil, for example, had a complex and conflictual trade relations with the United States, because of the existence of conflicts on issues such as protectionist measures on goods such as shoes, steel, textiles, the negotiations of services in the General Agreement on Tariffs and Trade (GATT) rounds and the reserve of the market of science and technology, just to mention some conflictive issues.[7]

Regional factors were also significant. The risk of a military conflict between Argentina and Chile on the Beagle Channel was high in 1978. In this context, Argentina could not maintain at the same time confrontational fronts with both Brazil and Chile. Brazil, in the meantime, feared that due to its "swinging strategy" in the conflict over the Itaipú Dam, Paraguay could turn to Argentina, thus affecting the Brazilian national interests.[8]

All these factors created conditions that allowed the improvement of relations between Argentina and Brazil. The first actions in this process back to the year 1976, when the Argentine president Jorge Rafael Videla, appointed Oscar Camilión, specialist in Brazil, as Ambassador of Argentina in Brasilia. Camilión backed the idea of improving relations with Brazil. However, bilateral relations took a new real turn since 1979, when Brazil began to give priority to its links with Argentina because "a stable and strong connection" with that country would "improve conditions of stability in the region and increase the margins of predictability Argentina's international action."[9]

The signing in 1979 of the Tripartite Treaty on the Itaipú Dam between Argentina, Brazil and Paraguay in Puerto Stroessner (currently Ciudad del Este, Paraguay) was also a milestone in the process. This agreement represented the most important rapprochement between Brazil and Argentina since the signing of Uruguaiana agreement in 1961. However, it was feared that, as in previous agreements, the Itaipú agreement was just a one-time act of cooperation, which would not be sustained over time. These fears were not confirmed, since the Brazilian president João Batista Figueiredo went to Buenos Aires in 1980 and furthered a series of cooperation agreements with the Argentine government. This was the first visit of a Brazilian president to Argentina since 1935. Videla also visited Brazil that year. According to Gian Luca Gardini[10], "the conclusion of nuclear and military agreements inaugurated a process of confidence-building that was to characterize bilateral relations throughout the 1980s. Commitment to periodical consultation between foreign ministers initiated a serious political dialogue on topics of international relevance. The creation of a *Grupo Binacional* [in Spanish in original] introduced integration as an issue for careful reflection." This was an important fact, even if it is difficult to measure the influence in the initiatives that took place later in the 1980s; however, as stated by Gardini[11], attention should be paid to at least two ideas from the Group.

The first was that the private sector should be invited to participate in the integration process. This important role of the private sector existed already during Figueiredo's presidential visit, expressed in the number of Brazilian entrepreneurs that signed a series of agreements with their Argentinean counterparts, for example, a complementation agreement in the automotive industry. This alliance between the private sectors of the two countries continued in the following years and represents another dimension of the path of integration that goes beyond the nation-state interactions. Thus, a meeting between Argentine and Brazilian entrepreneurs (in which the idea of promoting economic integration through sectoral agreements was raised) took place few months after the end of the Falklands War in São Paulo (Brazil). Similarly emerged an interest in an integration that would be deepened by sectoral agreements, progressive trade liberalization and security in the enforcement of bilateral industrial or trade projects in order to deal with possible changes of national economic policies."[12]

Despite this rapprochement that took place between 1979 and 1982, none of these initiatives constituted a decisive indication of undertakings cognate to Mercosur.[13] A crucial aspect was the re-democratization in the region. The first step in the re-democratization process took place in Argentina about a year before than in Brazil. The president of the new Argentinean democracy, Raúl Alfonsín, considered that relations with Brasilia should remain a priority for the country's foreign policy. This was part of a strategy developed by the Argentinean Minister of Foreign Affairs, at the time, Dante Caputo, who was the first in Alfonsín's administration to promote economic integration with Brazil. For Caputo, cooperation and economic integration was crucial for the creation of a democratic community in the Southern Cone.[14] Caputo, in an informal meeting in December 1983 with the Brazilian Minister of Foreign Relations Ramiro Saraiva Guerreiro, "proved 'to be very disposed to a practically immediate integration' but the Brazilian minister warned him about the difficulties and the degree of effort and patience that such an operation required."[15]

The first discussions on the economic integration of the two countries took place in January 1984. A Brazilian-Argentinean ministerial meeting to discuss economic issues of mutual interest was held in April that year. Gardini asserts that in a telegram found in Itamaraty archives, Brazilian officials evaluated the results of this meeting as follows: "promising results to open perspectives of enlargement of cooperation and integration between the two countries." As Gardini points out, Latin American summits often result in public and rhetorical statements stressing commitment to regional unity, but this was not the case because the telegram was a reserve correspondence between two Brazilian ministers, without the objective of being published widely.[16]

International factors also help to explain these initiatives. Among these, no doubt, the crisis of the external debt was of crucial importance. It was considered that the increase in interest rates by the administration of Ronald Reagan in the United States had been the trigger for the crisis, affecting the capacity of Latin American countries to pay their debt service and making inapplicable economic policies developed in the region since the 1950s. The crisis made react Brazil, one of the most indebted countries in the region. In his speech to the General Assembly of the United Nations, Brazilian president João Baptista Figueiredo asserted that "the economic policy of great powers destroys without building nothing instead."[17] This discontent increased because of the lack of interest demonstrated by the Reagan administration to find a solution to the crisis. The announcement of Mexico of its inability to pay its debt service 1982 caused a snowball effect throughout the region, but especially in Argentina and Brazil, both countries being part of the largest debtors in the region.

The economic recession generated by the debt crisis and by the blockage of access to foreign credit had a considerable impact. In the case of Brazil, its economy was already hit since the 1970s because of the first and second oil crises (1973 and 1979). Although the economy had grown during the first years of Figueiredo's government, serious problems of inflation persisted: the inflation rate rose from 77 percent in 1979 to 100 percent in 1980. At the beginning of the 1981, Brazil was at the heart of the largest depression the country had experienced in sixty years, registering a 10 percent drop in industrial production and an inflation rate of 120 percent[18]. The crisis was exacerbated by the increase in interest rates in the United States and the negative effect that the short recession that took place between 1979 and 1982 in developed countries caused the Brazilian exports. The environment of insecurity that the debt crisis produced led to an accelerated flight of capitals and a general economic crisis, which resulted in a process of hyperinflation that reached 200 percent in 1984. [19]

The crisis led to a review of the model of development in Brazil that since the post-war had been influenced by the developmental ideas of Raúl Prebisch and CEPAL. This is crucial to understand the Brazilian strategy of regional integration and cooperation. Despite the crisis generated in the 1970s by the rising of oil prices, easy international credit allows the governments of Ernesto Geisel (1974–1979) (and Figueiredo's) to continue the inward development strategy. Brazilian debts grew rapidly in those years as accessibility to recycled petrodollars made international borrows from private banks easy. Thus, the external debt increased US $ 10 billion between 1974 and 1979, with an additional US $ 10 billion increase in the period 1979–1981[20]. Without this easy access to international credit, it would have been almost impossible for Brazil to continue its programs of industrial development and import substitution. The consequences of the rise in interest rates by the Reagan administration on Brazilian debt were immediate, increasing the amounts payable for the repayment of outstanding loans. Thus, between 1980 and 1982, the interest payments on the debt represented 70 percent of the deficit of the current account, and only for the year 1982, the debt service represented 72 percent of export earnings in Brazil.[21]

The end of the easy access to foreign credit seemed to impede the Brazilian economy to pursue its "developmentalist model." Moreover, the continuing crisis forced to implement adjustment policies that aimed to curb hyperinflation and to restart economic growth. However, Figueiredo's government avoided to resort to financial assistance of the International Monetary Fund (IMF) because it involved the implementation of a structural adjustment program. This was also a condition that the international private bank established to renegotiate existing debt and granting of new credits. Despite this reluctance, the Brazilian government finally decided to negotiate an adjustment program with the IMF in December 1982. The program involved policies such as increasing the real exchange rate, reducing demand by promoting a decrease in private consumption, reduction of investments and public spending, and higher taxes. However, this program was difficult to implement and Brazil had to negotiate later seven letters of intent with the IMF[22]. This was to a large extent due to the refusal of Brazil to abandon the developmentalist project that, if the measures recommended by the IMF had been fully implemented, could not be prosecuted.

The crisis also had an impact in Argentina, creating conditions to further cooperation with Brazil. External debt and failed economic policies of the military governments caused an economic recession that led to hyperinflation. Certainly, under the responsibility of José Alfredo Martínez de Hoz, the Argentinean military governments between 1976 and 1982 implemented economic programs based on free market–oriented policies, while maintaining some sectoral interventionist mechanisms. However, because of tariff reduction, the liberalization of financial markets as well as the maintenance of sectoral policies, Argentina had an important fiscal deficit. The consequences of the Malvinas War were also important and aggravated the economic crisis.

On the one hand, the conflict caused a political distance from the United States, an important socioeconomic partner of Argentina and, on the other hand, the European Economic Community approved economic sanctions that affected the export sector of the economy, already weakened. The decision of President Leopoldo Fortunato Galtieri to retake the archipelago could not come at a worse time for the Argentine economy: the foreign debt reached $ 40 billion, representing 60 percent of the Gross National Product.[23]

However, the Falklands War had consequences on the relationship with Brazil. Despite the problems caused by the unexpected action of Argentina, Brasilia backed Argentina by condemning the embargo declared by the European Community against its neighbor and by encouraging for an immediate cease of fire and a negotiated solution of the conflict. The government of General Reynaldo Bignone, that replaced Galtieri in July 1982, tried to end the crisis by implementing a new economic emergency plan, but with no more success than its predecessor. Inflation continued its unstoppable rise, reaching 134 percent in 1983, while fixed investment dropped precipitously in the context of a speculative movement against the peso and a share purchase, real states acquisitions or any other thing that could retain its value.[24]

In these difficult economic conditions, the two countries began a process of transition toward democracy, an important factor to understand the development of future bilateral integration. Certainly, as already mentioned in this chapter, the first step toward greater cooperation between Argentina and Brazil was developed under the military government. When the possibility of bilateral integration began to be put on the negotiating table, Brazil was still ruled by the military. However, one cannot deny the fact that democracy was an important factor in the trigger of the bilateral integration. The signing of trade agreements had not only an economic objective, but those agreements also "sought to establish mechanisms which would prevent the return of military regimes by directly linking their countries' economic future to the endurance of democratic rule."[25]

All these factors created conditions to gradually promote a relationship of trust between the Argentina and Brazil, a process that had gradually begun with the signing of the Treaty of Itaipú, continued with the signing of a Treaty of Nuclear Cooperation and led to the creation of the Binational Group that consists of officials of Ministries of Economy and Foreign Affairs of the two countries.

During the transition to democracy in Brazil, the bilateral process was strengthened. The new president José Sarney clearly supported bilateral integration, which prepared the ground for the Summit at Foz de Iguaçu. The international environment had not changed at the time of this Summit. The debt crisis was at its peak as well as the economic recession affecting both countries. Bilateral integration seemed undoubtedly to be a way to deal with this unfavorable international situation. According to Luigi Manzetti, the initiative to promote bilateral integration was "also envisaged as part of the Alfonsín administration's new development strategy."[26]According to this pundit, Argentine political leaders thought that both the import substitution programs implemented from 1930 to 1976 and the neoliberal reforms imposed by the military from 1976 to 1982 had proved to be detrimental to long-term economic growth. A new development strategy could be "achieved instead by reorienting manufactures (traditionally produced to supply domestic demand) toward the export market through bilateral agreements that seemed best-suited to this end."[27] Therefore, Alfonsín aimed to develop an intermediate model between import substitution and the indiscriminate liberalization of the international market. In this context, a strategy to sign bilateral agreements seemed to be more effective than previous multilateral integration initiatives. These bilateral agreements were intended "to promote close relations with some countries, which could boost economic development following a model of regulated liberalization, and give the signatory countries the ability to protect themselves from adverse external conditions generated by their exposure to the world economy."[28]

For the new Brazilian democracy, the changing regional and global situation required to adapt its foreign policy by trying to overcome the suspicions that the autarkic policies of military governments had generated in the region. In this context, Latin America began to gain more importance in the Brazil's foreign policy. Without abandoning the universalist paradigm that characterized the previous foreign policy strategy, the new democratic government began to perceive its neighbors as a "privileged space for its political-diplomatic and economic action."[29] Moreover, for Brazil, the alliance with Argentina was very different to the alliances promoted by the military governments with Japan and Germany in the previous decade. It was a more symmetrical alliance and based on the convergence of interests and economic objectives. One of those objectives was the promotion of joint economic development as part of a process of economic integration, on the one hand, from the interactions of the productive sectors and, on the other hand, from initiatives in strategic sectors such as energy, transport and telecommunications.[30]

For all these reasons, when the Brazilian president-elect Tancredo Neves went to Buenos Aires, he took the initiative to deepen relations with Argentina with the aim of successfully eliminating the causes of possible conflicts. When Neves died in 1985, Sarney took his succession to power and demonstrated the same interest to improve the bilateral relations with Argentina. All these factors caused a series of diplomatic consultations that concluded with the presidential summit in Foz Iguaçu, in November 1985. In July 1986, the Act for Argentine-Brazilian integration was subscribed and the Argentine-Brazilian Program for Economic Integration and Cooperation (PEIC, known in Spanish as PICE[31]) was launched. Twelve bilateral protocols were signed in the framework of PICE in areas such as capital goods, wheat, food supply reciprocity, expansion of trade, bilateral enterprises, financial affairs, investment funds, energy, biotechnology, economic research, nuclear cooperation and aeronautics.

The process of integration was advanced in 1988, when the Treaty of Integration, Cooperation and Development between Argentina and Brazil was signed. Although some conditions that existed when the Program of Economic Integration and Cooperation was signed had not changed, others were undergoing major transformations. International transformations such as the birth or rebirth of integration initiatives in different areas of the world, such as the relaunch of European integration after the Single European Act in 1986 and the signing of a free trade agreement between the United States and Canada in 1988. In addition, the transformation of the process of production was accelerated due to the scientific and technological progress. Another factor that had an impact in Latin America was the maintenance of protectionism in developed countries, despite negotiations of the Uruguay Round of GATT[32].

All these factors had an impact on the strategy of bilateral regional integration initiated in 1985, which could not ignore the demands of trade liberalization that were growing in the late 1980s. This led to a transformation in the logic of the integration process by incorporating the objective of establishing a bilateral free trade area within 10 years, as a first step in building a common market. This shift in the model of integration was also related to the failure of the heterodox programs implemented by both Sarney and Alfonsín to address the economic recession.

The new direction of the bilateral integration was confirmed in 1990 with the signing of the Act of Buenos Aires. International conditions had suddenly changed, especially after the fall of the Berlin Wall and the demise of communist governments in Eastern and Central Europe. This had consequences for Latin America in general, because it was argued that once the East-West conflict was ended, issues such as security and the fight against communism were not priorities in the national political agenda and in the relations with the United States. In this context, the opportunities for cooperation and integration in the continent were opened. This was closely related to an increasing of regionalization of the world economy and a commitment of the United States to regionalism that led to begin negotiations to establish a North American Free Trade Agreement (NAFTA) with Mexico and Canada. This project was expected to be widened to the whole Western Hemisphere, as it was announced by President George H. Bush in June 1990 in his proposal of the Initiative Enterprise for the Americas (IEA). This initiative showed the interest of the United States in promoting a regional bloc of which would be the leader. The IEA proposed to create a free trade area from Alaska to Tierra del Fuego, in which goods, services and capital could move freely.

The neoliberal hegemony in Latin America was already established in the early 1990s. In consequence, the attempts to find a solution to the economic crisis by implementing heterodox economic programs, such as those implemented in Argentina and Brazil by the governments of Alfonsín and Sarney, vanished, and instead of it, structural adjustment programs recommended by the IMF and the World Bank began to be adopted throughout the region. The hegemony of the Washington Consensus led to a regional convergence around the solution to the crisis in which interventionist policies or import substitution were put aside and replaced with a strategy focused on free trade, economic deregulation, liberalization and integration to the international economy. Even if the debt problem had not been resolved definitively, it had ceased to be the main issue of the regional agenda. The announcement of the Brady Plan in 1989 allowed refinancing of debts but that was conditioned to the increasing implementation of adjustment programs. This had an impact on the process of Argentine-Brazilian bilateral integration. The rise to power of Carlos Saul Menem in Argentina in 1989 and Fernando Collor de Mello in Brazil in 1990, both committed to the Washington Consensus, implied a change of the economic policy of the two countries and produced an ideological convergence that created the conditions for a shift of paradigm in the bilateral integration process.

In the case of Argentina, Menem took office in 1989 in a country plunged into a deep economic crisis. Alfonsín's government sought to solve the crisis by implementing heterodox programs such as the "Plan Austral" (1985), the "Plan de Julio" (1987) and "Primavera Plan" (1988), which included measures such price controls, elimination of wage indexation and monetary reform. None of these programs succeeded, and, the country experienced in 1989 a hyperinflation with a rate of 5,000 percent inflation, a significant scarcity of foreign exchange, and a 20 percent drop in per capita income and 50 percent in national investment.[33] During his mandate, Menem, diverse Ministers of Economy tried to address the crisis but it was not until 1991 when Domingo Cavallo proposed the Convertibility Plan, whose clear neoliberal orientation was adopted by Menem. The new strategy involved the resolution of bilateral disputes with developed countries, including the United States, a country with which the Menem wanted to have a special relationship, described by the Minister of Foreign Affairs Guido Di Tella as *relaciones carnales*, that is to say, brotherly relations. Furthermore, greater harmonization with international financial institutions and foreign investors took place.

In the case of Brazil, the economic situation was also critical. During the second half of the 1980s, several stabilization programs were implemented, as the Cruzado Plan (1986), the Plano Bresser (1987) and Plano Verão (1988), which included measures such as price controls that caused an immediate but temporary fall of prices, but soon after inflation returned. When Fernando Collor de Mello took office in 1990, the economic situation was grave. As a result, Collor approved a program of structural adjustment in line with the recommendations of the IMF but not similar to that implemented by Menem in Argentina. Although, Collor approved measures such as liberalization of prices and foreign exchange, he was more cautious in the process of privatization, for example. However, the idea of a better insertion into the global markets was clearly a goal to be achieved and, in this context, the deepening of regional integration with Argentina was crucial.

This movement toward regional integration between Brazil and Argentina caused reactions in the neighboring countries. Uruguay was the first state interested in being part of bilateral process furthered by Argentina and Brazil. The reason was very simple: since the 1970s, Uruguay had signed preferential trade agreements with its two neighbors. In 1974, the country subscribed with Buenos Aires the Argentine-Uruguayan Economic Complementarity Agreement (CAUCE in Spanish), whereas with Brazil, existed since 1975 the Protocol for Trade Promotion (PEC in Spanish and Portuguese) between Uruguay and Brazil. Both agreements were very important for Uruguay. Because of CAUCE, Uruguay sent 65 percent of their total exports to Argentina between 1982 and 1984, and 90 percent of industrial exports from Uruguay to Argentina were done in the framework of CAUCE. The importance of the PEC with Brazil was lower because in the same period, Uruguay sent 16.8 percent of the total exports in the framework of that agreement.[34] For these reasons, President José María Sanguinetti and his Minister of Foreign Affairs Enrique Iglesias showed since 1985 great interest in promoting integration with the two neighbors. In a summit held on May 19, 1985 between Alfonsín and José María Sanguinetti, the Act of Colonia that fostered economic and social integration between Uruguay and Argentina was signed and CAUCE was updated. The PEC in force with Brazil was also used in various protocols signed within the framework of ALADI. All this led to the signing in 1988, in Brasilia, of the *Alborada Act*, by which the incorporation of Uruguay in the integration process was formalized, although it was begun in the transport sector. [35]

After the signing of the Act of Buenos Aires in 1990, a bilateral negotiation between Argentina and Brazil began to construct a common market to be set up in 1994. However, the bilateral process became a regional process when Uruguay, Paraguay and initially Chile entered into the negotiations. These events triggered a process that led to creation of Mercosur in March 1991, a process that raised high expectations when created. The Brazilian commitment to this regional bloc meant the success of the approach proposed by Jaguaribe in the 1950s according to which integration should start with the integration with Argentina and the following step would be integration with countries of the Southern Cone.

In consequence, Mercosur meant the success of those who backed the path of integration. As a direct heir of the bilateral integration with Argentina, Mercosur was for Brazil a mechanism to deal with a global and regional uncertain scenario characterized by the transition to democracy in South America, the end of the Cold War and the deepening of the process of globalization. In this sense, it is important to analyze the reasons that led Brazil to promote Mercosur.

Two concepts are crucial to understand the Brazilian approach to Mercosur. These are the concepts of universalism and autonomy that have defined the Brazilian foreign policy for decades. As a project of integration, Mercosur should be compatible with these two concepts.

The idea of universalism is summarized in the search for a comprehensive projection of Brazil that led the country to deploy its diplomatic actions at different stages of world politics, both at the subregional level as the Mercosur and South American, hemispheric, interregional and multilateral levels. The idea of autonomy meant that the country must continue to keep the fundamental control of its own decisions.

The compatibility of universalism and autonomy was not an easy goal to achieve in the early 1990s. Universalism began to adopt a largely economic dimension, in the sense that it was likened to the insertion into the international economy and it was related to open regionalism and the need to overcome all forms of Third World Speech and promote the insertion into a world described as free of East-West and North-South ideological conflicts. As a result of the end of the Cold War, the consensus on the failure of the import substitution strategy and the growing economic and financial globalization, there was no alternative but the promotion of a strategy of economic reform and conquest of world markets and, at the political level, setting up alliances with the Western "market democracies" led by the United States.

The problem was that to achieve the desire international integration, the Brazilian government had to adopt policies that weakened its autonomous national development project. This was particularly true concerning trade and financial liberalization. Fernando Collor de Mello understood this dilemma and proposed to develop a policy of reform and trade liberalization that would reestablish the country's credibility after years of economic crisis and hyperinflation. This was accompanied by a desire to transform the image of Brazil from underdeveloped and Third World country to a reliable partner in the developing world. However, to succeed in this strategy "to enter into modernity," Brazil should adopt policies that involved a certain redefinition of its sovereignty and national development project. In this framework, it began to be argued that Brazil would find a space to redefine its international strategy by promoting integration with its South American neighbors.

On the one hand, the support the Brazilian government gave to the proposals of bilateral integration and Mercosur did not entail to neglect the principle of universalism but its reformulation. As Tullo Vigevani argues, Mercosur was an effort to produce a convergence of the national and regional interests in the Southern Cone. By doing so, the national interest would be best served as part of an integration process. Mercosur was aimed to reinforce the universalist principle of international insertion promoted by the Brazilian government by promoting free trade, but without establishing strong regional institutions or interventionist policies.[36]

On the other hand, the idea of autonomy meant for Brazil to seek mechanisms to maintain its autonomous decision-making capacity vis-à-vis the world centers of power in an unfavorable international context. Thus, the participation in Mercosur was not seen in Brazil as limitation of autonomy, but rather as an alliance of interests that would increase its external capacity.[37] Therefore, a link between regional integration and the traditional values of the Brazilian foreign policy was established. In the case of Mercosur, the defense of autonomy also implied the defense of a development model that, while accepting most of the principles of the Washington Consensus, did not allow the dismantling of its industrial development strategy. For the Brazilian government, the defense of its "industrial strategy" is the defense of its national development project, based on industrial restructuring and enlargement of the internal market. On this aspect, Brazil differs significantly from its Mercosur partners, including Argentina. After the military dictatorships, several Brazilian governments became the fundamental agents of the economic activity: the resources were invested in infrastructure, and foreign investment was directed toward the areas of industry, while protecting the domestic market and supporting industries through subsidies. As a result, the Brazilian industrial structure was able to expand and diversify, and the country became a newly industrialized economy.[38]

Although in different segments of the Brazilian state and society prevailed in the early 1990s, a view which involved the construction of a new national project and recognized the obsolescence of the economic model in force until the mid-1980s, at the same time it was still hegemonic the idea of maintaining the complex and diversified industrial structure of the country. The defense of this strategy of industrialization was maintained during the difficult years of the debt crisis for being deemed a pillar of the national economic autonomy. Insertion into the global economy and participation in regional integration agreements should not affect the industrial development.[39]

In other words, in the establishment of Mercosur, any project that caused a dismantling of the Brazilian national development plan (that for decades was based on industrialization) was excluded, as would have happened if Mercosur had adopted radically the Asia-Pacific style open regionalism approach, the prescriptions of the Washington Consensus or the NAFTA style of regional economic integration. Brazil succeeded in keeping the main tenets of its national project and this explains why Brazil was one of the countries that most progressively implemented the structural reform without abandoning some regulatory mechanisms.

The neoliberal reform implemented during the two administrations of Fernando Henrique Cardoso did not modify this aspect of the Brazilian development model, and the state's developmentalist approach remained as a pillar of the economic strategy[40]. In this sense, although Collor and Cardoso put in place policies of economic reform, trade liberalization, privatization and state reform, but did not deliberately promote a process of deindustrialization.[41] Lula's government has largely continued this strategy even if his commitment to greater interventionism was, at least in discourse, stronger than during the two previous administrations. Amado Cervo and Flavio Sombra Saraiva describe the Lula government's strategy as a "logistical state" in which state action is used to build a global systemic capacity. Once again, one can observe a reluctance to adopt the neoliberal idea of radical liberalization[42].

The preservation of interventionist policies had consequences on the design of Mercosur. As Nicola Phillips has pointed out, the Brazilian approach to Mercosur was primarily linked to national industrialization and the contribution that regional integration could bring in terms of improving the competitiveness of national industry and attracting foreign investments.[43] Raúl Bernal Meza[44] agrees with that argument, by asserting that for Brazil, Mercosur was an intermediary step toward an economic liberalization, a less traumatic transition from a closed economy to an economy that must accommodate to the demands of the international economic system. Mercosur was perceived as an intermediate alternative between keeping nationalist policies and the liberal economy prevailing in the world market.[45]

In any case, the defense of autonomy was a key element of Brazil's international strategy with significant consequences in the construction of Mercosur. During the government of Fernando Henrique Cardozo, this goal of autonomy was linked to the world economy and politics. It was then replaced the strategy of "autonomy by the distance" that characterized Brazilian politics during the Cold War by an "autonomy through participation."[46] On this aspect, the idea of autonomy is juxtaposed with that of universalism.

The principle of universalism is manifested by a reluctance about the possibility of creating a regional bloc in the Americas led by the United States, reluctance even greater if such an agreement was envisaged to further a model of integration that could affect the Brazilian developmentalist strategy. The Brazilian unwillingness was based on the asymmetry that existed between the United States and South America, both in the economic structure and the bargaining power. Fears of an "invasion" of US products and the risk that due it stronger bargaining position, the United States could impose WTO-plus disciplines', that that Brazil hesitated to support at multilateral level were important. This is crucial to understand the model of regional integration and cooperation adopted in Mercosur that was to some extent a response to the US proposal to establish a free trade area in the Americas.

After the announcement by President George H. Bush of the IEA, the Brazilian government showed little enthusiasm for the idea of creating a free trade area from Alaska to Patagonia. This hemispheric trade area would be created by signing bilateral agreements between the United States and Latin American countries that would be based upon the NAFTA model of economic integration. In contrast to other Latin American governments, the Brazilian government showed no particular enthusiasm for the announcement of the Bush proposal. *Plano Alto* described the IEA as "devoid of concrete content." The limited goals of the proposal (certainly centered on free trade and investments) were also criticized because it did not consider aspects such as the transfer of technology. In addition, Brazil was opposed to a negotiation strategy based in the signing of bilateral agreements.[47] Although the United States and Mercosur signed the "Rose Garden" agreement in June 1991 that established just the basis of a free trade agreement, the progress of its implementation was minimal, due to a large extent to the Brazilian lack of interest. Moreover, this agreement was intended responding to many issues raised in the Bush's proposal, in particular to avoid the approval of norms that could represent an undue intrusion in areas such as intellectual property and services.[48]

President Bill Clinton convened in December 1994 a Summit of Heads of State and Government in Miami to discuss, among other issues, the creation of hemispheric free trade area. Before the summit, Brazil began to develop a diplomatic strategy to influence on the model of integration that will be adopted in the hemispheric agreement, avoiding so that this letter would only be based on the US views. Thus, Brazil led Latin American countries on the discussions of the agenda of the Miami Summit in a preliminary ministerial meeting held in Virginia (United States), few months before the summit. Brazilian diplomacy succeeded in amending the proposal of the United States that included the negotiation of issues such as environment or labor. Similarly, Brazil secured to establish a more progressive and less restrictive schedule for adoption of a free trade area.[49] President Itamar Franco eventually participated in the Miami Summit, but his participation was modest, which showed the Brazilian "lukewarm enthusiasm" for the project.

After the beginning of "pre-negotiation period" of the Free Trade Area of the Americas (FTAA) that took place at the Ministerial Meetings of Denver (1995) and San Jose (1998), differences between Brazil-Mercosur and the United States on the agenda and the terms of negotiation of the trade agreement were significant. These differences remained during the "negotiation period" that began after the second Summit of the Americas held in Santiago de Chile in 1998. The differences remained when a first draft of the FTAA treaty was made public in 2001 and led eventually to the collapse of the hemispheric negotiation at the Summit of Mar del Plata in 2005.

The reluctance regarding the FTAA was based upon the Brazilian perception that that project was contrary to its national interests. Two factors should be considered when deciding to participate in such agreements. On the one hand, Brazil was a "global trader," namely, a country with a diversified trade pattern. On the other side, the proposal of the FTAA was a North-South integration modality, to which the Brazilian government was reluctant due to the economic asymmetry with the United States. In this sense, Luiz Alberto Moniz Bandeira, pointed out that integration with the United States would lead to a dismantling of the Brazilian industrial park "that would turn into scrap yard."[50] The ambassador Samuel Pinheiro Guimarães, one of the promoters of the bilateral integration with Argentina in 1987, when he was Chief Adviser of the Economic Integration Division of Itamaraty, described the US proposal as a strategy to preserve its hegemony in the region. Guimarães also stated that with the FTAA, the United States "would achieve its historical goal of a subordinated incorporation of Latin America to its economic territory and its sphere of military and political influence":[51]

Initially the FTAA forced Brazil to develop a defensive strategy, but later the US free trade initiative led the Brazilian government to further an "offensive strategy" that involved the development of a wider regional cooperation and integration in the whole America South subcontinent. This was the beginning of a process of construction of a new South American regionalism that eventually will led to the establishment of UNASUR in 2008, a new circle in the integration strategy recommended by Jaguaribe.

Thus, the creation and consolidation of Mercosur and its enlargement to the rest of South America were for Brazil part of a strategy to defend a model of economic integration that mixed interventionism in industrial issues and trade liberalization, which led to describe this model as strategic regionalism.[52] Brazilian political and economic sectors believed that the excessive neoliberal approach of the FTAA would affect Mercosur and would destroy the principle of autonomy. In addition, the FTAA would subordinate the economy of Brazil to the United States, affecting so the principle of universalism.

The commitment to the principles of autonomy and universalism will have two major effects. The principle of autonomy and in particular the defense of industrial development project imply the refusal of any economic regional agreement based on a deep integration agenda. In principle, the implementation of a program of trade liberalization is not rejected, since the regional integration would be "a space for learning and an adaptation of the private sectors to economic liberalization and foreign competition."[53] However, going beyond this program of tariff reductions to regulate issues such intellectual property, government procurement, labor or environmental issues was not a goal of the Brazilian government. However, what is crucial for our analysis is the strategy adopted in the 1990s which shows that Brazilian elites thought that the country could not deal "alone" with the challenges imposed by a changing global environment. Those challenges could be more effectively managed through the join actions with its neighbors in the framework of regional institutions. That was a victory for the path of integration.

FROM MERCOSUR TO THE WHOLE SOUTH AMERICA: THE PATH TO UNASUL

The initial success of Mercosur in the early years of implementation of the Treaty of Asunción and the perception that the FTAA and its NAFTA model of economic integration entailed risks for the Brazilian international strategic based on the principles of universalism and autonomy led to the promotion of a new regional project that included the whole South American region.

The Brazilian diplomacy decided to promote the concept of South America as a crucial element of its foreign policy strategy and as alternative to the idea of Latin America. In a study on this issue, Luiz Alberto Moniz Bandeira[54] argues that the idea of South America was historically relevant in the Brazilian diplomacy, but it was since the government of Collor that "South America" takes precedence over "Latin America" to describe Brazil's relations with its neighbors. Cepik and Farias[55] argue that in the search for an operational concept for action in the region, since the government of Collor the concept of Latin America was described as an invention of Napoleon III, during its imperial adventure in Mexico. By contrast, South America was a concept more adapted to the current "real" circumstances. This challenge to the notion of Latin America became much stronger after the signing of the NAFTA by Mexico. Since then, "Brazil's regional and international presence has been increasingly perceived as a process intimately connected to the emergence of 'South America' as a particular group in the international community."[56]

Due to the initial success of Mercosur, the government of Itamar Franco decided to promote a similar process in northern South America: the first step was the Amazon initiative, announced at the Summit of the Rio Group held in Buenos Aires in December 1992. The goal was to generate a rapprochement with the countries of the Treaty for the Amazonian Cooperation and complement in the north of the South American subcontinent the integration process that was being developed in the Southern Cone.[57] Another proposal was the creation of a Northern Common Market (known in Spanish as Merconorte). This idea of creating a northern axis in the Brazilian South American strategy was not new, because José Sarney had conceived a Brasilia-Caracas axis in the 1980s that would be the equivalent to the Brasilia-Buenos Aires axis promoted in Program Integration and Economic Cooperation between Brazil and Argentina. [58]

The Amazon Initiative and Merconorte were substituted by the project of creating a South American Free Trade Agreement (SAFTA). Firstly, SAFTA were largely a response to the FTAA and its NAFTA model, the changing global order and the creation of economic blocs. SAFTA was a project to create in South America a sort of counterbalance of NAFTA by establishing a regional space in which free trade would led to a closer interdependence among the South American countries. In this logic, SAFTA was a way to defend the autonomy from the FTAA. The Brazilian government began to perceive that SAFTA, even if was just a trade agreement, could also be used as an instrument to strengthen the bargaining power of South America in the FTAA negotiations. The original trade initiative became a political and strategic project that aimed to unify the South American countries in an integration process that would be achieved before the FTAA and would help increasing regional interdependence. The purpose was obviously to strengthen the region vis-a-vis the United States. Specialists such as Marcelo de Almeida Medeiros[59] consider that, by promoting SAFTA, Brazil proposed to erect a bulwark from which the region would have a single voice vis-à-vis the United States. Similarly, SAFTA rejected the US strategy to dilute Latin American regional groups by encouraging initiatives such as the FTAA. Medeiros also believes that from the Brazilian perspective SAFTA could increase South American negotiating power vis-à-vis its Asian and European partners and also allow the consolidation of intraregional economic relations.

However, the agenda of SAFTA should be minimal, limited to trade issues. In other words, the South American regionalist project originally promoted by Brazil had a "minimalist" agenda so that it was consistent with the strategy of autonomy "through integration." For this reason, Brazil did not further the creation of supranational institutions, the promotion of regional industrial projects (as the Andean Pact did in 1970s) or the establishing of regional social policies. This agenda was not accepted by Brazil for being considered too ambitious and not consistent with its foreign policy strategy. Based on this approach, between 1993 and 1999 the Brazilian government sought to negotiate a free trade agreement between Andean Community and Mercosur in order to establish SAFTA. However, the SAFTA project stagnated after 1998 because of the difficulties that both Mercosur and the Andean

Community experienced in those years. The Brazilian economic crisis produced by the devaluation of real in Brazil had impact on the development of Mercosur. At the same time, the Andean Community lost the dynamism that had characterized 1990s and in particular, the axis Caracas-Bogotá, began to show signs of fracture. As a result, the negotiation process between the Andean Community and Mercosur to establish the SAFTA stagnated.

In this regional context, President Fernando Henrique Cardoso convened in September 2000 to the Presidents of the countries of the Andean Community and Mercosur at a regional summit in Brasilia to discuss peace, democracy, stability and development in South America. Chile, an associate member of Mercosur, and Suriname and Guyana, two countries that, despite being part of the Amazon Cooperation Treaty, have traditionally been isolated in the region, were historically closer to English-speaking Caribbean, were also invited to the Summit.

In this Summit proposals beyond free trade were furthered, when the idea of SAFTA was replaced by the more ambitious scheme: The South American Community of Nations (SACN). The logic of SACN was based on the idea that the construction of a South American regional bloc required first the creation of a free trade zone between the two subregional blocs: the Andean Community and Mercosur, namely, SAFTA. This would be the beginning of the integration process, but SACN would not be just free trade. The presidents established four pillars in the construction of the new South American space: the defense of democracy; physical integration and infrastructure; the combat against drug trafficking; and the development knowledge and technology. Four major decisions were made in the Brasilia Summit: to set up a South American system of economic and political cooperation among its members that essentially meant the creation of a free trade area; to implement in a 10-year period an action plan for Program of Regional Infrastructure in South America (known in Portuguese and Spanish as IIRSA); to consider democracy as a prerequisite to be part of the system; and to develop measures to combat organized crime, including drug trafficking.[60]

Cardoso's plan was to relaunch the Brazilian strategy of South American integration. SACN meant an evolution toward a "more interventionist model," a shift that Brazil was also furthering in Mercosur by promoting an agenda to relaunch the regional bloc that included proposals very similar to those approved at the Summit of Brasilia. By transforming SAFTA into SACN, Cardoso also aimed to distinguish between a "South American agenda" beyond trade and the "FTAA agenda" centered on trade. While the FTAA mainly addressed the negotiation of tariffs and the new trade-related issues (intellectual property, services, government procurement, etc.), SACN (although include trade) proposed to develop a regional space by investing in infrastructure, energy, telecommunications and border development, etc.[61]

The South American leaders met again in September 2002, in the city of Guayaquil, Ecuador. After the Summit of Guayaquil, a Free Trade Agreement between the Andean Community and Mercosur was signed in December 2003 as foresaw in the SAFTA project. Afterward, a treaty that formally established the SACN was signed at a meeting of South American presidents held in Cusco, Peru in December 2004. In the Declaration of Cusco was announced as goals of the new regional bloc: a) the political and diplomatic coordination to enhance the South American region as a differentiated and dynamic actor; b) deepening of the convergence between Mercosur, the Andean Community and Chile in a free trade area, to which Surinam and Guyana might join; c) physical, energy and communications integration in South America and the promotion of IIRSA; d) harmonization of policies for rural and agricultural development;) technology transfer and horizontal cooperation in all fields of science, education and culture; and the increasing interaction between business and civil society in the dynamics of integration.

The First Summit of Presidents and Heads of Government of SACN was held in Brasilia in September 2005. In the Presidential Declaration and Priority Agenda, the final document of the summit, the areas to be developed in the SACN were set up: political dialogue, physical integration, environment, energy integration, the establishment of South American financial mechanisms and promoting social cohesion and justice.[62]

Thus, the Brazilian strategy in the SACN was clear. The SACN was based on the Brazilian leadership and a minimalist agenda consistent with the principle of autonomy "through integration" promoted by Brazil. The new globalized economic reality, in particular the process of trade liberalization, did not allow continuing a strategy to defend the autonomy based on the promotion of autarky. The structural changes in the global and hemispheric economic structure forced Brazil to further a deeper integration into a world increasingly competitive. However, as beforehand mentioned, when analyzing Mercosur, a radical liberalization would have meant a de facto resign to the concept of autonomy, to which Brazil did not want to give up. The answer to this dilemma was given by the government of Fernando Henrique Cardoso by proposing an "autonomy through integration."[63]

The strategy of the emerging Brazilian Transnational Firms and the role of the South American countries in the strategy of internationalization of those firms are also crucial to understand the promotion of a new regionalism in South America. Thus, the Mercosur experience was invaluable to the Brazilian Transnational Firms as an initial space in the process of internationalization of their activities. According to De Gouvea Neto, "depending on the source, one-third to one-half of all Brazilian companies involved in international business started their international operations in Mercosur."[64] It is valid to argue that if the creation of a regional market in Mercosur favored the expansion of the activities of the Brazilian firms, these latter would support the establishment of a wider South American space in which to continue their process of internationalization. In fact, this was the continuation of the involvement of the private sector in the promotion of regional integration and cooperation as established in the Argentine-Brazilian bilateral process in the 1980s. There has been a significant expansion of the activities of Brazilian companies in the sector of service, especially in the area of construction, such as Odebrecht, a firm that promoted major infrastructure projects in Venezuela and the Interoceanic Highway that will link Brazil with Peru's ports in the Pacific.[65] The SACN was conceived as a project that would allow Brazilian firms to continue the expansion of their activities, which explain why one of its pillars was the IIRSA, a mechanism to improve infrastructure needed for free trade. Once built this regional infrastructure, Brazilian firms would benefit of the new roads that facilitate the trade of goods and reduce freight costs, facilitating a further expansion of their activities in the region.[66]

From 2004 onward, political changes in the region became a crucial variable to explain the changes in the construction of the South American project and the transformation of SACN into UNASUR. After his victory in the recall referendum in August 2004, Hugo Chavez government in Venezuela began to play a major role in the construction of the South American regionalism. The Venezuelan foreign policy differed greatly from Brazil's international strategy, by fostering goals such as the promotion of a multipolar order, South-South cooperation and the Bolivarian integration. To understand Venezuelan foreign policy, it was crucial to consider the idea of the "fight against a unipolar order," the way the Venezuelan government describes the post-Cold War world. Chávez proposed to replace that unipolar world with a multipolar order in which various poles of power were created to build a more balanced international order. For Chávez, South America should become one of the new poles of power in that multipolar order. In this context, integration became an element to promote "autonomy" in the sense of transforming the region into a political actor not subordinated to the US unipolarism. Thus, Chávez developed a strategy to include in the South American regional project objectives such as the creation of a regional bloc of power and the construction of a "non-liberal" integration model based on complementation and solidarity. By doing so, the South American integration was instrumental to the objectives of the Chavist Venezuelan foreign policy.

In this context, Chávez certainly backed the Brazilian project of creating a South American regional bloc as a new actor in the hemispheric and global affairs. However, he criticized some aspects of the Brazilian project. Firstly, he rejected the idea of a Community of Nations because for him South America was one single nation. In consequence, he preferred the term "Union of the South." Secondly, Chávez criticized the fact that one of the pillars of SACN was the convergence of the Andean Community and Mercosur. According to him, these two processes of integration were based on neoliberalism and did not promote real integration of peoples. For the Venezuelan president, "the South American Community must go beyond Mercosur and the Andean Community, and these institutions should disappear. If not, we are doing nothing."[67]

As a result, emerged a sort of low-intensity struggle for leadership (or at least competition) between Brazil and Venezuela related to the integration model that the new South American regionalism should adopt. In reality, as Sean Burges[68] has argued, behind this competition existed a "divide between the overt importance placed upon policy pragmatism and attempts at ideological purity." The crux of the matter was the way that each country perceives its insertion into the global political economy, "which in turn [pointed] to antithetical visions for Latin American and Southern relations with the global system."[69] Burges described this situation in the following terms:

> Brazil is self-interestedly looking to create economic opportunities for itself, which might offer opportunities to regional "partners." The goal is to make South America a vibrant market for Brazilian products and a source for the energy resources that the country's economy needs. This pragmatic and self-servingly market-friendly attitude is not neoliberal at its core—it deploys the state in support of national firms exploiting regional and global opportunities—but it does stand in contrast to the avowedly socialist vision being advanced by Hugo Chavez. The Venezuelan president is rapidly taking his country down a statist path that will concentrate economic decisions in the hands of the state. Everything is to be subsumed to the prerogative of human and societal development according to a socialist ethos as understood by Chávez.[70]

According to that view, the Brazilian commitment to integration in South America was just a self-interested action without regional objectives but eventual opportunities that could emerge for the South American countries of the Brazilian growing economic presence in the region. It could be argued that this is a new way to present the path of separation. Obviously, Brazil promoted its national interests by promoting regionalism as Germany and France did in the 1950s when fostering European integration or the United States did when furthered NAFTA in the 1990s. However, both Mercosur and UNASUR are for Brazil more than spaces to create economic opportunities or promote trade and investments. The transformation of SAFTA into SACN validates this argument. If the goal was just to expand the market for Brazilian firms, it is legitimate to ask why Cardoso included in the regional initiative goals as the defense of democracy, the consolidation of South America as a zone of peace or the combat of drug trafficking. In reality, the SACN was an attempt to create a new regional actor to influence in hemispheric and global affairs.

This Brazilian view is confirmed if one considers the criticisms Chavez made to the SACN project. Andres Serbin argues[71] that substantial differences exist between the process of ALBA, led by Venezuela, and SACN project led by Brazil. For Serbin, there is a clear-cut difference between the conceptual and ideological basis Venezuelan and Brazilian projects. The principles of economic and market liberalization and open regionalism have not been rejected, a point on which SACN was not too far from the FTAA's views on free trade and investment; SACN's main objective remained associated to the strengthening of regional capacity to insert the region efficiently into the international economy. The victory of the center-left governments in countries such as Argentina, Brazil and Uruguay has led to greater state intervention in the regulation of markets and the promotion of social policy but not a radical break with the principles of liberalization and open regionalism[72]. By contrast, in the Venezuelan projects, the nation-state plays a leading role as organizer of society, based on firstly an endogenous development strategy and later in the 21st-century socialism strongly critical to globalization (understood as a neoliberal process).[73]

These differences in the integration model became more evident since the Summit of SACN held in Brazilian in 2005 and the following Summit in Cochabamba in 2006. The shift toward the modification of the nascent SACN process took place at the First Energy Summit of South America held in 2007 in Margarita Island, Venezuela, where SACN was renamed UNASUR. The presidents at the summit decided to initiate negotiations for a treaty that would establish the goals, mechanisms and institutional structure of UNASUR. This agreement was signed at a South American summit held in Brasilia in May 2008. The UNASUR treaty implied the transformation of the South American project from a minimalist, pragmatic project (represented by SAFTA and the SACN) to a maximalist, ambitious project with trade, social, productive, environmental and political goals. As a result, trade disappeared, infrastructure became secondary and UNASUR became an agreement, the main goals of which are cooperation and political dialogue, defense and some financial and social issues. This proved to be the lowest common denominator resulting from the positions led by Brazil and Venezuela and shared for other South American countries.

In this context, UNASUR became for Brazil a space to build a South American area of dialogue and political cooperation, especially on matters concerning regional security. This explains the proposal to create a South American Community of Defense and the role given to UNASUR in the solution of conflicts that may arise between member countries. It can be argued that these will be the aspects of UNASUR in which Brazilian diplomacy will invest the most resources. This does not mean that Brazil has given up on achieving goals such as IIRSA and SAFTA, but perhaps to achieve these goals, UNASUR is no longer needed. The convergence between the Andean Community and Mercosur in a free trade zone has been taking place since the signing of Economic Complementation Agreement no. 59. In addition, IIRSA is an initiative that has its own momentum and its continued progress in the creation of a South American infrastructure advance beyond the formalization of SACN and UNASUR.

CELAC AND THE RETURN OF LATIN AMERICA

As Helio Jaguaribe recommended since the 1950s, after the consolidation of integration and cooperation with Argentina, the Southern Cone and South America, Brazil should further closer relations with the rest of Latin American countries. This would be the largest circle in the strategy of concentric circles Brazil should implement. The establishment of the Latin American and Caribbean Community of States (CELAC), in which Brazil was actively involved, was the manifestation that the concept of Latin American is still important for the Brazilian foreign policymakers.

Certainly, as beforehand mentioned, since the 1990s some sectors in Itamaraty decided to further South America as a category that influence on the design of the Brazilian regional integration policy and strategy. The process that started with the SAFTA proposal and ended with UNASUR exemplified that strategy. This notwithstanding, Brazil never stopped its participation in old Latin American integration such as the SELA, LAIA and the Rio Group.[74] In other words, despite its South American strategy, Brazil was also actively involved in the Latin American regional dynamics.

This is not only a matter of participating in old regional schemes, but new initiatives were fostered during the government of Lula. Thus, Brazil became an observer of the Caribbean Community in 2004 (CARICOM) and Lula participated in the CARICOM Summit in 2005 held in Paramaribo, Surinam. Later, A Brazil-CARICOM Summit was held in Brasilia in 2010. Similar activism has been shown toward Central America. In 2008, President Lula participated in the Summit of Central American Integration System and Brazil became an observer of this integration process.[75]

It is this context that Lula conveys a Latin American and Caribbean Summit (known in Spanish and Portuguese as CALCS) in Salvador, Bahia, Brazil in December 2008. In that Summit, Lula asserted: "This Summit has a simple but fundamental message: we only overcome the challenges of integration and development if we undertake our Latin American and Caribbean vocation."[76] Lula also assert that: it was needed "the collective action of the countries of the South in order to transform the international order by modifying the international norms in force and the search for a global balance through the construction of regional poles of power."[77] The Mexican representative proposed the creation of a Latin American and Caribbean Union based on the experience of regional cooperation in the Rio Group. The Mexican approach was to create a regional institution with far-reaching and ambitious goals ranging from the promotion of economic and social development to the commitment to construct a fairer and equitable international order. From the conjunction of the Brazilian and Mexican proposals, the creation of a Latin American and Caribbean Community of States was proposed. This was formally discussed in the second Summit of CALCS held in Cancun, Mexico, in February 2010, Where negotiations to subscribe a treaty to establish a new regional scheme were approved.[78]

In the meantime, the Brazilian involvement in Latin American affairs continued in 2010. After the earthquake in Haiti that year, Brazil decided to coordinate the United Nations Stabilization Mission in Haiti (UNSTAMIH, known in Spanish and Portuguese as MINUSTAH). Similarly, Brazil was quite involved in political crisis in Honduras after the coup d'état to President Manuel Zelaya.

CELAC was formally established in a Summit of Presidents and Head of Governments held in Caracas in December 2011. As Michael Shifter argues, the creation of CELAC shows the changes in the region's politics in the first decade of the new millennium[79]. Despite the vagueness of its objectives and the weak institutional design, CELAC supposed the creation of regional institution that excluded the United States and Canada but included Cuba, a country excluded from the OAS since the 1960s. Rojas Aravena also highlights that the foundation of CELAC is an attempt to overcome political fragmentation and strengthen the Latin American's voice by establishing mechanism of political coordination among the countries of the region.[80]

The Brazilian participation in the promotion and development of CELAC is certainly an expression of the Latin American dimension of its recent foreign policy. Being part of CELAC is consistent with the principle of universalism but at the same time reveals the importance given to a better political coordination among the Latin American countries. Similarly, the participation in CELAC reinforces the principle of "autonomy through diversification" promoted during the Lula da Silva's administration. This is a category proposed by the Brazilian scholars Tullo Vigevani and Gabriel Cepaluni. For these pundits, although there were no significant ruptures from the paradigms of Brazilian foreign policy during the Lula era, there was a change in the emphasis given to certain options opened previously in the Cardoso administration. "Both administrations (Cardoso and Lula) used different foreign policy means, trying not to sway too far from the constantly pursued aim of developing the country economically while maintaining a certain political autonomy."[81] While Cardoso furthered an autonomy by integration, Lula "opted for an autonomy through diversification in adherence to international norms and principles by means of South-South alliances, including regional alliances, and through agreements with non-traditional partner (...) trying to reduce asymmetries in external relations with powerful countries."[82] Arguably, the participation in CELAC was part of this strategy. That is particularly true if one consider the exclusion of the United States and Canada and the idea or creating an exclusive Latin American and Caribbean space for political dialogue and conflict resolution.

Teixeira Gonçalves argues that the participation in CELAC reveals a redefinition, at least partially, of the Brazilian foreign policy. Certainly, South America remains as a priority but the integration and cooperation in that region become a platform to expand the Brazilian involvement beyond, in Central America and the Caribbean. This is certainly a change compared to the strategy fostered in the 1990s and the first decade of 2000s when South America was the main concern. In Lula's administration, the whole Latin American and Caribbean region was considered important.[83] Teixeira Gonçalves goes further and asserts that evidence are enough to demonstrate that this is a long-term structural process and not a conjectural moment based on specific Brazilian interests. This Brazilian expert even considers that the actions in Central America and the Caribbean as well as the creation of CELAC are more important for the Brazilian foreign policy than its partnerships in Africa, Asia or the Middle East.[84]

NOTES

1. Bruno Allyon, "Aspectos conceituais da diplomacia universalista do Brasil: as relações bilaterais e a integração regional (1945–2000)," *Carta Internacional* (2005), 22.

2. See José E. Mindlin, "Desenvolvimento Brasileiro e a crise da ALALC", *Revista de Administração de Empresas*, vol. 13, no. 2, (1973), 75–80.

3. George Lott, "Latin American Economic Integration," *Lawyer of the Americas*, vol. 10, no. 2, (1978), 549–575.

4. Georges D. Landau, "The Treaty for Amazonian Cooperation: A Bold New Instrument for Development," *Georgia Journal of International and Comparative Law*, vol. 10, no. 3, (1980), 472.

5. Gian Luca Gardini, "Making Sense of the Rapprochement between Argentina and Brazil, 1979–1982," *Revista Europea de Estudios Latinoamericanos y del Caribe*, no. 80 (2006), 58.

6. Ibid., 58.

7. Luiz Alberto Moniz Bandeira, *O eixo Argentina- Brasil. O Processo de Integração de América Latina* (Brasilia: Editorial Universidade de Brasília, 1987), 74.

8. Gian Luca Gardini, "Making Sense of the Rapprochement," 58.

9. Mónica Hirst, "La participación de Brasil en el proceso del Mercosur: evaluando costos y beneficios," in Francisco Rojas Aravena and William C. Smith (eds.), *El Cono Sur las transformaciones globales* (Santiago de Chile: FLACSO, North South Center, CLADE, 1994), 319.

10. Gian Luca Gardini, "Making Sense of the Rapprochement," 60–61.

11. Ibid., 61.

12. Amado Luiz Cervo, *Relações Internacionais da América Latina. Velhos e novos paradigmas* (Brasilia: Ed. Saraiva, Instituto Brasileiro de Relações Internacionais, 2ª edição, 2007), 209–210.

13. Gian Luca Gardini, "Making Sense of the Rapprochement," 67.

14. Gian Luca Gardini., "Two Critical Passages in the Road to Mercosur," *Cambridge Review of International Affairs*, vol. XVIII, no. 3 (2005), 410.

15. Ibid., 410.

16. Ibid., 411.

17. Quoted in Luiz Alberto Moniz Banderira, *O eixo Argentina- Brasil. O Processo de Integração de América Latina*, 72.

18. Wilber Albert Chaffee, *Desenvolvimento: Politics and Economy in Brazil* (Boulder, CO: Lynne Rienner, 1998), 137.

19. Ibid., 136.

20. Ibid., 134.

21. Werner Baer, *The Brazilian Economy: Growth and Development* (Westport, CT: Praeger, 2001), 100.

22. Ibid., 101.

23. William C. Smith, *Authoritarianism and the Crisis of the Argentine Political Economy* (Stanford: Stanford University Press, 1991), 246.

24. Ibid., 247.

25. Jorge Schvarzer, "Mercosur: The Prospects for Regional Integration," *NACLA Report on the Americas*, vol. XXXII, no. 6 (1998), 26.

26. Luigi Manzetti, "Argentine-Brazilian Economic Integration: An Early Appraisal," *Latin American Research Review*, vol. XXV, no. 3 (1990), 114.

27. Ibid., 114.

28. Alcides Costa Vaz, *Cooperação, integração e processo negociador. A construção do Mercosul* (Brasilia: FUNAG, IBRI, 2002), 76.

29. Ibid., 74.

30. Ibid., 79.

31. PICE means Programa de Integración y Cooperación Económica entre Brasil and Argentina.

32. Maria Cândida, Galvão Flores, *O Mercosul nos discursos do governo brasileiro (1985–94)* (Rio de Janeiro: Editora FGV, 2005), 53.

33. Nicola Phillips, *The Southern Cone Model: The Political Economy of Regional Capitalist Development in Latin America* (London – New York: Routledge, 2004), 66.

34. Leopoldo Marmora and Dirk Messner, "La integración de Argentina, Brasil y Uruguay"; *Nueva Sociedad*, no. 113 (1991), 133.

35. Roberto Ruiz Díaz Labrano and Ramón Silva Alonso, *El Mercosur: marco jurídico institucional, análisis y perspectivas de sus normas derivadas* (Asunción: Universidad Nacional de Asunción, Intercontinental Editora, 1993), 23.

36. Tullo Vigevani, Gustavo de Mauro Favaron, Haroldo Ramanzini Júnior & Rodrigo Alves Correia, "O papel da integração regional para o Brasil: universalismo, soberania e percepção das elites," *Revista Brasileira de Política Internacional*, vol. LI, no. 1 (2008), 6.

37. Ibid., 6.

38. Miguel Teubal, "Regional integration processes in Latin America: Argentina and MERCOSUR," in Alex E. Fernández Jilberto and André Mommen (eds.), *Regionalization and Globalization in the Modern World Economy: Perspectives on the Third World and Transitional Economies* (London: Routledge, 1998), 243.

39. Mónica Hirst, "La participación de Brasil," 316–317.

40. Nicola Phillips, *The Southern Cone Model*, 77.

41. José Alexandre A Hage, *As relações diplomáticas entre Argentina e Brasil no MERCOSUL. Princípios de hegemonia, dependência e interesse no Tratado de Assunção* (Curitiba: Jurúa editora, 2004), 129.

42. José Flavio Sombra Saraiva, "Um novo ensaio estratégico argentino- brasileiro: possibilidades e limites," in Fausto, Ayrton and José Flavio Sombra Saraiva (eds.), *Diálogos sobre a Pátria Grande* (Brasilia: FLACSO-Brasil, 2004), 89. Amado Luiz Cervo, "Estado logístico: la inserción internacional sistémica de Brasil en el siglo XXI," in José Briceño-Ruiz y Alejandro Simonoff (eds.), *Integración y Cooperación Regional en América Latina: Una relectura a partir de la teoría de la autonomía* (Buenos Aires: Editorial Biblos, 2015), 163–188.

43. Phillips, Nicola, *The Southern Cone Model*, 100.

44. Raúl Bernal Meza, *Sistema Mundial y MERCOSUR. Globalización, Regionalismo y Políticas Exteriores Comparadas* (Buenos Aires: Nuevohacer/Universidad Nacional del Centro de la Provincia de Buenos Aires, 2000), 382.

45. Sean W Burges, "Consensual Hegemony: Theorizing Brazilian Foreign Policy after the Cold," *Internacional Relations*, vol. XXII, no.1 (2008), 76.

46. Tullo Vigevani and Marcelo Fernandes De Oliveira, "Brazilian Foreign Policy in the Cardoso Era: The Search for Autonomy through Integration," *Latin American Perspectives,* vol. XXIV, no. 5 (2007), 63.

47. Tullo Vigevani and Marcelo Passini Mariano, "A ALCA e a política externa brasileira," in Henrique Altemani, and Antonio Carlos Lessa (eds.), *Relações Internacionais do Brasil*, vol. 1 (Brasilia: FUNAG, Editora Saraiva, Instituto Brasileiro de Relações Internacionais, 2006), 339.

48. Celso Amorim and Renata Pimentel, "Iniciativa para as Américas: O acordo do Jardim das Rosas," in Albuquerque, J. A. Guilhon, *Sessenta anos de política externa brasileira* (São Paulo: Cultural/Nupri/USP/Fapesp, 1996), vol. 2, 118.

49. This process is analyzed in Sean, Burges, "Without Sticks or Carrots: Brazilian Leadership un South America During the Cardoso Era, 1992–2003," *Bulletin of Latin American Research*, vol. XXV, no. 1 (2004), 30–32.

50. Luiz Alberto Moniz Bandeira, "O Brasil e a América do Sul," in Altemani, Henrique and Antonio Carlos Lessa (eds.), *Relações Internacionais do Brasil,* vol. 1 (Brasilia: FUNAG, Editora Saraiva, Instituto Brasileiro de Relações Internacionais, 2006), 278.

51. Quoted in Moniz Bandeira, "O Brasil e a América," 278.

52. José Briceño-Ruiz, "El regionalismo estratégico en las interacciones entre Estados Unidos y Brasil en el ALCA: Un análisis desde el liberalismo intergubernamental," in Shigeru Kochi, Philippe de Lombaerde and José Briceño-Ruiz (eds.), *Del regionalismo latinoamericano a la integración interregional* (Madrid: Siglo XXI editores, 2008), 99–136.

53. Vaz, *Cooperação, integração e processo*, 88.

54. Luiz Alberto Moniz Bandeira, "O Brasil e América," 267–297.

55. Marco Aurélio Chaves Cepik and Carlos Aurélio Pimenta de Faria, "Brasil y América Latina: Bolivarismos antiguos y modernos," *Análisis Político*, no. 49 (2003),74.

56. María Regina Soares de Lima and Monica Hirst, "Brazil as an Intermediate State and Regional Power," *International Affairs*, vol. 82, no. 1 (2006), 29.

57. Marco Aurélio Chaves Cepik and Carlos Aurélio Pimenta de Faria, "Brasil y América Latina," 49.

58. Amado Luiz Cervo, *Relações internacionais da América Latina*, 206–207.

59. Marcelo da Almeida Medeiros, *La genèse du MERCOSUD* (Paris: L'Harmattan, 2000), 380.

60. Andrés Serbin Bartosch, "El largo (y díficil) camino hacia una integración sudamericana," in Consuelo Ahumada y Arturo Cancino (eds.), *Comunidad Andina y Mercosur en la perspectiva del ALCA* (Bogotá: Memorias del Observatorio Andino, Centro Editorial Javeriano, 2003), 35.

61. Lincoln, Bizzozero, "Los cambios de gobierno en Argentina y Brasil y la conformación de una agenda del Mercosur ¿Hacia una nueva cartografía sudamericana/ interamericana?," *Nueva Sociedad*, no. 186 (2003), 132.

62. Declaración Presidencial y Agenda Prioritaria, 2005, available at: http://walk.sela.org/attach/258/EDOCS/SRed/2010/09/T023600002368–0-Declaracion_Presidencial_y_Agenda_Prioritaria_-_Comunidad_Sudamericana_de_Naciones.pdf (accessed: September 17, 2016).

63. Tullo Vigevani and Marcelo Fernandes de Oliveira, "Brazilian Foreign Policy," 58–80.

64. Raul De Gouvea Neto, "Mercosur: Fostering Regional Economic Integration," *Thunderbird International Business Review*, vol. 40, no. 6 (1998), 591.

65. As known, Odebrecht was later involved in a huge case of corruption in diverse Latin American countries.

66. Rita Giacalone, "La Comunidad Sudamericana de Naciones: ¿Una alianza entre izquierda y empresarios?," *Nueva Sociedad*, no. 202 (2006), 81–82.

67. Chavez quoted in Yañez, Antonio, "Comunidad Sudamericana de Naciones ¿con impronta venezolana o brasileña?", *La Onda Digital*, no 256, 04/10/2005 al 10 October 2005, available at: http://www.laondadigital.com/laonda/laonda/201–300/256/B21.htm (accessed: October 31, 2009).

68. Sean Burges, "Building a Global Southern Coalition: The Competing Approaches of Brazil's Lula and Venezuela's Chávez," *Third World Quaterly*, vol. 28, no. 7 (2007), 1343–1344.

69. Ibid., 1344.

70. Ibid.

71. Andrés Serbin, "Entre UNASUR y ALBA: ¿Otra integración (ciudadana) es posible?," *Anuario de integración regional de América Latina y el Gran Caribe*, no. 6 (2007), 183–207.

72. Ibid., 196.

73. Ibid., 197.

74. The Contadora Group was created in 1983 by Colombia, Mexico, Panamá and Venezuela in a Ministerial Meeting held at the Contadora Island in Panamá with the aim of promoting a peaceful solution to the political crisis in Central America. The Rio Group was the result of the so-called Support Group (*Grupo de Apoyo* in Spanish), a regional space created in 1986 as a mechanism to support the actions of the Contadora Group. The Support Group and Contadora Group were renamed in 1990 as the Rio Group.

75. Felipe Teixeira Gonçalves, *A CELAC, o SELA e a agenda do Brasil para América Latina e Caribe, Boletim de Economia e Política Internacional*, vol. 8 (2011), 51.

76. Ibid., 51.

77. Lula da Silva, quoted by María Regina Soares de Lima, "La Política Exterior brasileña y los desafíos de la gobernanza global," *Foreign Affairs Latinoamérica*, vol. 9, no. 2 (2009), 29.

78. Francisco Carrión Mena, "Política Exterior de América Latina y las Cumbres de la CELAC," in Adrián Bonilla Soria and Isabel Álvarez Echandi (eds.), *Desafíos estratégicos del regionalismo contemporáneo: CELAC e Iberoamérica* (San José; Costa Rica: FLACSO, 2013), 120.

79. Michael Shifter, "The Shifting Landscape of Latin American Regionalism," *Current History*, vol. 111, no. 742 (February 2012), 56.

80. Francisco Rojas Aravena, *Global Shifts and Changes in Latin America*, available at http://library.fes.de/pdf-files/iez/10344.pdf (accessed: October 29, 2016).

81. Tullo Vigevani and Gabriel Cepaluni, "Lula's Foreign Policy and the Quest for Autonomy through Diversification," *Third World Quarterly*, vol. 28, no. 7 (2007), 1310.

82. Ibid., 1333.

83. Felipe Teixeira Gonçalves, *A CELAC, o SELA e a agenda do Brasil para América Latina e Caribe*, 53.

84. Ibid., 53.

Conclusion

The historical analysis made throughout the diverse chapters of this book shows that there has certainly been a "path of separation" between Brazil and its neighboring countries in Latin America. It is therefore with good reason this view has been quite influential in academic, political and economic sectors in Brazil, as well as with pundits outside the country. This notwithstanding, there is another story of Brazil's relationship with the region that is not frequently told. As our book addresses, there is also a path of integration that goes as far back as colonial times, a period when Brazil would generally have been described as isolated or hostile vis-à-vis its Hispanic neighbors. We hold that this path of integration persisted into the 19th century, with stronger forms of interaction between Brazilian political events, and that which would later be known as Latin America. Research on the issue fails to recognize these facts. Thus, recent Brazilian historiography accounts for the influence of Hispanic American independence movements on the political process that was initiated in Brazil in the early 1820s, as showed in chapter 2 of this book. Similarly, a review of Brazilian diplomatic correspondence shows that despite not participating in the American International Congresses that began in Panamá in 1826, the Brazilian government followed with attention the previous negotiations that led to these meetings.

In chapter 3, we show that the Brazilian rapprochement with Latin American was even more intense in the 20th century, with initial steps such as the second ABC initiative made by President Peron and his rapprochement with Argentina and other Latin American countries. Later on, we also point out the Brazilian involvement in CEPAL and its proposal to create a Latin American Common Market that led to the establishment of LAFTA. We also mention subsequence events, such as the signing of the Amazonian Cooperation Treaty in the 1970s and the success to work out the differences on issues such as nuclear cooperation and the development of the Itaipú Dam in the Parana River. As shown in chapter 4, the path of integration-oriented initiatives continued and reached historically high levels during the 1980s. Some starting points were the bilateral cooperation and integration with Argentina that was triggered in Foz de Iguaçu in 1985, the creation of Mercosur in 1991 and the process that began with the proposal of setting up a South American Free Trade Area (SAFTA), which concluded with the creation of the UNASUR in 2008. Even if much of the research surrounding this issue holds that the path of integration was born in the 1980s, our study suggests that this path of integration with Latin America was not a novelty in Brazilian foreign policy.

Despite strong evidence concerning integration-oriented lines of action, the idea of Brazil as something specific and separate from Latin America still appears dominant, both in Brazil and among non-Brazilian pundits. In our view, there is no doubt that Brazil is an integral part of Latin America, sharing all the virtues and defects of other Latin American societies. The question as to why Brazilian society has a different answer to this may seem quite obvious for an observer beyond the region. People such as Manuel Bomfin, Joaquim Nabuco, Manuel de Oliveira Lima, Darcy Ribeiro, Paulo Freyre and many other important national intellectual and political influential personalities have, at different moments, answered positively to the question. The same would be the case concerning many of their peers, in both Spanish-speaking America and the rest of the continent. This national attachment to a regional identity does not, however, mean a rejection of a Brazilian national definition (s) or other kind of particularities. Moreover, it does not need to contradict other kinds of cultural, economic or geopolitical supranational formations, as is the case with Christian civilization, South America, the "South," America, Pan-America or Western.

There are of course those who have found, to the contrary, that Brazil is incompatible with the Latin American dimension due to its having a different language and particularities related to a Portuguese origin of the "Brazilian civilization," in addition to a historical accumulation of cleavages leading to the formation of antagonist economic and geopolitical interests and strategies. From this vantage point, Brazilian foreign policy convergences might go along a Western, American, Pan-American, national and policy alignment, but not a Latin American one.

We described the first position as the "path of integration" and the second as the "path of separation." These two trends, as mentioned beforehand, have coexisted in the long history of relations between Brazil and Latin America. In this book, our efforts have been to show the initiatives based upon the path of integration in order to overcome simplistic explanations, according to which Brazil has always been distant regarding Latin America, or Brazilian particularities have made cooperation and integration with Latin American countries impossible. The issue is more complicated because, as described in the diverse chapters of this book, interactions have not only always existed but in some particular historical moments been considered crucial in the international projection of Brazil.

There are, of course, often no clear-cut differences between those two views, since policies and identities many times overlap depending on the various themes (economy, security, foreign policy, culture and identity) and the people that have been behind by them. Moreover, scholars and policies might change position within their own life time, something that should raise a caveat as far as pointing out names is concerned. That was the case, for example, with Joaquim Nabuco and Manoel Bonfim, who took pro-Latin American positions in earlier writings and then turned toward a more negative view.

Our caveat can be extended even further, for example, regarding what is meant by "Latin America," and even "Brazil" or other concepts, at different moments of time. The earlier voices referring to these concepts often had an elitist point of view, which were in some cases pejorative with respect to certain ethnic groups. The word "race" was often used, although in a different meaning than that related to biological linkages. The *raza Latina* was, for example, a concept that referred to a broader cultural group, with links to Hispanic and Iberian roots. The word was used in that way by, for example, the Chilean Francisco Bilbao, one of the first pundits who used the expression Latin America. Even if that was not the case of Bilbao, other scholars that promoted the idea of a *raza Latina* neglected the ethnical diversity and even tensions that might exist among the groups which they grouped in this definition. Other pundits, such as José Vasconcelos, Arturo Uslar Pietri or Néstor García Canclini, tried, for example, to find a homogenous perception that highlighted the ideals of hybridization and what in Spanish is called *mestizaje*. In the case of Brazil, earlier ideas on this subject can be found in the abolitionist writing of Joaquim Nabuco, who argued that Brazil should be reconstructed around working toward a free union of races in liberty.[1] This idea inspired later scholars, such as Gilberto Freyre, who found comparative advantages in societies that could promote cultural interaction and hybridization.[2]

With the advent of the 20th century, the concept of Latin America acquired a stronger position, including a consolidation of the perception of regional diversity in cultural terms. At the same time, the idea of Latin America went beyond identity and culture, becoming increasingly associated with common (regional) perceptions of security and economics, particularly in relation to the notions of autonomy and development. The incorporation of Brazil into this dimension is part of the acceptance of a kind of *e pluribus unum*.

Despite evident setbacks, and at times strong opposition, the long-term tendency seems to go along the path of integration. As we argued in the introduction, most studies of Brazil and its neighbors emphasize the actions and people who go along the path of separation. Sometimes scholars discuss some of the elements we presented in our study by pointing out pro-integration positions and ideas. Yet, since these are generally presented in disassociation with the historical process that led up to them, these are treated as "exceptions" or anomalies in the image of the Brazilian "island." In our study, we choose another path. The focus has been on presenting the continuities in the "path of integration." Of course, not everything along this track has been about "integration," just as not everything along the other path has been related to "separation." In some cases, there were advanced proposals of friendship, common understanding, rapprochement, free trade agreements and other looser forms of approximation. However, this position is in some cases part of deeper intentions regarding integration while in others part of unionist proposals.

We admit that our book might be perceived as having a bias toward the path of integration. That is a risk we take, with the goal of showing that integrationist initiatives and supranational identities are not "exceptional" elements in Brazilian foreign and development oriented policies. These did not emerge in the 1990s, as some suggest, and will not disappear due to circumstantial crises in processes of regional integration. Our point is to address that those policies represent deep forces, ideological currents and interests of social groups, with strong historical roots in both Brazil and the rest of Latin America. In our view, they can be traced back to colonial times, where both intellectuals and politicians found an important acquis of ideas and initiatives from which to sustain this position.

Nothing of this, however, means that integration will be successful or that it will develop into more ambitious forms of union. As we have shown, the path of integration, at the moment when first pursued within the framework of the Spanish and Portuguese empires, had its own particularities, in national terms and with regard to the forces behind it. The same is true for later unionist ideas in the River Plate Basin during the early post-colonial period, which were mostly based on pro-monarchist and anti-popular positions. However, later, as recent Brazilian historiography shows, the Hispanic American independence movement influenced some aspects of Brazil. By the late 19th century, the cultural identity, or whatever we prefer to call a regional dimension, took another dimension, as did the forces promoting the path of integration. It was, however, not until the so-called national popular governments initiated by Getulio Vargas that the political forces promoting the path of integration were more linked to popular movements. By the 1960s, Latin Americanism also had socialist and other kinds of linkages, such as a Catholic trend associated with Alberto Methol Ferré, which transformed it into a very different approach to "integration" and "nationhood" than those promoted by earlier political, economic and social forces. In some moments and by some groups, common forms of projection and convergence with, for example, Catholic and conservative groups were found. Indeed, this is not an issue that can be understood from contemporary right and left, or conservative and progressive, dichotomies.

In the same way, we cannot sustain the position that pro-integrationist forces will remain the same, or that these will pursue the same frameworks of regional integration. It might be that old categories re-emerge and again take central stage, such as America or Pan-America, or that new ones emerge, such as South America. Based on the analysis of historical tendencies and the resilience of ideas, political forces and interests of state, there are reasons to believe that the path of integration will continue to be part of Brazilian foreign policy initiatives toward its neighboring countries.

NOTES

1. Joaquim Nabuco, O *abolicionismo* (Recife: FUNDAG-Editora Massangana, 1988), 19.
2. Enrique Rodríguez Larreta, "Cultura e hibridación sobre algunas fuentes latino-americana," *Anales Nueva Época*, no. 7-8, 2005, 107-123; 116-117.

Bibliography

Aleixo, José Carlos Brandi. *Visão e atuação internacional de Simón Bolívar, Revista de informação legislativa*, vol. 20, no. 80 (1983), 25–52.

Allyon, Bruno. "Aspectos conceituais da diplomacia universalista do Brasil: as relações bilaterais e a integração regional (1945–2000)," *Carta Internacional* (2005), 15–25.

Almeida, Paulo Renan de. *Perón – Vargas – Ibáñez. Pacto ABC. Raízes do Mercosul* (Porto Alegre: Edipucrs, 1998).

Altemani, Enrique de Oliveira & Alburquerque Guilhon, José Augusto (eds.). *A política Externa Brasileira na Visão dos seus Protagonistas* (Rio de Janeiro: Editora Lumen Juris, 2005).

Amorim, Celso & Pimentel, Renata. "Iniciativa para as Américas: O acordo do Jardim das Rosas," in Albuquerque, J. A. Guilhon, *Sessenta anos de política externa brasileira* vol. 2 (São Paulo: Cultural/Nupri/USP/Fapesp, 1996), 103–133.

Anderson, Benedict. *Imagined Communities. Reflections on the origin and spread of nationalism* (London-New York: Verso, 2006).

Andrada e Silva, José Bonifácio. "Os Brasileiros querem ter liberdade," in Andrada e Silva, José Bonifácio, *Projectos para o Brasil*, edited by Dolhnikoff, Miriam (São Paulo: Editora Schwarcz Ltda, 2005), 200–204.

———. A disoluçâao da Asambleia foi mais que um crime, foi um erro palmar," in Andrada e Silva, José Bonifácio, *Projectos para o Brasil*, edited by Dolhnikoff, Miriam (São Pulo: Editora Schwarcz Ltda, 2005), 212–218.

Anjos, João Alfredo dos. *José Bonifácio, primeiro Chanceler do Brasil* (Brasília: Fundação Alexandre de Gusmão, 2007).

Aranda Bustamante, Gilberto & Pavez Rosales, Lucas. "El Legado del ABC: un *Southfalia* Suramericano para la Convergencia en la Diversidad," in Matus, Maria Ignacia Matus & Gilberto Aranda Bustamante. *A 100 Años del ABC: Desafíos y Proyecciones en el Marco de la Integración Regional* (Santiago: CESIM-IEI, 2016).

Araujo, Andre Leite & Carlos Gustavo Poggio Teixeira. "A posição do Brasil no sistema diplomático, da Bacia do Prata entre 1969 e 1974," *Boletim Meridiano 47*, vol. 16, no. 148 (2015), 10–17.

Ardao, Arturo. "Panamericanismo y Latinoamericanismo," in Zea, Leopoldo (ed.), *América Latina en sus ideas* (México: Siglo XXI, 1986), 157–171.

———. *América Latina y la latinidad* (México: UNAM, 1993).

Ardenberg, R. M. "Rio Branco e a Emergência do Ambiente Científico no Brasil," in Cardim, carlos Henrique & João Almino (eds.), *Rio Branco a América do Sul e a Modernização do Brasil* (Rio de Janeiro: EMC – Edições, 2002).

Arrighi, Giovanni. *The Long Twentieth Century* (London: Verso: 2006).

Azcuy Ameghino, Eduardo & Birocco, Carlos Maria. "Las colonias del Río de la plata y Brasil: geopolítica, poder, economía y sociedad (siglos VIII y XVIII)," in Rapoport, Mario & Cervo, Amado Luiz (comp.). *El Cono Sur. Una historia Común* (Buenos Aires: Fondo de Cultura Económica de Argentina, S.A., 2001), 11–70.

Azevedo, Jõao Lúcio. *O Marquês de Pombal e a Sua Epoca* (São Paulo: Alameda, 2004).

Backheuser, Everardo. *Curso de Geopolítica Geral e do Brasil* (Rio de Janeiro: Gráfica Laemmert Limitada 1948).

Barbosa, Francisco de Asses. "José Bonifácio e a política internacional," *Revista do Instituto Histórico e Geográfico Brasileiro*, vol. 260 (1963), 258–284.

Barrios, Miguel Ángel. *El Latinoamericanismo en el pensamiento político de Manuel Ugarte* (Buenos Aires: Editorial Biblos, 2007).

Bernal Meza, Raúl. *Sistema Mundial y MERCOSUR. Globalización, Regionalismo y Políticas Exteriores Comparadas* (Buenos Aires: Nuevohacer/Universidad Nacional del Centro de la Provincia de Buenos Aires, 2000).

Bethell, Leslie (ed.), *Colonial Brazil* (Cambridge: Cambridge University Press, 1987).

———. "Brazil and 'Latin America,'" *Journal of Latin American Studies*, no. 42 (2010), 457–485

———. *Brazil. Empire and Republic, 1822–1930* (Cambridge: Cambridge University Press, 1993 [1989]).

Bilbao, Francisco. *La iniciativa para la América, Idea de un Congreso General de las Repúblicas,* Universidad Nacional Autónoma de (México: Centro de Estudios Latinoamericanos – Facultad de Filosofía y Letras – Unión de Universidades de América Latina, Cuadernos de Cultura Latinoamericana, núm. 3, 1979). Original 1856.

Bizzozero, Lincoln. "Los cambios de gobierno en Argentina y Brasil y la conformación de una agenda del Mercosur ¿Hacia una nueva cartografía sudamericana/interamericana?," *Nueva Sociedad*, no. 186 (2003), 128–142.

Bolívar, Simón Bolívar, Reply to Louis Souza Díaz, Envoy Extraordinary and Minister Plenipotentiary of His Majesty the Emperor of Brazil. Bogotá, 30 March 1830, in UNESCO, *Simón Bolívar: The Hope of the Universe* (Paris: United Nations Educational, Scientific and Cultural Organization, 1983), 305.

Bolívar, Simón. *The Jamaica Letter: Response from a South American to a Gentleman from This Island,* in Bushnell, David (ed.), *El Libertador: Writings of Simón Bolívar* (Oxford: Oxford University Press, 2003), 12–30.

———. Bolívar a Santander, Lima 23 de enero de 1825, in *Archivo Santander*, vol. 12 (Bogotá: Aguila Negra Editorial, 1917), 219–220.

Bomfim, Manoel. *América Latina: males de origem*, (Rio de Janeiro: Centro Edelstein de Pesquisas Sociais, 2008).

———. *O Brasil na América: Caracterização da Formação Brasi*leira, 2ª edição (Rio de Janeiro: Topbooks, 1997).

Bonifácio Andrada e Silva. José Jose Bonifácio a Correa da Câmara, Rio, 30 May 1822, in Caldeira, Jorge (ed.), *José Bonifácio Andrada e Silva* (São Paulo: Editorial 34, 2002), 147–150.

Boxer, Charles Ralph. *O Império Colonial Português* (São Paulo: Edições 70, 1969).

Brands, Hall. "Third World Politics in an Age of Global Turmoil: The Latin American Challenge to U.S. and Western Hegemony, 1965–1975," *Diplomatic History*, vol. 32, no. 1 (2008), 105–138.

Braudel, Fernand. *The Perspectives of the World. Civilization & Capitalism, 15th–18th Century*, vol. 3 (New York: Harper & Row, Publishers, 1979).

Briceño-Ruiz, José. "El regionalismo estratégico en las interacciones entre Estados Unidos y Brasil en el ALCA: Un análisis desde el liberalismo intergubernamental," in Shigeru Kochi, Philippe de Lombaerde & José Briceño Ruiz (eds.). *Del regionalismo latinoamericano a la integración interregional* (Madrid: Siglo XXI editores, 2008), 99–136.

Buarque de Holanda, Sérgio (ed.), *História Geral da Civiliza*ção *Brasileira. A* È*poca Colonial. Administração, Economia, Sociedade,* Tomo I (São Paulo: Difusão Eur-péia do Livro, 1960).

Bueno, Clodoaldo, Vigevani, Tullo; Ramazini Junior, Haroldo. "Latin American Integration: a Brazilian View," in Andrés Rivarola Puntigliano, José Briceño-Ruiz (org.). *Resilience of Regionalism in Latin America and the Caribbean* (London: Palgrave Macmillan, 2013).

Bulmer-Thomas, Victor. *The Economic History of Latin America Since Independence*, Second edition (Cambridge: Cambridge University Press, 2003).

Bunge, Alejandro. *Una Nueva Argentina* (Buenos Aires: Ed. Guillermo Kraft Ltd., 1940).

Burges, Sean W. "Consensual Hegemony: Theorizing Brazilian Foreign Policy after the Cold," *International Relations*, vol. 22, no.1 (2008), 65–84.

———."Without Sticks or Carrots: Brazilian Leadership in South America during the Cardoso Era, 1992–2003," *Bulletin of Latin American*, vol. 25, no. 1 (2004), 23–42.

———."Building a Global Southern Coalition: The Competing Approaches of Brazil's Lula and Venezuela's Chávez," *Third World Quarterly*, vol. 28, no. 7 (2007), 1343–1358.

Burns, E. Bradford. *The Unwritten Alliance: Rio-Branco and Brazilian-American Relations.* (New York: Columbia University Press, 1966).

Calógeras, João Pandiá. *A Política Exterior do Imperio*, vol. 1 (Brasilia: Senado Federal, 1998), 14.

Calvo, Carlos. *Colección Completa de los Tratados, Convenciones, Capitulaciones, Armisticios y Otros Actos Diplomáticos de todos los Estados de la América Latina Comprendidos entre el Golfo de Méjico y el Cabo de Hornos Desde el Año de 1493 Hasta Nuestros Días*, Tomo Tercero (Paris: Libreria de A. Durand, 1862).

Campos, Roberto. *A Laterna na Popa*, Memórias 2 (Petrópolis RJ: ParkGraf Editora Ltda, 2004).

Cardim, Carlos Henrique. "O Barão do Rio Branco e Rui Barbosa," in Cardim, Carlos Henrique e João Almino (eds.), *Rio Branco a América do Sul e a Modernização do Brasil* (Rio de Janeiro: EMC – Edições, 2002).

Carmona, Rolando. "Bonifácio, gênese do pensamento nacional," *World Tensions*, vol. 9, no. 16 (2013), 196–215

Carneiro, Glauco. *Lusardo. O último Caudillho*, vol. 2. (Rio de Janeiro: Editora Nova Fronteira S.A., 1977).

Carrión Mena, Francisco. "Política Exterior de América Latina y las Cumbres de la CELAC," in Bonilla Soria, Adrián and Isabel Álvarez Echandi (eds.), *Desafíos estratégicos del regionalismo contemporáneo: CELAC e Iberoamérica* (San José, Costa Rica: FLACSO, 2013), 113–128.

Castilho, Alessandra Beber. "O golpe de 1964 e a politica externa brasileira dentro do contexto repressivo," *Revista NEIBA Cadernos Argentina – Brasil*, vol. 2, no. 1 (2014), 57–68.

Castro, Flávio Mendes de Oliveira. *Dois Séculos de História da Organização do Itamaraty, Volume 1, 1808–2008*. Vols 1 y 2 (Brasilia: Fundação Alexandre de Gusmão, 2009).

Cepik, Marco Aurélio Chaves & Faria, Carlos Aurélio Pimenta de. "Brasil y América Latina: Bolivarismos antiguos y modernos," *Análisis Político*, no. 49 (2003), 63–82.

Cervo, Amado Luiz & Bueno, Clodoaldo. *História da Política Exterior do Brasil* (Brasilia: Editora UNB – Instituto Brasileiro de Relações Internacionais, 2002).

Cervo, Amado Luiz. *Relações Internacionais da América Latina. Velhos e novos paradigmas* (Brasilia: Ed. Saraiva, Instituto Brasileiro de Relações Internacionais, 2ª edição, 2007).

————."Estado logístico: la inserción internacional sistémica de Brasil en el siglo XXI," in José Briceño-Ruiz y Alejandro Simonoff (eds.), *Integración y Cooperación Regional en América Latina: Una relectura a partir de la teoría de la autonomía* (Buenos Aires: Editorial Biblos, 2015), 163–188.

Chaffee, Wilber Albert. *Desenvolvimento: Politics and Economy in Brazil* (Boulder, CO.: Lynne Rienner, 1998).

Chami, Pablo. *Gloria y fracaso del Plan de Operaciones ¿Quién escribió el plan atribuido a Mariano Moreno?* (Buenos Aires: Prometeo, 2012).

Cortesão, Jaime. *Alexandre de Gusmão e o Tratade de Madrid*, Parte I – Tomo I (1695–1735) (Rio de Janeiro: Ministério das Relações Exteriores-Instituto Rio-Branco, 1952).

Costa, Darc. *Fundamentos para o Estudo da Estratégia Nacional* (São Paulo: Paz e Terra, 2009).

Crespo, Regina Aída. "Cultura e política: José Vasconcelos e Alfonso Reyes no Brasil (1922–1938)," *Revista Brasileira de História*, São Paulo, vol. 23, no. 45 (2003), 187–208.

De Carvalho, Delgado. *Historia Diplomática do Brasil* (São Paulo: Companhia Editora Nacional, 1959).

De la Reza, Germán A. *El Ciclo Confederativo. Historia de la Integración Latino-americana en el siglo XIX* (Lima: Fondo Editorial de la UNMSM, 2012).

De Marco, Manuel Ángel. *Belgrano. Artífice de la Nación, Soldado de la Libertad* (Buenos Aires: Emecé, 2012).

De Monteagudo, Bernardo. *Ensayo sobre la necesidad de una Federación General entre los Estados hispanoamericanos y Plan de su organización*, in Bernardo de Monteagudo, Escritos Políticos (Buenos: Aires, EMECE, 2009).

Declaración Presidencial y Agenda Prioritaria, 2005, available at: http://walk.sela.org/attach/258/EDOCS/SRed/2010/09/T023600002368-0-Declaracion_Presidencial_y_Agenda_Prioritaria_-_Comunidad_Sudamericana_de_Naciones.pdf (accessed: 17 September 2016).

Del Valle, José Cecilio. "Proyecto de Confederación Americana. 1822. Soñaba el Abad de San Pedro: Y yo también se soñar," Del Valle; José Cecilio, *Obra Escogida* (Caracas: Biblioteca Ayacucho, 1982).

Del Vecchio, Angelo. "Política e Potência no Regime Militar Brasileiro," *Projeto História, São Paulo,* vol. 2, no. 1 (2004), 169–196

Díaz Labrano, Roberto Ruiz and Ramón Silva Alonso. *El Mercosur: marco jurídico institucional, análisis y perspectivas de sus normas derivadas* (Asunción: Universidad Nacional de Asunción, Intercontinental Editora, 1993).

Disney, A. R. *A History of Portugal and the Portuguese Empire: From Beginnings to 1807,* Volume 1 (Cambridge: Cambridge University Press, 2009).

———. *A History of Portugal and the Portuguese Empire: From Beginnings to 1807* Volume 2 (Cambridge: Cambridge University Press, 2009).

Dosman, Edgard J. *The Life and Times of Raúl Prebisch 1901–1986* (Montreal: McGill-Queen's University Press, 2008).

Falla aos Americanos Brazilianos, em nome d'America por seus irmãos aos habitantes das vastas Províncias do Rio da Prata, available in https://archive.org/details/fallaaosamerican00unkn (accessed: 20 July 2016).

Fernandes, Ana Claudia. "A revolução de Pernambuco nas páginas do Correio Braziliense e do Correo del Orinoco: linguagens, conceitos e projetos políticos em tempos de independência (1817–1820)," *Almanack Braziliense*, no. 9, May 2009, 144–153.

Fernandes, Tiago Coelho. "Entre Bolívar e Monroe: o Brasil nas relações interamericanas," in Suárez Salazar, Luis and Tania García Lorenzo (eds.) *Las relaciones interamericanas: continuidades y cambios* (Buenos Aires: CLACSO, 2008), 213–240.

Ferreira Filho, Arthur. *História Geral do Rio Grande do Sul* (Porto Alegre: Editora Globo, 1978).

Flores, Maria Cândida Galvão. *O Mercosul nos discursos do governo brasileiro (1985–94)* (Rio de Janeiro: Editora FGV, 2005).

Frazão Conduru, Guilherme. "O Subsistema Americano, Rio Branco e o ABC". *Revista Brasileira de Política Internacional*, vol. 41, no. 2 (1998), 59–82.

Freyre, Gilberto. *O Brasileiro Entre os Outros Hispanos: Afinidades, Contrastes e Possiveis Futuros nas suas Interrelações* (Rio de Janeiro: Livraria José Olympo Editora, 1975).

Friedrich, Tatyana Scheila and Guimarães, Guilherme Athaides. "Ensaios de integração: Brasil e Argentina no século XX, pontos de aproximação e de afastamento até a formação do Mercosul," *Estudos Internacionais*, vol. 3, no. 1 (2015), 115–140.

Furtado, Celso. *A Fantasia Desfeita* (Rio de Janeiro: Paz e Terra, 1989).

Gardini, Gian Luca. "Making Sense of the Rapprochement between Argentina and Brazil, 1979–1982," *Revista Europea de Estudios Latinoamericanos y del Caribe*, no. 80 (2006), 57–71.

————."Two Critical Passages in the Road to Mercosur," _Cambridge Review of International Affairs_, vol. 18, no. 3 (2005), 405–420.

Giacalone, Rita. "La Comunidad Sudamericana de Naciones: ¿Una alianza entre izquierda y empresarios?," _Nueva Sociedad_, no. 202 (2006), 74–86.

Gobat, Michel. "The Invention of Latin America: A Transnational History of Anti-Imperialism, Democracy, and Race," _The American Historical Review_, vol. 118, no. 5 (2013), 1345–1375.

Gonçalves, Luiz Eduardo Fonseca de Carvalho. _As relações Brasil-CEPAL (1947–1964)_ (Brasília: Fundação Alexandre de Gusmão, 2011).

Guimarães, Argeu, _Bolívar e o Brasil_ (Paris: Edição do "Livre Libre," 1930).

Hage, José Alexandre A. _As relações diplomáticas entre Argentina e Brasil no MERCOSUL. Princípios de hegemonia, dependência e interesse no Tratado de Assunção_ (Curitiba: Jurúa Editora, 2004).

Herrick, Jane. The Reluctant Revolutionist: A Study of the Political Ideas of Hipólito da Costa (1774–182), _The Americas_, vol. 7, no. 2 (1950), 171–181.

Hirst, Mónica. "La participación de Brasil en el proceso del Mercosur: evaluando costos y beneficios," in Rojas Aravena, Francisco & William C. Smith (eds.), _El Cono Sur las transformaciones globales_ (Santiago de Chile: FLACSO, North South Center, CLADE, 1994), 315–331.

Hogan, J. W. "Remoulding the critical conjecture approach," _Canadian Journal of Political Science/ Revue canadienne de science politique_, vol. 39, no. 3 (2006), 657–679.

Huntington, S. _The Clash of Civilizations and the Remaking of World Order_ (London: Simon & Schuster UK Ltd., 2002 [1997]).

Ianni, Octavio. "A Questão Nacional na América Latina," _Estudos Avançados_, vol. 2, no. 1 (1988), 5–40.

Iñiguez, Carlos Piñeiro. _Perón. La Construcción de un Ideario_ (Buenos Aires: Siglo XXI Editora, 2010).

Jaguaribe, Helio. "Brasil y la América Latina," in Tomassini, Luciano (com.), _Las Relaciones Internacionales de la América Latina_ (México, DF: Fondo de Cultura Económica 1981), 417–446.

Joaquina, Carlota. _Manifiesto Dirigido a' los Fieles Vasallos de su Magestad Católigca el Rey de las Españas é Indias_ (Rio de Janeiro: Impressão Régia, 1808).

Johannesson, Fredrik. _Det Panamerikanska Problemet 1829–1920. En studie i Modern Politik_ (Norrköping: Norrköpings Tidningars Aktiebolags Tryckeri, 1922).

Johnson, H. B. "Portuguese settlement, 1500–1580," in Leslie Bethell (ed.), _Colonial Brazil_, (Cambridge: Cambridge University Press, 1987).

Júnior, Antônio Manoel Elíbio. "De Vargas e Geisel: as Estratégias da Política Externa Brasileira para a Criação do Tratado de Cooperação Amazônica - TCA (1940–1978)," _Cadernos do Tempo Presente_, no. 10 (2012), 1–10.

Junior, Floriano Guwzynski. Hipólito Da Costa e as independências na América Espanhola: O caso venezuelano, _Oficina do Historiador_, vol. 2, no. 1 (2010), 78–96.

Landau, Georges D. "The Treaty for Amazonian Cooperation: A Bold New Instrument for Development," _Georgia Journal of International and Comparative Law_, vol. 10, no. 3 (1980), 463–489.

Lessa, Antônio Carlos Moraes. "Instabilidade e mudanças: os condicionantes históricos da política externa brasileira sob Geisel (1974–1979)," *Revista de Informação Legislativa*, vol. 34, no. 133 (1997), 73–81.

Lewis, Martin W. & Wigen, Kären E. *The Myth of Continents. A Critique of Metageography* (Berkeley: University of California Press, 1997).

Lima, María Regina Soares de and Hirst, Monica. "Brazil as an Intermediate State and Regional Power," *International Affairs*, vol. 82, no. 1 (2006), 21–40.

Lima, María Regina Soares de. "La política exterior brasileña y los desafíos de la gobernanza global," *Foreign Affairs Latinoamérica*, vol. 9, no. 2 (2009), 25–32.

Lima, Néstor dos Santos. *A imagen do Brasil nas cartas de Bolívar* (Brasilia: Verano Editora, 2001).

Lott, George. "Latin American Economic Integration," *Lawyer of the Americas*, vol. 10, no. 2 (1978), 549–575.

Lynch, John. *Latin America between Colony and Nation. Selected Essays* (Houndmills: Macmillan Press, 2001).

Manzetti, Luigi. "Argentine-Brazilian Economic Integration: An Early Appraisal," *Latin American Research Review*, vol. 25, no. 3 (1990), 109–140.

Marmora, Leopoldo and Messner, Dirk. "La integración de Argentina, Brasil y Uruguay," *Nueva Sociedad*, no. 113 (1991), 130–145.

Mauro, Fréderic, "Political and Economic Structures of Empire, 1580–1750," in Leslie Bethell (ed.), *Colonial Brazil* (Cambridge: Cambridge University Press, 1987).

Medeiros, Marcelo da Almeida, *La genèse du MERCOSUD* (Paris: L'Harmattan, 2000).

Médici, Emílio Garrastazú. *Nosso Caminho* (Brasilia: Departamento de Imprensa Nacional, 1972).

Mello, Evaldo Cabral de. *A outra independencia. O federalismo pernambucano de 1817 a 1824* (São Paulo: Editora 34, 2014).

Mendonça, Filipe Almeida do Prado & Miyamoto, Shiguenoli. "A Política Externa do Governo Geisel (1974-1979)," *Século XXI*, vol. 2, no. 2 (2011), 11–29.

Mendonça, Renato. *História da política exterior do Brasil: do período colonial ao reconhecimento do Império (1500–1825)* (Brasília: FUNAG, 2013).

Mindlin, José E. "Desenvolvimento Brasileiro e a crise da ALALC," *Revista de Administração de* Empresas, vol. 13, no. 2 (1973), 75–80.

Moniz Bandeira, Luiz Alberto. "América Latina o Sudamérica? *Diario Clarin.com*, Buenos Aires, 16 may 2005, available at: http://edant.clarin.com/diario/2005/05/16/opinion/o-01901.htm (accessed: 11 November 2016).

———. "O Brasil e a América do Sul," in Altemani, Henrique and Antonio Carlos Lessa (eds.), *Relações Internacionais do Brasil*, vol. 1 (Brasilia: FUNAG, Editora Saraiva, Instituto Brasileiro de Relações Internacionais, 2006), 267–293.

———. "O Brasil e a America do Sul," in Altemani, Hernique de Oliveira & Antônio Carlos Lessa (eds.). *Relacões Inernacionais do Brasil. Temas e Agendas*, vol. 1. (São Paulo: Editora Saraiva, 2006).

———. *O eixo Argentina- Brasil. O processo de integração de América Latina*, (Brasília: Editorial Universidade de Brasília, 1987).

Moravcsik, Andrew. "Bringing Constructivist Integration Theory of EU out of the Clouds: Has it Landed Yet?" *European Union Politics*, vol. 2, no. 2 (2001), 226–240.

Moreno, Mariano. *Plan de Operaciones, in Plan de Operaciones, Mariano Moreno, Prologo Esteban de Gorri. Estudios críticos Noberto Piñero y Paul Groussac. Investigación bibliográfica Mario Tesler* (Buenos Aires: Biblioteca Nacional, 2007).

Mörner, Magnus. *The Political and Economic Activities of the Jesuits in the La Plata Region. The Hapsburg Era* (Stockholm: Library and Institute of Ibero-American Studies, 1953).

Moura, Gerson. *Autonomia na dependência. A política externa brasileira de 1935 a 1942* (Rio de Janeiro: Editora Nova Fronteira, 1980).

Neto, Raul De Gouvea. "Mercosur: Fostering Regional Economic Integration," *Thunderbird International Business Review*, vol. 40, no. 6 (1998), 585–604.

Neumann, Iver B., "A Nordic and/or a Baltic Sea Region? The Discursive Structure of Region-Building," in Wellmann, Christian (ed.), *Baltic Sea Region: Conflict or Cooperation?* (Kiel: Kiel Peace Research Series, 1992), 69–70.

———. *Uses of the Other: "The East" in European identity* (Manchester: Manchester University Press: 1999).

Newcomb, Robert Patrick. "José Enrique Rodó: 'Iberoamérica,' the Magna Patria, and the question of Brazil," *Hispania*, vol. 93, no. 3 (2010), 368–379.

Perón, Juan Domingo. *Los Estados Unidos de América del Sur* (Buenos Aires: Ediciones Corregidor, 2008 [1982]).

Phelan, John Leddy. "Pan-Latinism, French Intervention in Mexico (1861–1867) and the genesis of the Idea of Latin America," in *Conciencia y autenticidad históricas. Escritos en homenaje a Edmundo O'Gorman* (México: UNAM, 1968), 279–298.

Phillips, Nicola. *The Southern Cone Model: The Political Economy of Regional Capitalist Development in Latin America* (London – New York: Routledge, 2004).

Pierson, Paul. *Politics in Time. History, Institutions and Social Analysis* (Princeton: NJ: Princeton University Press, 2004).

Pimenta, João Paulo G. & Salay Leme, Adriana. "Imperador de toda a América do Sul". D. João no Brasil e o Rio da Prata," *Revista USP*, São Paulo, no. 79 (2008), 34–43.

Pimenta, João Paulo G. *Brasil y las Revoluciones de Hispanoamérica (1809–1822)* (Bogotá: Universidad de Externado de Colombia, 2006), 347–364.

Pimenta, João Paulo G. *Las independencias cruzadas de Brasil e Hispanoamérica: el problema de las sincronías y diacronías*, in Thibaud, Clément, Entin, Gabriel, Gómez, Alejandro and Morelli, Federica (eds), *L'Atlantique révolutionnaire. Une perspective Ibero-Américaine* (Becherel: Les Perséides), 289–299.

———. *Tempos e espaços das independências: a inserção do Brasil no mundo ocidental (c.1780–c.1830)* Tese de Livre Docência (São Paulo: Universidade de São Paulo – Faculdade de Filosofia, Letras e Ciências Humanas.

Pimentel, José Vicente de Sá (ed.), *Pensamento Diplomático Brasileiro Formuladores e Agentes da Política Externa (1750–1964)* (Brasilia: Fundação Alexandre de Gusmão, 2012), 89–119.

Pinheiro Guimarães, Samuel. *Desafios Brasileiros na era dos Gigantes* (Rio de Janeiro: Contraponto, 2006).

Poggio Texeira, Carlos Gustavo. *Brazil, the United States, and the South American Subsystem. Regional Politics and the Absent Empire* (Lanham: Lexington Books, 2012).

Preuss, Ori. "Brazil into Latin America: The Demise of Slavery and Monarchy as Transnational Events," *Luso-Brazilian Review* vol. 49, no. 1 (2012), 96–126.

———. "Discovering "Os Ianques do Sul": Towards an Entangled Luso-Hispanic History of Latin America," *Revista Brasileira de Política Internacional*, vol. 56, no. 2 (2013), 157–176.

———. *Bridging the Island: Brazilians' Views of Spanish America and Themselves, 1865–1912* (Madrid: Iberoamericana – Vervuert, 2011).

Puig, Juan Carlos. *Integración Latinoamericana y Régimen Internacional* (Caracas: Universidad Simón Bolívar, 1987).

Ramos, Jorge Abelardo. *Historia de la Nación Latinoamericana* (Buenos Aires: Senado de la Nación, 2006).

Rapoport, Mario & Madrid, Eduardo. *Argentina- Brasil. De Rivales a Aliados* (Buenos Aires: Capital Intelectual, 2011).

Reyes Abadie, Washington. *Artigas y el Federalismo en el Río de la Plata, 1811–1820* (Montenvideo: Ediciones de la Banda Oriental, 1987).

Riberio, Darcy. *O Povo Brasileiro* (São Paulo: Companhia das Letras, 2006).

Rivarola Puntigliano, Andrés & Briceño-Ruiz, José (eds.). *The Resilience of Regionalism in Latin America and the Caribbean: Development and Autonomy* (London: Palgrave Macmillan, 2013).

Rivarola Puntigliano, Andrés. "De CEPAL a ALALC: tres vertientes del pensamiento regionalista en Latinoamérica," in Briceño-Ruiz, José, Rivarola Puntigliano, Andrés & Casas-Gragea, Angel (eds.). *Integración Latinoamericana y Caribeña. Política y Economía. Política y Economía* (Madrid: Fondo de Cultura Económica de España, 2012).

———. "'Geopolitics of Integration' and the Imagination of South America," *Geopolitics*, vol. 16, no. 4 (2011), 846–864.

Rock, David. "Latin America and the United States," in Rock, David (ed.), *Latin America in the 1940s. War and Post-war Transitions* (Berkeley: University of California Press, 1994).

Rodó, José Enrique. "Iberoamérica," in Rodó, José Enrique, *Obras Completas* (Madrid: Aguilar, 1967), 689–690.

———. "Ibero-America," in Vaccaro, José Alberto (ed.), *Obras Competas de José Enrique Rodo* (Buenos Aires, Ediciones Antonio Zamora, 1948).

Rojas Aravena, Francisco, *Global Shifts and Changes in Latin America*, available at http://library.fes.de/pdf-files/iez/10344.pdf (accessed: 29 October 2016).

Rojas Mix, Miguel. "América Latina: integración e identidad," available at: http://miguelrojasmix.net/wp/?p=127 (accessed: 16 April 2014).

———. "Bilbao y el hallazgo de América Latina: Unión continental, socialista y libertaria," *Cahiers du monde hispanique et luso-brésilien*, no. 46 (1986), 35–47.

———. *Los cien nombres de América* (Barcelona: Editorial Lumen, 1991).

Rosenthal, Gert, "ECLAC: A Commitment to a Latin American Way toward Development," in Berthelot, Yves (ed.), *Unity and Diversity in Development Ideas. Perspectives from the UN Regional Commissions* (Blomington: Indiana, Indiana University Press, 2004).

Rugai Bastos, Elide. *Gilberto Freyre e o Pensamiento Hispânico. Entre Dom Quixote e Alonso el Bueno* (Bauru: EDUSC/ANPOCS, 2003).

Santos, Luís Cláudio Villafañe G. *A América do Sul no discurso diplomático brasileiro* (Brasília: FUNAG, 2014).

Santos, Luis Claudio Villafañe Gomes. *O Brasil entre a América e a Europa: O Império e o Interamericanismo (do Congresso de Panamá ao Congresso de Washington)* (São Paulo: Editora UNESP, 2004).

———. *O Imperio e as República do Pacifico: as relações do Brasil com Chile, Bolívia, Peru, Equador e Colômbia – 1822–1889* (Curitiba: Editora UFPR, 2002).

Scheidt, Eduardo. "Representações da Revolução Americana no ideário de Francisco Bilbao," *Estudos Ibero-Americanos*, vol. 36, no.1 (2010), 48–66.

Scheman, L. Ronald. "The Alliance for Progress: Concept and Creativity," in Scheman L. Ronald (ed.), *The Alliance for Progress. A Retrospective* (New York: Praeger, 1988), 3–63.

Schmitt, Carl. *The Nomos of the Earth in the Law of the Jus Publicum Europaeum* (New York: Telos Press, Ltd, 2003 [1950]).

Schvarzer, Jorge. "Mercosur: The Prospects for Regional Integration," *NACLA Report on the Americas*, vol. 32, no. 6 (1998), 25–27.

Seckinger, Ron L. "The Chiquitos Affair: An Aborted Crisis in Brazilian-Bolivian Relations," *Luso-Brazilian Review*, vol. 11, no. 1 (1974), 19–40.

Segreti, Carlos S. A. *El Plan atribuido a Mariano Moreno* (Córdoba: Centro de Estudios Históricos, 1996).

Serbin Bartosch, Andrés. "El largo (y díficil) camino hacia una integración sudamericana," in Consuelo Ahumada y Arturo Cancino (eds.), *Comunidad Andina y Mercosur en la perspectiva del ALCA* (Bogotá: Memorias del Observatorio Andino, Centro Editorial Javeriano, 2003), 15–54.

Serbin, Andrés. "Entre UNASUR y ALBA: ¿Otra integración (ciudadana) es posible?" *Anuario de integración regional de América Latina y el Gran Caribe*, no. 6 (2007), 183–207.

Shifter, Michael. "The Shifting Landscape of Latin American Regionalism," *Current History*, vol. 111, no. 742, (February 2012), 56–61.

Smith, William C. *Authoritarianism and the Crisis of the Argentine Political Economy* (Stanford: Stanford University Press, 1991).

Sodré, Nelson Werneck. *Formação Histórica do Brasil* (São Paulo: Editora Brasiliense, 1973).

Sombra, José Flavio Saraiva. "Um novo ensaio estratégico argentino- brasileiro: possibilidades e limites," in Fausto, Ayrton and José Flavio Sombra Saraiva (eds.), *Diálogos sobre a Pátria Grande* (Brasilia: FLACSO-Brasil, 2004), 83–98.

Süssekind, Flora, "Shifting Frontiers – Manuel Bonfim and A América Latina: An Introduction," *Journal of Latin American Cultural Studies: Travesía*, vol. 11, no. 1 (2002), 65–76.

Teixeira Gonçalves, Felipe. *A CELAC, o SELA e a agenda do Brasil para américa Latina e Caribe, Boletim de Economia e Política Internacional*, vol. 8 (2011), 49–60.

Teubal, Miguel. "Regional integration processes in Latin America: Argentina and MERCOSUR," in Fernández Jilberto, Alex E. & André Mommen (eds.), *Regionalization and Globalization in the Modern World Economy: Perspectives on the Third World and Transitional Economies* (London: Routledge, 1998), 230–250.

Thorp, Rosemary. "The Latin American Economies in the 1940s," in Rock, David (ed.), *Latin America in the 1940s. War and Postwar Transitions* (Berkeley: University of California Press, 1994).

Trías, Vivan. *Las Montoneras y el Imperio Británico* (Montevideo: Ediciones Uruguay, 1961).

———. *Imperialismo y Geopolítica en América Latina* (Montevideo: Ediciones del Sol, 1967).

Ugarte, Manuel. *El porvenir d América Española* (Valencia: Prometeo Sociedad Editorial, 1910).

———. *La Nación Latinoamericana* (Caracas: Biblioteca Ayacucho, 1978).

Vaz, Alcides Costa. *Cooperação, integração e processo negociador. A construção do Mercosul* (Brasilia: FUNAG, IBRI, 2002).

Vigevani, Tullo & Marcelo Passini Mariano. "A ALCA e a política externa brasileira," in Altemani, Henrique, & Antonio Carlos Lessa (eds.), *Relações Internacionais do Brasil,* vol. 1 (Brasilia: FUNAG, Editora Saraiva, Instituto Brasileiro de Relações Internacionais, 2006), 321–356.

Vigevani, Tullo & Cepaluni, Gabriel. "Lula's Foreign Policy and the Quest for Autonomy through Diversification," *Third World Quarterly,* vol. 28, no. 7 (2007), 1309–1326.

Vigevani, Tullo & Oliveira Marcelo Fernandes De. "Brazilian Foreign Policy in the Cardoso Era: The Search for Autonomy through Integration," *Latin American Perspectives,* vol. 25, no. 5 (2007), 58–80.

Vigevani, Tullo, Favaron, Gustavo de Mauro, Ramanzini Júnior, Haroldo & Correia, Rodrigo Alves. "O papel da integração regional para o Brasil: universalismo, soberania e percepção das elites," *Revista Brasileira de Política Internacional,* vol. LI, no. 1 (2008), 5–27.

Werner Baer. *The Brazilian Economy: Growth and Development* (Westport, CT: Praeger, 2001).

Williams, Mark Eric. *Understanding U.S.-Latin American Relations. Theory and History* (New York: Routledge, 2012).

Winand, Érica Christina Alexandre. "A Rivalidade como sentimento profundo: Origem, evolução histórica e reflexos contemporâneos do padrão de rivalidade entre Brasil e Argentina" *Historia e Cultura,* vol. 4, no. 1 (1995), 68–94, 72.

Wise Randig, Rodrigo. "Argentina, primer país en reconocer la independencia de Brasil," *Archivos del Presente. Revista Latinoamericana de Temas Internacionales,* n/d, 107–118, available at;http://www.archivosdelpresente.com/site/assets/files/1186/wiese_randig.pdf (accessed: 4 April 2017).

Yañez, Antonio. "Comunidad Sudamericana de Naciones ¿con impronta venezolana o brasileña?," *La Onda Digital,* no 256, 4 October 2005 al 10/10/2005, available at: http://www.laondadigital.com/laonda/laonda/201-300/256/B21.htm (accessed: 31 October 2009).

Index

About the Authors

José Briceño-Ruiz is associated professor at the Faculty of Social and Economic Sciences of the University of the Andes, Mérida, Venezuela. He holds a PhD in Political Science from the Institut d'Etudes Polí:tiques d'Aix-en-Provence (Science Po Aix), France. His research areas of expertise include Latin American regionalism, comparative regionalism, international political economy and foreign policy. He has been visiting scholar at the University of São Paulo, Universidad Nacional Autónoma de México, Stockholm University, Aoyama Gakuin University in Tokyo, Universidad de Sonora (México), Universidad de Buenos Aires. He has edited several articles and books on Latin American regionalism, the more recent of them: *Post-Hegemonic Regionalism in the Americas: Toward a Pacific–Atlantic Divide?* (London: Routledge, 2017, in collaboration with Isidro Morales Moreno) and *The Resilience of Regionalism in Latin American and the Caribbean. Autonomy and Development* (Palgrave, 2013, in collaboration with Andrés Rivarola Puntigliano).

Andrés Rivarola Puntigliano is associate professor in Economic History, senior lecturer in Latin American Studies, and director of the Institute of Latin American Studies, at Stockholm University. Rivarola Puntigliano's research is focused on regional integration in Latin America, international political economy, development studies, geopolitics and foreign policy. He has been visiting scholar and lecturer at universities in different countries as well as published several articles and books. Among the most recent are: "21st century geopolitics: integration and development in the age of 'continental states'," *Territory, Politics, Governance*, Vol 3, No 3., 2016; "Thinking big from the periphery: Raúl Prebisch and the World System", Matias E. Margulis (ed), *The Global Political Economy of Raúl Prebisch* (London: Routledge, 2017); and *The Resilience of Regionalism in Latin American and the Caribbean. Autonomy and Development* (Palgrave, 2013, in collaboration with José Briceño Ruiz).

www.ingramcontent.com/pod-product-compliance
Lightning Source LLC
Chambersburg PA
CBHW021817270326
41932CB00007B/224